Win Your Day

The Blueprint for Human Reinvention

By Jason A. Safford, Sr.

Copyright Page

Win Your Day: The Blueprint for Human Reinvention

Copyright © 2025 by Jason A. Safford, Sr.

All rights reserved.

Library of Congress Cataloging-in-Publication Data

Cataloging-in-Publication data is available upon request.

For permissions, inquiries, or speaking engagements, contact:
public.relations@exceptionalresultsnow.com

Win Your Day: The Blueprint for Human Reinvention
/ by Jason Andrew Safford, Sr.
ISBN: 979-8-9941119-0-1
Printed in the United States of America
10 9 8 7 6 5 4 3 2 1
First Edition

Epigraph

The root of happiness grows in justice.
The root of justice thrives in strength.
The root of strength lives in mastery of self.
— Inspired by Kautilya

"Crisis is not the end of you.
It is the beginning written in fire.
When the world strips you bare,
what remains is not weakness,
it is the code of your becoming."
~ Resilience Architecture™ Principle

To Camlin, Andrew, & Austin

And to all who have walked through the furnace of crisis and chosen not just to survive, but to rise, this book is for you.

Table of Contents

About This Book

This book is for people who cannot afford to collapse.
People others rely on.
Those carrying weight in silence.
Leaders who need structure when emotion surges.

If you want comfort, this book will challenge you. If you want strength, it will build you.

You hold more than a book. A code for winning rests in your hands. Reading alone never unlocks it. Training begins the moment pages turn. Mind, heart, and body strengthen together through deliberate practice. Every story reflects strength already present.

Two operating codes guide the work. The Winning Formula stands first. Winning equals effort multiplied by completion, recovery, and awareness. Action matters. Finishing matters more. Rest restores capacity. Attention directs power.

Practice all four and the day bends in your favor. External verdicts lose authority. Failure stops posing as an enemy. Both outcomes become training ground. Each attempt sharpens capability. Progress compounds through consistency.

The Flow Formula defines how life moves when alignment replaces resistance. Flow means every energy moving together with purpose. Five forces shape that movement. Mind directs. Heart commits. Body executes. Spirit grounds. Creativity adapts. Unity brings lightness and clarity. Action follows without strain. That state is flow.

Alignment begins the moment inner conflict ends. Energy stops pulling apart and forms one team. Life responds with momentum instead of friction. Progress feels natural rather than forced. Direction sharpens as effort eases.

This work builds your Resilience Architecture as an internal design for strength and focus. Training unfolds across four strands with intent. Leader stories reveal real people who fell and rose. Universal laws govern every collapse and climb. Daily algorithms install winning habits into the body. Client mirrors prove the system works now.

Together these strands turn stress into structure. Failure converts into fire and chaos resolves into clarity. Collapse signals reset rather than ending. Measurement follows through attention to day, focus, and flow. Energy reveals itself as architecture in motion.

Comfort never serves the mission. Entertainment stays outside the design. Building requires pressure and truth. Crisis never breaks you. Ignition begins here.

This is your blueprint to rise, rebuild, and Win Your Day.

Preface

This book formed inside the furnace of my own collapse. Breath came hard on many days. Crisis stripped certainty, title, and identity without mercy. Truth surfaced in those moments. Resilience is not luck or grit. Choice builds it through ritual practiced daily.

Fire gave birth to Win Your Day. A blueprint took shape instead of slogans. Shallow motivation never entered the design. The aim stayed practical and alive. An operating system emerged for those exhausted by survival. Crisis became fuel rather than sentence.

Pages here reject abstraction in favor of lived proof. Stories follow men and women who entered fire and emerged forged. Roosevelt fought for air in darkness. Mandela stood unbroken inside a narrow cell. Oprah rose from silence and poverty into voice. These arcs reflect mirrors rather than entertainment.

Training continues alongside each journey. Twelve Universal Laws govern collapse and ascent without exception. Resilience Pillars decide collapse or stability under pressure. Daily algorithms sharpen response through short disciplined rituals. Fifteen minutes each morning rewires confusion into clarity.

This work speaks directly to you. Not the polished version presented to the world. The real self feels cracks and weight. Doubt whispers about rising again. That question carries an answer. Yes remains available.

Crisis has always engineered transformation across history. Permission arrives through pressure rather than comfort. Turn these pages with honesty and courage. Make a decision without retreat. Whatever brought you here will not mark your ending. Fire will ignite a beginning.

Welcome to Win Your Day.

Acknowledgements

No book is written alone.
Every page carries the fingerprints of those who walked beside me, believed in me, and lifted me when I faltered.

To my loving wife Camlin, thank you for being the anchor of strength for our family.
Your patience, your faith, and your courage made this book possible.

To my two extraordinary sons, Andrew & Austin, your laughter, curiosity, and resilience remind me each day why this mission matters.
May this book one day remind you that every crisis can be converted into creation.

To my Father Edwin, my sister Sherna, and all my family and friends, thank you for showing me that resilience is never a solitary act, but a shared vibration of hope, encouragement, and love.

To Beatrice Pierce who has stood by my side through countless collapses and rebuilds, I rise again as the Phoenix with your intrepid belief in my abilities to become more. Thank you.

To the mentors and teachers who shaped me, some through wisdom and others through challenge, your lessons became the architecture of this work.

To the leaders and visionaries whose stories fill these chapters. Roosevelt, Mandela, Oprah, Jobs, Musk and countless others, your lives stand as proof that human resilience is the most powerful force in existence.

And finally, to you, the reader.
This book is not complete without you.
Your willingness to turn these pages, to lean into the fire of your own crisis, and to rise again is the very reason these words exist.
You are the continuation of this transmission.

With gratitude,

Jason Andrew Safford, Sr.

Transforming Your Crisis

Crisis comes without warning or permission. It arrives as a late-night call that fractures sleep or a diagnosis that steals breath. Betrayal cuts fast. Loss lands heavy. One heartbeat can turn a stable life into ash. Most people believe that moment ends the story.

It does not.

Another truth waits beneath the wreckage. Collapse can begin the narrative instead of sealing it. Doorways hide inside ruins. Crisis never spreads chaos at random. Construction starts the instant illusion burns away.

Pressure strips titles, comfort, and disguise until only truth remains. Fire consumes the temporary and spares what cannot break. Something survives inside the wreckage. An ember endures. That ember carries resilience. This book teaches you how to breathe it into flame.

You will walk beside those who entered the furnace and refused erasure. Theodore Roosevelt gasped for air in the Badlands and advanced anyway. Nelson Mandela endured iron bars without surrender. Oprah Winfrey rose from poverty and fracture and became sovereign. Suffering granted them permission to become more.

Resilience Architecture provides the framework for that ascent. Pressure converts into power through ritual and law. Tools replace despair with direction. Reading alone never completes the work. Application rebuilds the self.

Each chapter shifts your internal frequency toward command. Survival gives way to creation through disciplined action. Collapse transforms into authority earned through fire. The crisis before you carries ignition, not finality.

Your furnace will not mirror Roosevelt's or Mandela's. It belongs to you alone. That reality changes nothing. The fire you face holds enough heat to forge strength. Transformation begins here. Victory follows one deliberate day at a time.

The Story of Resilience

Dawn of Man

Light climbed across raw earth.
Heat split ice. Stone cracked.
Fire learned its name.
A human form stepped forward as fear tightened the
chest.
Resilience moved beside that fear and refused
extinction.

Flint struck bone. Sparks leapt.
Beasts circled the edge of vision.
Cold pressed close. Night swallowed sound.
Hands steadied. Bodies stayed.
Resilience held the line when instinct begged retreat.

Ancient footprints fade into dust.
What carried them forward did not disappear.
Resilience remains inside you.

The First Bond

Hunger scraped the land bare.
Wind tore through open fields.
Mothers wrapped children in breath and bone.
Fathers guarded flame while wounds sealed under
smoke.
Resilience hardened love until it could carry pain.

Storms shattered roofs. Rivers claimed the living. Crops failed. Names vanished.
Tears soaked soil where memory refused erasure.
Resilience rose inside grief and taught humanity to rise with it.
Loss did not end the line.

The Thread Crosses

Resilience thinned itself into thread and crossed distance.
Tribes gathered where it pulled.
Songs climbed new skies.
Trust fractured. Knives flashed. Lines broke.

A father buried his son.
Dawn still found him hunting.
A widow fed children from guarded embers.
Ships split wide seas under iron skies.
Marchers carried justice with Resilience beating in their blood.

What held then holds now.
Resilience gathers strength where trust once shattered.

The Cut

Illusion collapsed.
Smoke cleared.
Resilience sharpened.

A boy gasped through midnight asthma while neighbors doubted his future.

Resilience steadied his ribs and pulled breath from dark.
A soldier crouched in mud and smoke with a letter
pressed to his chest.
Resilience closed his hand around belief.

Crisis burned disguise from will.
Wounds shaped force.
The blade that once saved now cuts weakness away.

The Whisper Behind the Wall

Resilience spoke without sound.
Direction arrived in bone.

Generals fell to loss. Resilience lifted them altered.
Concrete trapped prisoners until cracks mapped escape.
Widows woke to ruin and rebuilt life from vows
Resilience kept alive.
Sick bodies fought for breath while Resilience steadied
the pulse. Refugees crossed fire as Resilience carried
fathers through endless nights.

Children lifted hope like a shield.
Faith stepped beside Resilience and named more than
pain. Together they carried humanity through nights
that tried to end everything.

Now they carry you.

The Wide Open

Resilience loosened survival's grip.
Old forms collapsed.
Embers learned flame.

Soldiers refused fracture as Resilience drove them forward.
Explorers crossed fevered jungles under its quiet command.
Prisoners walked free with Resilience stronger than steel bars.
Comfort fell first. Pride followed. Illusion collapsed last.

Endurance thickened into strength.
Strength rose into creation.
Resilience advanced beyond survival and began to build.

It shaped code.
Shaped marrow.
Carved growth.

Creation replaced endurance.

The Final Whisper

This moment carries the story of Resilience.
It carries the story of humanity.
It carries your own.

Resilience leans close without sound.
You hold more than belief allows.
Fall breaks nothing Resilience teaches to rise.

Seven times down.
Eight times standing.
Resilience remains.

Threshold: Win Your Day

This book does not exist to inspire you.
Resilience already did that.

It exists to teach command.

Resilience responds when you move first.
It sharpens when you choose early.
Organizes itself around decisive action.

Every day resets the field.
Morning decides who holds ground.
Hesitation hands advantage to chaos.

This book shows how pressure rewires identity through
lived action.
How unseen laws govern effort, energy, and outcome.
Structure replaces emotion when emotion fails.

The pillars you will build do not comfort.
They stabilize.
Turn stress into leverage.

Ritual does not soothe collapse.
It converts collapse into direction.

Others learned this in deserts, trenches, silence, and
wild land.
You learn it where you stand now.

Tomorrow does not belong to hope.
It belongs to whoever claims it first.

Wake with intent.
Move with clarity.
Finish what matters.

Crisis does not block the path.
Resilience builds it.

This is how you win your day.

Are you ready to climb?

Part I

The Crisis Advantage: Why Pressure Creates the Elite Leader

Chapter 1: Crisis as Catalyst, Not Collapse

"Do what you can, with what you have, where you are."

~ Theodore Roosevelt

The Furnace of Rock Bottom

Collapse arrives before the mind can brace. Order snaps. Ruin hits fast. Breath tightens in your chest. Thought scatters like ash. The path ahead disappears.

A sound cuts the air. Truth lands hard. A number falls. A promise breaks. Your map burns. Your compass goes cold. Confusion spreads.

Good.

The furnace opens here. Heat strips comfort. Fire rips the masks off. You stand in bright light with nothing to hide. Truth rises through the smoke.

Despair circles low and patient. It calls surrender "rest." It sells drift as relief. Silence invites collapse.

Stand anyway. Rise anyway. The fall does not finish you. The furnace starts you. Cause meets effect. Choice meets impact. One breath sparks the climb.

Leaders get made here. Flame makes them. Loss carves them. Will remains when everything else leaves. Roosevelt learned it. Mandela learned it. Jobs, Schultz, Oprah learned it.

Now it's your turn. Choose. Breathe. Step. Move while the world pulls down. That step starts the rise.

Crisis enters like an engineer. It clears rot. It exposes weak beams. Fire rebuilds your frame. Heat sharpens your sight. Courage hardens in the forge.

The furnace stands ready. Heat waits. Step with purpose. Step with strength. Step toward the version of you that begins here.

Theodore Roosevelt: The Furnace of Confrontation

The Boy Who Refused to Die

Midnight pressed against the windows. Oil lamps shook. Shadows dragged along the walls. A small boy lay rigid on a narrow bed. His breath came broken and sharp. Each inhale scraped like metal on stone.

Theodore Roosevelt balanced at the edge of death. Blue crept across his lips. His chest convulsed upward. Fingers crushed the sheets. Air denied him. Neighbors gathered for the ending. Their whispers carried surrender.

His mother knelt close. Her hands trembled as they cooled his burning skin. Prayer fractured under fear. His father paced the floor. Each step struck with force. Power filled his frame. Helplessness hollowed his eyes. Doctors spoke with care. They marked the boy too weak for manhood.

Silence seized the room. The lamp hissed. The world narrowed to a motionless chest. Breath vanished. His parents froze. They listened. Nothing answered.

Time stretched thin. Panic thickened the air. His mother leaned in. His father bent low. They waited for proof of life.

The proof came violently. Roosevelt's body snapped upright. A savage gasp tore his throat open. Air flooded his lungs. His mother cried out. His father caught him with shaking hands. One breath shattered death's claim.

The furnace ignited there.

Asthma did not retreat. It returned every night. Darkness became a battleground. He met it breath by breath. Dawn arrived as stolen territory. Pain trained him. Air taught discipline. Survival became repetition.

Years later, his father spoke without comfort. "Theodore, you must make your body." The sentence carried no mercy. It carried truth.

Roosevelt answered with action. Iron scorched his arms. Hills burned his legs. Weakness met resistance and failed. Strength never appeared as gift. He dragged it from opposition.

The fragile boy hardened into a man who moved toward storms.

Everything began in choking silence. In lungs that chose defiance.
I will not die tonight.

Asthma pressed its verdict. He confronted it. Effort replaced ease. Will replaced fear. Motion replaced collapse.

Crisis never blocked his path.
Crisis built it.

From one stolen breath, he forged a life that advanced into resistance and never yielded.

The Valentine's Day Massacre of the Soul

The boy survived.
Night after night he wrestled breath from darkness.
Morning arrived as stolen ground. Collapse never finished him. Collapse trained response.

Furnaces do not rest.

February 14, 1884. Valentine's Day.

Morning light slid across the house on East 20th Street. Roses scented the air. Clean linen softened the rooms. Upstairs, a newborn cried. The sound carried promise. Alice lay pale beneath blankets. Childbirth drained her strength. Down the hall, his mother Mittie burned with fever. Typhoid tightened its grip.

Roosevelt moved between the rooms. Joy struck one moment. Fear followed the next. He kissed his wife's hand. He counted his mother's breaths. Life waited on one side of the hall. Death gathered on the other. The house held both without mercy.

By noon the air shifted. Mittie's breathing thinned. Her eyes lost focus. Strength drained away. Roosevelt knelt beside her. He held her hand. Her chest stilled. Loss hit without warning or restraint.

He rose and crossed the hall.

Alice lay quiet. Her voice no longer answered. Complications stole her strength. Her heart failed. Roosevelt stood helpless as life left her body. He spoke too late. Silence answered first.

Mother gone.
Wife gone.
One house.
One day.
Nothing left standing.

He opened his journal. He wrote one line.

The light has gone out of my life.

The book closed. The world followed.

Walls pressed inward. Streets narrowed into cages. Memory struck from every corner. Breath failed him indoors. Breath failed him in the city. He chose distance over decay.

Roosevelt fled west. He left his infant daughter with his sister. He rode toward the Dakota Badlands.

He did not wait to heal.
He turned and met the wound.

The West did not comfort him. It measured him. Its land offered no language for grief, only tests that required proof. He rode into that open verdict with sorrow bound tight against his ribs.

Collapse did not seal him shut.
It summoned him.

Loss taught him balance under load. Pain showed him where to plant his feet. Breath returned only after he stopped circling suffering and stepped directly into its center.

Grief struck once and stayed.
What remained stood harder.

The furnace deepened. The man stepped forward.

The Wilderness Forge

The Dakota Badlands offered no retreat.
They demanded proof.

Cliffs split the sky. Wind dragged grit across the plains. Rock lay exposed like bone. Each mile stripped comfort from the body. Each night tested resolve.

Roosevelt arrived carrying grief tight against his chest. He asked nothing from the land. He came for judgment. Locals watched him closely. They named him a soft Easterner. They measured him against winter and waited for failure.

The country answered first.

Storms rolled hard through the hills. Wind tore at his coat. Ice locked the rivers. Heat cracked the ground. Law thinned to distance. Risk followed every step.

One night he entered his cabin and found three thieves waiting inside. They wanted silence. Roosevelt met them without hesitation. His rifle held steady. His eyes did not move. The men froze. Dawn came cold and slow. He marched them across frozen ground to the nearest town. The law spoke praise. Roosevelt spoke nothing. Duty needed no defense.

Another day the weather closed its fist.

Snow rose without warning. Wind cut like wire. Ice burned his face raw. His horses collapsed in drifts. Men vanished in storms like this. Roosevelt pressed forward. He crawled through brush. He shielded fire through the night.

Morning found frost locked in his beard. Blood split his lips. His lungs burned. He stood alone and laughed once. The storm released him.

Work followed without ceremony. Wood split his palms. Cattle dragged him through mud and thunder. Hunger stretched days thin. Sleep came broken. Strength gathered slowly. Breath deepened. The frail body disappeared under use.

Silence finished what hardship began.

No audience watched him. No reward waited. The land stripped him down and rebuilt him without instruction. Crisis no longer startled him. Exposure had trained his instincts.

When he rode east again, nothing rattled. His frame held. His breath stayed steady. His will moved before thought.

The wilderness did not save him.
It made retreat impossible.

He learned the truth only men under pressure discover. Survival belongs to those who ride forward when everything else turns back.

The Rough Rider's Charge

By 1898, restlessness lived in Roosevelt's bones.
The Badlands had hardened him. Politics had steadied him. Something remained unfinished. War answered that hunger. Spain held Cuba. The nation called. Roosevelt moved.

He resigned his post in Washington and raised a volunteer cavalry. Cowboys rode beside Ivy League athletes. Ranch hands stood next to city men. Critics laughed. They called him a performer. They accused him of chasing legend. Roosevelt ignored the noise and built readiness.

Cuba greeted them with heat and smoke. Air pressed heavy on the lungs. Bullets cracked across open ground.

Soldiers flattened themselves against the earth. Fear pinned the line. Movement stopped.

Roosevelt mounted his horse and faced the hill. Spanish rifles lined the ridge. He raised his voice once. Forward. Then he rode into fire.

The men followed without order or pause. Smoke swallowed the climb. Fear broke under motion. Boots tore into dirt. Will pulled them upward.

Gunfire shredded the air. Earth burst at their feet. The slope fought every step. Roosevelt did not slow. He drove ahead with measured force. The line surged. The ridge gave way. The hill fell.

The child who once gasped for breath now led men through bullets. The widower who once fled grief now stood steady before death. The man shaped by storms and solitude advanced without hesitation.

Every furnace converged on that climb. Asthma trained endurance. Loss forced motion. Wilderness forged instinct. Nothing here surprised him.

San Juan Hill broke. Roosevelt stood at the crest. Sweat ran. Smoke drifted. Calm held. Crisis met action. Danger met direction.

The charge did not make him legendary.
It revealed what confrontation had already built.

Resilience never lived in theory for him.
It lived in motion, under fire, without retreat.

The Presidency Under Siege

The presidency offered no reward.
It delivered exposure.

In 1901, at forty-two, Roosevelt entered the Oval Office through violence. An assassin's bullet ended McKinley's life. The nation staggered. Grief flooded the streets. Roosevelt stepped forward without rehearsal. The weight of the country struck all at once.

Crisis followed without pause.

Winter tightened its grip. Coal bins emptied. Homes froze. Miners demanded safety and fair pay. Owners refused movement. Roosevelt summoned both sides to the White House. He issued one line. Settle this dispute or I seize the mines. His voice carried decision. His will carried consequence. The strike ended.

Power answered back.

Monopolies strangled markets. Titans bent prices and crushed competition. Wall Street expected compliance. Roosevelt chose confrontation. He wielded the Sherman Antitrust Act without hesitation. Lawsuits followed. Untouchable men found limits. Newspapers cried recklessness. Roosevelt advanced without noise.

Danger pressed close.

Threats crowded his mail. Shadows followed his movements. Crowds offered applause and risk in equal measure. His staff watched carefully. Roosevelt walked steady. Breath held firm. A lifetime of pressure had stripped fear of novelty. Weapons did not move him. He had met worse in silence.

The presidency burned daily.

Each front demanded decision. No cover waited. No retreat existed. His past answered every test. Asthma taught him control under strain. Grief taught him posture after devastation. The Badlands taught him endurance without escape. San Juan Hill taught him movement through fear.

Roosevelt acted.

He spoke plainly. He drew lines and held them. When the nation shook, he stood forward. Crisis did not fracture him. It clarified him.

The furnaces had already written the code.
The presidency exposed it.

Power did not change him.
It revealed what confrontation had forged.

The Final Furnace: The River of Doubt

By 1914, Roosevelt had already lived several complete lives. War tested him. Power exposed him. History recorded him. Most men at that summit chose comfort. They chose reflection. They chose distance from risk.

Roosevelt chose confrontation.

He accepted an invitation into unmapped jungle. Locals spoke in lowered voices. They named the river the River of Doubt. He brought his son Kermit. He brought soldiers and guides. Certainty stayed behind.

The jungle answered immediately.

Heat crushed the air. Insects carried sickness. The river hid death beneath dark water. Food vanished. Morale splintered. Men mutinied. Illness spread. Every mile stripped strength and patience.

Roosevelt moved ahead one morning. Stone tore into his leg. Blood followed. In that jungle, infection meant execution by time. Fever seized him. Pain hollowed his body. He drifted between waking and dark dreams in a hammock strung above mud.

He spoke plainly. Leave me here. Save the expedition.

He did not dramatize it. He accepted consequence.

Kermit refused.

The son did not leave.
 He closed the distance and took the weight.

Hands dragged a failing body forward. Water burned its way past cracked lips. An arm locked around a collapsing frame and refused release. Each step arrived on borrowed strength.

Roosevelt surged back in fragments. Vision cleared. Then darkness returned. His body folded. Words broke from him. He asked for rest. He asked for release.

The jungle remained still.
 So did Kermit.

Breath offered nothing here.
Grief carried no currency.
Authority dissolved on contact.
The body failed first.
What stayed answered everything.

Against expectation, Roosevelt endured. Scars followed. Strength did not return. Survival arrived stripped of illusion.

The spirit held.

He carried wounds forward. He carried a final clarity. Resilience did not require victory. It required choice under failure.

The child who once fought for air now surrendered nothing to the jungle. The man who buried grief in open land faced mortality without disguise. The leader who confronted nations now confronted his own limits.

Each collapse struck first.
Every response followed as decision.
Decision shaped effect.

Together they formed the man who met the end without retreat.

Universal Law: Cause & Effect

When crisis strikes, your response becomes the cause that shapes your destiny, and every breath you choose under pressure creates the effect that forges who you become.

Core Lesson

Roosevelt built strength in the heat of crisis. Asthma pressed his lungs as a boy. Grief carved him open after the deaths of his mother and wife. The Badlands cut his hands and hardened his frame. San Juan Hill tested his courage under fire. The presidency demanded resolve as nations strained. The River of Doubt pushed him past exhaustion. Each furnace burned away comfort and revealed the next layer of command. Crisis shaped him into a man who welcomed pressure and forged capacity.

Another truth rose with each trial. Collapse forced choice. Choice shaped structure. Structure produced a stronger self. Roosevelt advanced because he acted while others waited. He built his body through discipline. He deepened his heart through loss. He strengthened his will through frontier labor. He steadied his spirit through national danger. He expanded his creativity through exploration. He treated hardship as architect and turned pressure into power.

A simple pattern emerges. Crisis sets the blueprint. Choice lifts the framework. Repetition strengthens the beams. Identity rises from the structure that follows.

Roosevelt proved the path. Leaders grow inside the furnace. Leaders build themselves in the fire.

Client Story: From Ruin to Relentless

Erik walked blind into the storm.

In 2019, real estate bent to his steady hand and fast stride. Deals closed inside bright glass towers. Handshakes carried wealth and certainty. A German car waited below with fresh leather and quiet pride. Investors followed. Checks cleared faster than signatures. Days moved clean and sharp.

Then the ground split.

COVID erased deals before morning meetings ended. Banks locked doors as tenants vanished. Properties bled value until numbers cut deep. Calls stopped. Dinners fell silent. Former allies dodged his voice. Marriage cracked under a fear he could not name.

A small apartment replaced the towers. Paint peeled in long strips. Sleep came on a sagging mattress heavy with regret. Accounts drained. Confidence followed. Mornings arrived with tight lungs and added weight. The phone glowed without answers. Nights stretched. Days folded together. Courage narrowed to lifting the blinds. Collapse pinned him in place.

Ignition came on a Tuesday call.

His voice broke as he asked for help he felt unworthy to receive. Shame bent him lower than debt ever could. I listened, then cut through the fog. Humiliation is not identity. Collapse never defines. Collapse trains. Stillness burns. Work forges.

Resistance shook his head. Discipline became the rope. Listening struck the first spark.

Reframing arrived without theory or filler. A code formed in one session and stayed simple enough to hold. Five a.m. arrived before despair spoke. Three lines entered a journal. Fear named. Lesson claimed. Action chosen before noon. Movement followed through pushups, squats, and sharp morning runs. Sweat marked return. One action landed each day. Perfection died. Motion ruled. Nights closed with one question: did I climb or collapse? The frame held.

Nothing changed outside in those early weeks. Accounts stayed empty. Silence lingered. Labels stuck.

Inside, gears turned.

Leverage replaced loss. Self-study replaced blame. Reframing finished its work.

Three months later, leanness returned. Eyes sharpened. Shoulders carried intent instead of shame. Small income streams formed and held. Effort replaced opinion. Speech tightened. Boundaries reset. Value stood clean.

Six months brought strength into every step. One year delivered clarity. Two years built a business anchored in systems, not ego. Applause lost appeal. Mastery took its place.

Legacy followed without announcement.

Life rebuilt into the man required, not the role once played. Discipline held. Deliberation guided. Breakage lost authority. Clients now learn the same code. Boardrooms receive counsel earned through fire. Leadership rises from scars, not slogans.

Collapse did not destroy Erik.
Collapse built him.

Tools & Tactics: The Resilience Rope

A 4-Step Tool for Climbing Out of Collapse

Breathe. Write. Move. Reflect. Repeat.

When crisis hits, you do not rise by chance.
You rise by activation.

This rope is not poetic.
It is not comfortable.
It is functional.

Grip it daily.
Climb with intention.

Crisis does not announce itself.
It does not wait for confidence.
It rewards readiness.

Use this tool every day.
When collapse comes, you will not fracture.
You will climb.

Step 1: The Decision Breath

Mental Mastery

Purpose: Interrupt panic. Reclaim command.

Execution:
Sit still. Close your eyes.
Take one deliberate inhale, even if shallow.
Whisper once: *I choose to rise.*

Why it works:
Choice always comes before strength.
The breath hard-codes that choice into the nervous system.
Control returns here.

Step 2: The Collapse Journal

Emotional Mastery

Purpose: Convert chaos into clarity.

Execution:
Each morning, write two lines only:

• What collapsed me yesterday?
• What choice strengthens me today?

Why it works:
Cause becomes visible.
Effect becomes intentional.
Response replaces reaction.
Emotion loses power the moment it is named.

Step 3: The Furnace Move

Physical Mastery

Purpose: Prove to the body that you do not fold.

Execution:
Move until heat appears.
Walk hard. Push. Lift. Run.
No optimization.
No negotiation.

Why it works:
Motion rewires belief faster than thought.
Pressure met with action teaches resilience at the speed of the body.

Step 4: The Night Check

Spiritual + Creative Mastery

Purpose: Lock the day into identity.

Execution:
Stand in silence before sleep.

Ask one question only:
Did I collapse today, or did I climb?

Do not justify.
Do not explain.

Why it works:
Honest reflection converts experience into wisdom.
Wisdom compounds.
Tomorrow strengthens because tonight was faced.

The Law of the Rope

You do not build resilience during collapse.
You reveal it.

Train daily.
Grip the rope before you need it.

When the ground disappears, you won't search for strength.
You'll already be climbing.

Algorithm: Collapse to Command

(15 Minutes)

Name It. Breathe It. Choose It. Move It. Seal It.

This is the rope out of collapse.
Use it every morning.
Rise on command.

1. Name the Problem (2 minutes)

Close your eyes.
Say one clear sentence:

"The problem is..."

Stop there.

Do not explain.
Do not justify.
Do not blame.

Clarity creates strength.

2. Choose with Breath (2 minutes)

Sit still.
Take one slow inhale.

Whisper once:
"I choose to rise."

Repeat three times.

The body learns the decision before the mind argues.

3. Pick Action → Pick Result (5 minutes)

Write two short lines:

Action: The one thing I will do today.
Result: What that action helps create.

One action.
One result.
Nothing else.

Simplicity produces force.

4. Move the Body (5 minutes)

Move with effort.

Push-ups.
Squats.
March in place.

Continue until warmth appears.

The body learns a single truth:
I push back.

5. Seal the Day (1 minute)

Stand tall.
Say out loud:

"Hard things make me stronger."

Carry that posture forward.

The Rule

Do not wait to feel ready.
Act first.
Strength follows.

Reflection Questions

- When pressure hit today, did I inhale or freeze?
- What cause did I choose, and what effect followed?
- If collapse is ignition, what fire in me is waiting?

Pillar Activation: The Five Pillars of Resilience Architecture

Game Plan

This chapter proves resilience is built, not wished for. Roosevelt survived repeated crisis by activating five internal engines. Those same engines live inside you, ready for command.

The Five Pillars:
1. Mental Precision
Crisis tried to scatter Roosevelt's focus.
Asthma, grief, war, and wilderness demanded clarity.
He reduced noise to one question.
Forward action restored direction.

Activation: Cut to one decision. Move.

2. Emotional Power
Loss surged. Fear pressed hard.
Roosevelt refused emotional drift.
He named the feeling and moved his body.
Breath and motion converted emotion into drive.

Activation: Name it. Move it.

3. Spiritual Alignment
Meaning anchored him when scale threatened collapse.
Purpose grew larger than pain.
Gratitude steadied resolve.
Belief tied effort to service beyond self.

Activation: Remember who this serves.

4. Physical Mastery
Endurance decided survival. Fatigue warned early.
Roosevelt answered with posture, water, breath, and
movement. The body carried the mission when will
alone could not.

Activation: Command the body. The mind will follow.

5. Imaginative Strategy
Old patterns failed under pressure. Adaptation saved
him. One new idea opened the path forward. Creativity
turned danger into advantage.

Activation: Ask what has not been tried.

Coach J's Challenge
You are not missing anything. These pillars already
exist inside you.
When crisis hits:
- Identify the signal.
- Activate the pillar.
- Restore command.

Discipline turns breakdown into momentum.

Locker–Room Reflection
Which pillar needs training today to move your life
forward right now?

Chapter 2: The Furnace of Setback

Where Resilience is Forged

"Sometimes life hits you in the head with a brick. Don't lose faith."

~ Steve Jobs

Pressure is the architect that shatters obsolete wiring so stronger design can emerge.
It arrives to audit. Strain climbs and exposes circuits that no longer carry the load.
What snaps first always required replacement.
The break reveals the blueprint.

If pressure keeps finding you, your current design is no longer built for the load you carry.

Heat rises inside before collapse announces itself. Breath shortens as systems drift out of sync. Muscle tightens where truth remains unspoken. Pain marks the joint that failed inspection. The forge activates when stability proves false.

Thought accelerates under demand.
Beliefs transmit silent commands into every decision.
Emotion magnetizes outcomes that match its charge.
Fear compresses perception until options vanish.
Discipline restores ground and returns choice.

Repetition hardens patterns into prisons.
Untested loops mature into invisible walls.
Stories calcify identity when comfort replaces truth.
New design breaks rooms that once defined limits.
Renewal begins the moment architecture faces scrutiny.

Exile cut Steve Jobs to bone.
Apple removed him and the world closed the book. He rejected their ending and accepted refinement instead. NeXT stripped excess and sharpened thought. Pixar trained his eye to see essence over noise.

Return followed signal, not timing.
Clarity walked back into Apple before profit ever did.
The iMac announced intention through form.
The iPod converted clarity into motion.
The iPhone rewired desire by redesigning attention.

Life obeys this law without exception.
Pressure amplifies fear when rhythm disappears.
Burnout smolders when pace outruns purpose. Silence
tightens the chest before collapse speaks. Each signal
marks circuitry prepared for upgrade.

Force rarely builds what lasts.
Clean signal moves more weight than effort.
Precision outperforms strain every time.
Courage forms when you end the loop draining power.
Strength appears when you install the loop that carries
load.

Truth clears fog without violence.
Collapse names the crucible.
Redesign marks ascent.
A stronger identity emerges only after the weaker
fractures.
Release becomes the gateway to growth.

Jobs released the world he built.
That release delivered the world he required.
Legacy expanded when control loosened.
The same doorway stands open now.
Step into the heat and rise.

Steve Jobs: The Furnace of Exile

In 1985, Steve Jobs stood at the summit.
A garage obsession had become a global revolution.
Apple ruled homes and offices.
Jobs ruled Apple.
Before thirty, belief alone bent markets to his will.

Vision burned behind his eyes.
Demands cut through comfort without apology.
Confidence wrapped him like armor.
The world leaned toward his signal.
Then the ambush arrived.

Behind sealed doors, doubt sharpened into weapons.
Too reckless.
Too volatile.
Too uncontrollable.
The room that echoed command hardened into
judgment.

The vote landed clean.
Fast.
Merciless.
One motion erased him.
One day, an emperor. The next, an exile.

He left Apple stripped of more than a title.
Identity collapsed with the badge.
Meaning vanished overnight.
The work that carried his name disappeared.
Power exited without ceremony.

This was not termination. The identity could no longer carry the weight.

The Public Execution

Humiliation followed him into daylight.
The press turned predator.
Prodigy became punchline.
Arrogant. Narcissistic. Impossible.
Headlines carved caricature where legacy once stood.

Rivals laughed openly.
His name became shorthand for excess and failure.
At night, silence pressed hardest.
Betrayal replayed without mercy.
Certainty fractured into noise.

Anger surged first.
Shame followed.
Confusion filled the gaps.
He broadcast collapse.
The world reflected it back with inked blades.

This was not setback.
It was annihilation of self.

The Wilderness of Exile

Exile does not erase leaders.
It disassembles them.

Jobs built NeXT with fury driving every decision.
He aimed to prove Apple wrong.

Machines rose sharp and beautiful.
Engineers admired them.
The market ignored them.

Brilliance no longer carried weight.
At the same time, he acquired a fragile animation studio
called Pixar.
Most dismissed it as indulgence.
A distraction for a fallen king.
They misjudged the furnace.

Animation demanded patience he lacked.
Thousands of frames.
Years of repetition.
Relentless revision under threat of collapse.
Money evaporated fast.

Failure circled close.
Jobs tried to sell Pixar for scraps.
No one wanted it.
That rejection cut deeper than Apple ever had.
Exile felt permanent.

The Rewiring

Something worked beneath the wreckage.
Failure burned arrogance to ash.
Waiting taught restraint.
Repetition trained precision.
Simplicity sharpened power.

Noise weakened force.
Focus multiplied impact.

Chaos refined into signal.
Jobs was not rebuilding companies.
He was rebuilding the man who would lead them.

Exile rewired him.

The Turn

In 1995, Pixar released *Toy Story*.
Mockery detonated into culture shock.
Audiences flooded theaters.
Records shattered.
Pixar went public.

The exile became wealthy again.
Then fate twisted harder.
By 1997, Apple hovered weeks from death.
Cash vanished.
Vision collapsed.

The board reached for the man they expelled.
Jobs returned to the halls that stripped him bare. Not as
a prodigy.
As a forged leader.
He returned without apology.

The Final Form

Jobs cut Apple to the bone.
Dozens of products collapsed into four.
Projects died.
Divisions vanished.
Noise fell silent.

Energy no longer scattered.
It struck with precision.
Design shifted toward humans, not engineers.
Machines became intimate.
Technology became identity.

The iMac.
The iPod.
The iPhone.
The iPad.
Each rewired how the world lived, worked, and
imagined the future.

Exile did not break Steve Jobs.
Exile finished him.

The Universal Law: Polarity

Every collapse contains its opposite, because crisis and
creation always arrive as twins, and the moment you
stand inside that truth you turn every fall into the force
that lifts you.

Core Lesson

Steve Jobs entered the world with sharp talent and
scattered alignment. Early brilliance carried force while
fragile emotion cracked beneath it. Pressure rose. The
board cut him from his own company. Silence filled the
void. Collapse cleared illusions. Identity broke open and
revealed a mind built for reinvention.

Exile shaped his next ascent. Pain carved discipline into his craft. NeXT became a forge. Pixar became a school of ruthless clarity. Long nights refined precision. New trials reshaped humility. Purpose shifted. The boy who chased glory faded. A creator with grounded vision stepped forward.

Return called him home. Apple opened its gates to a man rebuilt in fire. He answered with calm eyes and steady breath. Noise vanished under his knife. Systems tightened. Culture warmed. Products emerged like clean lines on white paper. iMac, iPod, iPhone, and iPad rose as extensions of a reordered soul.

His path became the pattern. Collapse stripped weakness. Exile built coherence. Return expressed mastery. Jobs climbed by rewiring his identity until each domain aligned with truth. His arc teaches one command. Fall with honesty. Rebuild with intent. Rise with clarity earned in the furnace.

Client Story: Polarity Furnace

Zak built a reputation as the man who never missed. Admiration followed his rise through corner offices and fast salaries.
Teams moved when he spoke.
Effort carved every step forward.
One belief ruled all. Outwork everyone.

The mindset carried him for years.
Success stacked like trophies.
Leaders leaned on him when projects turned grim.

Momentum hid its cost.
Every surge pulled a counterweight.

Collapse did not kick down doors.
It slipped beneath the surface.
Boredom struck first.
Meetings dulled sharp edges.
Projects drained spark.

Fatigue followed.
Training vanished.
Meals lost intention.
Sleep fractured into caffeine-soaked hours.
Mental static filled the gaps.

Thoughts looped without mercy.
Nothing matters.
I must keep running.
Stopping means failure.
Noise burned against his skull.

People sensed the shift.
His voice tightened.
Small questions triggered snaps.
Greetings passed unheard.
Focus evaporated.

Home grew heavier.
Silence pressed inward.
Evenings ended in darkness lit by a glowing phone.
His wife asked what pulled him under.
He answered tired. Truth ran deeper.

The reckoning arrived on a gray Tuesday.
Cold air hung still.
Hands crushed the steering wheel until pain registered.
Chest locked.
Breath thinned.

A voice cut through. Stop pretending.
Nothing changes.
Muscles refused command.
Shame carried him home an hour later.
The system had failed.

That night he called me.
Color drained from his voice.
He named the emptiness.
Grinding continued because stopping felt impossible.
Twelve words exposed collapse.

Our first meeting rejected old scripts.
Pushing harder built his prison.
Clarity replaced noise.
You are not broken.
Your wiring failed.

Exhaustion signals a burned circuit.
More effort will not save you.
Frequency will.
Confusion crossed his face.
Explanation followed.

Thought loops fire like electrical rhythms.

Change the current and outcomes shift.
Polarity always offers an opposite path.
Fear hides ascent.
Listening returned.

Rewiring began small.
One fear entered the page.
If I stop, I fall behind.
Its opposite followed.
If I stop, I breathe.

Shoulders loosened.
Old circuitry cracked.
Identification came next.
Five sentences revealed the storm.
They were current, not truth.

I cannot fail.
Nothing matters.
Options disappeared.
Stopping kills progress.
Rest equals danger.

Higher frequency replaced them.
Failure guides learning.
Purpose exists here.
Choice surrounds me.
Rest extends reach.

Repetition carved new grooves.
Action sealed change.
Gratitude entered mornings.

Silence preceded work.
One essential task replaced ten.

Meaning outranked urgency.
A ritual formed.
Forty-five minutes of deep work.
Fifteen minutes of hopeful creation.
One unit delivered daily.

A call.
One proposal.
An extra conversation.
Resistance screamed.
Old circuits fought.

Repetition won.
Static faded.
Clarity returned.
Energy stirred.
Authority softened.

Coworkers noticed calm presence.
Listening deepened.
Decisions arrived without fear.
Laughter returned at home.
Breath came easy again.

Zak learned the same law that lifted Steve Jobs from exile.
Collapse opens the return.

Three months passed.

The frozen man moved with purpose.
Grinding lost control.
Belief rewired at the core.
Teams felt direction, not tension.

Trust replaced force.
Presence returned at home.
Pressure still arrived.
Work still demanded strength.
Teeth unclenched.

Signal aligned.
Grit built the climb.
Frequency built the life.
Zak did not climb back.
Transformation took over.

Tools & Tactics: The Dual-Rail Daily Prompt

Use this every morning to convert tension into traction.

1. The Inverse Journal (5 minutes)

Write one sentence. No editing.

Fear:
"What I am afraid will happen today is..."

Now flip it. Write the inverse truth.

Inverse:
"If this fear exists, it means I am being invited to..."

Example:
"I will fail." → "I will discover what works."

This trains the mind to recognize that collapse and growth run on parallel rails.

2. Two-Hand Practice (60 minutes total)

Operate in polarity. Not comfort.

Hard Rail — 45 minutes
Attack the task you are avoiding.
The one that creates resistance.
No multitasking. No polishing. Just pressure.

Light Rail — 15 minutes
Create without constraint.
Sketch. Write. Map. Dream.
No outcome required. Only expansion.

One hand builds strength.
One hand builds vision.
Together, they prevent burnout and drift.

3. The Shipping Ritual (Non-negotiable)

Thought without output is stagnation.

Ship one unit today. Small counts.

- Send the email
- Publish the post
- Share the idea
- Deliver the draft

Momentum is proof of alignment.

4. Polarity Pause (As Needed)

When stuck, ask one question:

"What is the opposite signal available right now?"

- Anger → What do I care about?
- Fear → What do I want?
- Loss → What has been cleared?

This is not reflection.
It is navigation.

5. The Forge Reminder (Seal the Day)

Say this out loud before work begins:

"I can hold the dark and still move forward."

Repeat before speaking.
Repeat before acting.

Both rails exist.
You move by riding them. Not choosing one.

Algorithm: The Both-Hands Reset (15 Minutes)

Use this when you feel stuck or unsure.

Step 1. Find the Opposite (3 minutes)

Write one short sentence.

Fear or doubt:
"What I am worried about is..."

Now flip it.

Opposite truth:
"If this fear is here, it means..."

Example:
"I will be rejected."
→ "I will be redirected."

This helps your mind see a new path.

Step 2. Use Both Hands (10 minutes)

Hard Hand (7 minutes)

Work on the hardest task.

Rules:
· One task
· No breaks
· No fixing

64

Stay with it until time is up.

This builds strength.

Hopeful Hand (3 minutes)

Create something free and fun.

Pick one:
· Draw an idea
· Write a bold title
· List three dreams

No judging.

This opens imagination.

Step 3. Ship One Thing (2 minutes)

Send one small thing out.

· Post
· Send
· Share
· Demo

Small is good.
Done is better.

This restores forward motion.

Core Reminder

Hard and hopeful move together.
When one hand feels lost, the other leads you back.

You are not done.
You are in motion.

Reflection Questions

1. Which three thoughts hit you most when stress rises, and how do they shape your day?
2. What is the opposite truth of each thought, and which one challenges you the most?
3. What small daily action will you use to embody the new truth, and how will you stay consistent for seven days?

Pillar Activation: The Forge of Polarity

Game Plan

Collapse is not the end.
It is the forge.
Pressure exposes weak wiring so redesign replaces force.
What fails reveals where growth waits.
Polarity turns strain into leverage.

Pillar Activation

Mental Precision (Head)
Exile forced Steve Jobs to cut noise into signal.
Fewer products. Cleaner decisions. One focus.

Physical Mastery (Body)
Time rebuilt what speed destroyed.
Pixar trained patience and rhythm. Energy returned.

Emotional Power (Heart)
Anger and shame stayed.
Reaction ended. Resolve began.

Spiritual Alignment (Soul)
Ego fell away. Purpose surfaced.
Meaning stabilized the work.

Imaginative Strategy (Vision)
Simplicity sharpened impact.
Design served humans. Imagination shaped reality.

Coach J's Challenge
When pressure spikes, do not push harder.
Pause. Name the fear loop. Flip it. Work one hard task
with discipline. Create freely. Ship something small.
Ride both rails without burning out.

Locker-Room Reflection
Which fear is looping now, and which opposite truth
will you train today?

Chapter 3: The Reinvention Threshold

"In life, you can't have everything. But you can have the things that really matter to you."

~ Howard Schultz

Collapse does not knock.
It erases the ground you were standing on.
A quiet shift steals your balance before panic can speak.
One closed door denies a future you assumed secure.
A verdict lands and calm dissolves on contact.
Silence follows, and you must face what remains.

Silence met Howard Schultz when he returned to his creation.
The company still functioned, but its soul had thinned.
Espresso machines hissed while purpose fell quiet.
Speed replaced craft.
Growth blurred standards once held sacred.
Leadership no longer matched the mission it claimed.

Reinvention begins only here.
Pressure fractures old forms that once felt permanent.
Certainty loosens its grip and familiar stories lose authority.
Fear rises as comfort collapses and distraction tempts escape.
Most people retreat at this edge.
They trade truth for safety and call it survival.

Schultz stepped forward.
He shut down stores to retrain hands and restore ritual.
He listened beneath charts and forecasts others trusted blindly.
Tired eyes behind counters told him what numbers never could.
A living core still breathed, neglected but alive.
Crisis demanded essence, not the man he used to be.

Your collapse follows the same law.
Fire clears what blocks ascent.
Loss removes roles that no longer fit purpose.
Pressure strips what never carried truth.
A quiet signal rises through ash and doubt.
The doorway appears because the break carved the frame.

This moment marks the threshold.
Reinvention begins now.
Crisis does not take you.
Crisis shows you who remains.

Howard Schultz: The Furnace of Closed Doors

Howard Schultz never sold coffee.
He sold belonging.

Home, work, and a third place met inside each cup.
Names mattered. Smiles arrived before taste.
Customers felt seen before they were served.

That promise built an empire.

Growth followed feeling.
Scale rewarded intimacy.
Then momentum hardened into habit.

No alarm sounded when purpose blurred.

Early days carried quiet joy.
Stores became classrooms.
Baristas moved with rhythm and care.

Steam rose.
Grinders growled.
Warm light gathered strangers into pause.

People stayed longer than planned.

Friends lingered.
Arguments softened.
Dreams formed on tabletops.

Coffee anchored the moment.
It never stood alone.

Starbucks meant safety.
Ritual created loyalty.
Belonging became the currency.

The Year the Siren Lost Her Voice

By 2007, growth outran control.

New stores crowded old corners.
Speed replaced craft.
Machines rose between hands and faces.

Steel blocked connection.
Noise stayed constant.
Soul slipped away unnoticed.

Beans lingered too long.
Air lost its snap.
Burnt cheese smothered rooms built for pause.

Music blared.
Spaces filled.
Meaning emptied.

Then recession hit.

Five-dollar rituals cracked.
Lines shrank.
Sales slid.

Investors scattered.
The siren dimmed.
Schultz no longer held the chair.

He walked stores as a guest in his own home.

Timers owned attention.
Guests waited unseen.
Shots ran thin.

The air told the truth.

One memo followed.
No mercy.
No disguise.

"We lost the experience.
We lost the soul."

The wound showed.
The board summoned him back.
Collapse waited inside his creation.

Ignition

Most leaders hide fractures behind language.

Howard Schultz chose exposure.

Every U.S. store closed for one night.
Doors locked together.
Lights went dark.

Revenue stopped.
The company went silent.

Inside, partners trained.
Hands relearned the shot.
Craft reclaimed space from speed.

No customers entered.
Only skill mattered.

A hard line followed.

Espresso came first.
Nothing followed without it.

Analysts laughed.
Stock dipped.
Fear surfaced.

Retreat never appeared.

Ignition came through confrontation.
Schultz stepped into fire.
Repair began at truth's smallest unit.

From craft came trust.
In trust came motion.

Reframe

Ignition alone never saves a company.
Reframing does.

Schultz cut deep.

Hundreds of stores closed.
Teams cried.
Headlines declared decline.

He named the pain.
Called it pruning.

Breakfast sandwiches disappeared.
Coffee spoke again.
Air cleared.

Grinders returned to sight.
The bar reclaimed the stage.

Then the sentence landed.

"We are not a coffee company serving people.
We are a people company serving coffee."

No spin followed.
Soft edges did not survive.

The frame changed everything.

People reclaimed center.
Coffee became the medium.
Recovery found footing in identity restored.

Transformation

Truth held.
The climb began.

Partners rallied worldwide.
Language stayed clean.
Craft returned to speech.

Fresh beans replaced stale stock.
Shots landed true.
Eyes lifted behind the bar.

Menus slimmed.
Choices clarified.
Theater returned.

Single-cup brewers restored ritual.
Stores invited pause.
Idea walls welcomed unfiltered voice.

Dreams appeared.
Complaints followed.
Action came fast.

Innovation moved with restraint.

Pike Place honored roots.
VIA proved speed could keep soul.
Loyalty felt like membership.

Mobile ordering formed early.
Others copied later.

People stayed central.

Benefits held.
Stock grants remained.
One message echoed.

"We own the comeback."

By 2010, Starbucks stood lean.
Focus returned.
The future rose from the original vow.

Legacy

Resilience never began in a boardroom.

It began in Brooklyn.

A father fell at work.
A job vanished.
Dignity followed.

No safety net arrived.

A boy watched his father break.
The vow formed in silence.

When leadership came, people would matter.

Decades later, the vow held.

Markets demanded safety.
Schultz chose humanity.

Analysts measured risk.
He measured alignment.

Growth blinded craft.
Recession exposed truth.
A memo cut denial clean.

Stores went dark to relearn basics.
Leadership returned to fire.

Identity reset.

People reclaimed center.
Rot cleared.
Values stood plain.

Transformation followed through discipline.

Aroma returned.
Theater revived.
 Trust regained motion.

Digital rails formed without erasing touch.

The legacy arrived quietly.

A global brand still sells coffee.
It trades in dignity and belonging.

A vow from a small apartment guided a massive company.
Crisis opened the door.
Howard Schultz stepped through, and held it open.

The Universal Law: Vibration

The signal you broadcast becomes the reality that answers, because vibration always returns its source.

Core Lesson

Howard Schultz returned to truth when the company drifted. Clarity cut through noise as he named the fracture with no escape route. Stores closed. Craft restarted. Purpose rose from the floor and reclaimed its seat at the center. A leader rebuilt the frame by choosing people before product.

Shops regained breath as partners found pride again. Fresh grind filled rooms with honest scent. Light softened hard corners. Culture warmed as human care replaced speed. Guests felt seen. Connection returned as the core promise revived its pulse.

Change moved through the system like a clean tide. Rotten habits fell away. Standards sharpened. Innovation followed once alignment held steady. Craft regained weight. Trust grew cup by cup. The company shifted from drift to coherence through work, not wish.

Starbucks regained life because Schultz rebuilt from truth. He aligned purpose with action. He restored awareness across every level. He treated crisis as teacher. He built a culture that carried belonging as its true product. Resilience lived in that choice.

Client Story: The Architecture of Return

November 2020 sealed the world behind closed doors. Offices emptied overnight. Dining tables bent into desks. Families balanced screens, schedules, and suffocating isolation. Pressure settled everywhere without warning.

Daniel Cortez carried ten years of momentum in logistics leadership. A Senior Operations Director title followed him into every room. Teams called him the anchor. Chaos steadied when he arrived. Crises resolved under his watch. Trust formed his currency.

One call shattered that identity. Human resources spoke a single sentence about restructuring. Access denied before the exit doors opened. A frozen laptop marked the end of loyalty. Silence replaced a decade of service.

Night fell hard at the kitchen table. His wife searched his face and found fear. Two children lingered in the doorway and sensed the fracture. Reassurance refused to rise. Quiet filled the room and pressed inward.

The pandemic stripped purpose down to bone. Rejection letters stacked without mercy. Interviews closed with brittle smiles that cut deeper each time. Midnight checks yielded nothing but absence. Each refusal lowered his internal signal.

Fog swallowed the days. Wire tight nights stretched toward breaking. Without a title, worth felt uncertain. Children watched a quieter father. A spouse carried fear without words. Invisibility settled like gravity.

One sleepless hour broke the drift. A notebook opened under kitchen light. Across the page he carved a single question. What value disappeared, and what greater one demanded discovery. Ink soaked deep and refused comfort.

Truth surfaced before dawn. Worth had lived inside a title. When that title vanished, identity collapsed with it. The realization struck harder than the layoff itself. Management without mission revealed a hollow center.

That reckoning demanded action. Panic stayed off the table. Daniel tuned deliberately instead. Leaders who thrived in collapse became case studies. Mentors received calls shaped by curiosity rather than need. Morning pages mapped values he refused to abandon again.

Weeks lengthened into months. Title chasing lost appeal. Clarity replaced desperation. Conversations shifted tone and depth. Instead of asking for openings, he asked about unresolved problems. Attention sharpened around him.

Posture straightened. Voice steadied. Presence changed the room. Networks widened through resonance rather than reach. The signal carried coherence again.

Then the call returned from familiar ground. The same company faltered under remote strain. Systems fractured. Morale eroded. Leadership needed repair more than stability. The request carried urgency.

They did not offer his old seat. A larger one waited instead. The Chief Operating Officer role demanded architecture, not anchoring. Daniel returned changed.

Inside the same walls, a different man moved. Stability no longer defined him. Resilient systems replaced personal endurance. Teams learned to function through disruption. Coherence replaced control.

His journey followed an ancient pattern. Collapse removed the title and exposed the wound. Confrontation named misplaced worth and recalibrated energy. Climb rebuilt identity on values and returned power amplified.

Daniel Cortez never reclaimed what he lost. He built something stronger. Collapse did not end his signal. It tuned it.

Tools & Tactics: The Signal Rebuild System

Tool 1: The Truth Sentence

Take one sheet of paper.
Write one sentence you have been avoiding.

Name what you lost.
Say what happened next.
Add how it feels.
Do not explain.
Stop when it feels sharp.

Tactic:
Read the sentence once every morning.
Do this for three days.
Do not change it.

Why it works:
Truth breaks hiding.
Hiding stops action.
Action starts with truth.

Tool 2: Core Signal Rebuild

Think of one thing you stopped doing.
A skill.
A habit.
A value.

Pick only one.

Set a 15-minute timer each morning.
Work only on that one thing.
Do not check your phone first.

Tactic:
Ask one question when time ends:
"What did I make stronger today?"

Write one line.
Close the notebook.

Why it works:
Small signals build trust.
Trust brings chances.
Daily work rebuilds who you are.

Tool 3: The Two Wins Rule

Each day has two wins.
Only two.

One is for the body.
One is for direction.

Nothing else counts.

Tactic:
Body win: move and sweat for 10–20 minutes.
Direction win: finish one must-do task.

Try to finish both before noon.

Why it works:
The body wakes the mind.

The mind guides action.
Together they build momentum.

Tool 4: Nightly Signal Check

End the day with two short lines.
Write fast.
Be honest.

Tactic:
Answer this:
"What made me stronger today?"

Then answer this:
"What made me weaker?"

Pick one fix for tomorrow.
Only one.

Why it works:
Problems grow when ignored.
Seen problems can be fixed.
Small fixes add up.

The Operating Pattern

Notice where things broke.
Name it without fear.
Rebuild one signal each day.
Act early and clean.
Review each night.
Adjust once.

This pattern stays the same.
Lives change.
The rules do not.

Your signal shapes your world.
Tune it on purpose.
Then move.

The Algorithm: Retune the Signal (15 Minutes)

Step 1: Tell the Truth (2 minutes)

Sit down.
Take one breath.

Write one hard sentence.
Name the loss.
Say what it caused.
Say how it feels.

Stop.

Read it once.
Do not fix it.

Step 2: Strengthen One Signal (5 minutes)

Choose one thing you are rebuilding.
Only one.

Set a timer for 5 minutes.
Work on it without stopping.

No phone.
No switching.

When the timer ends, stop.

Write one line:
"I strengthened _____ today."

Close the notebook.

Step 3: Win the Body (3–5 minutes)

Stand up.

Move fast.
Push.
Squat.
Walk hard.
Breathe deep.

Work until warm.

Stop while you still have energy.

Step 4: Win Direction (3 minutes)

Choose one must-do task.
Only one.

Do the first real action.
Send it.
Start it.
Finish it.

No polishing.

Step 5: Seal the Signal (1 minute)

Say this out loud:
"My signal is getting stronger."

Picture tomorrow for five seconds.
Then move on with your day.

Night Check (Optional – 2 Minutes)

Write two lines.

"What made my signal stronger?"
"What made it weaker?"

Pick one fix for tomorrow.
Sleep.

Why This Algorithm Works

Truth clears fog.
Small work restores identity.
Movement wakes courage.
Action builds momentum.
Momentum changes outcomes.

No step is optional.
No step is complex.
This is how signal returns.

Reflection Questions

1. What collapse am I vibrating right now: fear, loss, or clarity?
2. How did my actions today shift my frequency: toward static or toward coherence?
3. What problem can I transmit into the world tomorrow that proves my new signal?

Pillar Activation: Doors to the Future

Game Plan
This chapter shows what happens when collapse strips away illusion and forces truth to the surface. Howard Schultz teaches us that crisis does not destroy leaders. It clarifies them.

Pillar Activation

Mental Precision (Head)
Schultz named the fracture without excuses. He stopped pretending systems mattered more than standards. Clear thinking returned when truth led every decision.

Physical Mastery (Body)
He shut every store and rebuilt craft by hand. Bodies relearned rhythm, repetition, and care. Energy returned through disciplined fundamentals.

Emotional Power (Heart)
Instead of hiding shame, he faced disappointment

head-on. Fear turned into resolve. Pride softened into responsibility.

Spiritual Alignment (Soul)
He remembered the vow formed in childhood. People always came first. Purpose anchored every painful cut and hard choice.

Imaginative Strategy (Vision)
He reframed the company's identity with one sentence. People before product changed everything. Innovation followed alignment, not the other way around.

Coach J's Challenge
When collapse hits your life, stop running. Name what broke. Strip away what no longer fits. Rebuild from the smallest true action you can control. Truth sharpens your signal. Consistency restores momentum.

Locker-Room Reflection
Where has drift replaced purpose in your life, and what truth are you ready to face today?

Chapter 4: Resilience Architecture™ Revealed

"Turn your wounds into wisdom."

~ Oprah Winfrey

Pressure does not break you. It exposes the parts that wait for alignment. Old memories cut because you reach for identities that no longer fit. Dust covers trophies that no longer match your purpose. Labels cling to your skin until you mistake them for truth. You rise when you stand as a complete system that moves with intent.

Most people fall out of sync. Thought runs fast while fear chases it. The body strains through fatigue. Emotion roars with no direction. Spirit sinks in private rooms that hold no light. Imagination builds worlds while discipline stays quiet. This split weakens structure. Collapse follows.

Crisis reveals the break. Storms hit without warning. Walls shake. Floors shift. Every fault comes into view. The Law of Correspondence speaks through this moment. Inner fracture produces outer ruin. Disorder inside your system spreads across your life. Alignment shifts the tide. Fire strips illusion. Light uncovers strength that formed in silence.

Resilience Architecture begins here. A blueprint waits behind every break. Skill does not grant it. Talent does not reach it. Alignment builds it. When mind, body, emotion, spirit, and imagination move as one, force turns into power that endures.

Oprah Winfrey embodies this truth. She carried wounds that threatened her future. She turned them into wisdom. She rebuilt her life from broken ground. She shaped her own identity through choice, clarity, and alignment. Her rise proves the core principle of this chapter. Inner order creates outer expansion. Alignment transforms collapse into ascent.

Oprah Winfrey: The Forge of Earned Power

Oprah Gail Winfrey did not enter power.
She entered fracture and learned how to stand.

Mississippi taught survival before comfort learned its name.
Dresses came from potato sacks.
Children laughed. Adults looked away.
Ridicule crowned her early.

Family offered no shelter.
A father rationed affection.
A mother disappeared into exhaustion.
Homes changed without warning.
Love arrived with conditions attached.

Violation followed.
Trust shattered at nine.
Silence hardened at ten.
Belonging turned predatory at twelve.
At fourteen, pregnancy arrived.
Weeks later, the child died.

Childhood burned to ash.
Foundation vanished.
Nothing grew clean.

Damage split inward and multiplied.
Survival became a system under siege.
Hunger mapped her ribs.
Shame locked her joints.
Memory carved itself into muscle.

Her mind moved faster than classrooms allowed.
Teachers waved her off.
Curiosity drew laughter.
Dreams returned as targets.

Emotion surged without warning.
Rage flashed. Shame settled.
Silence became craft.
Masks fooled rooms.
Night told the truth.

Faith stayed tangled in her hands.
Hymns promised worth.
Darker voices argued harder.
She stayed anyway.

The Law of Correspondence hovered near judgment.
Inner fracture predicts outer ruin.
Silence breeds silence.
Shame becomes destiny.

But the law cuts both ways.

Rebuild the interior, and the exterior must follow.
Change begins where no one watches.

The Suspense of Confrontation

Loss ends most stories.
Small coffins often close futures.

At fourteen, absence hollowed her bones.
No rescue came.
No hands reached down.
Silence delivered its verdict.

Broken.
Irrelevant.
Finished.

She nearly accepted it.

Another current stirred.
Quiet. Unlit.
A voice without witnesses spoke.

No one is coming.
I rise now.

Fear split from freedom.
Excuses burned.
A doorway opened.
She stepped through.

The Climb into Alignment

She rebuilt piece by piece.

Books became oxygen.
Dickens pulled her from dust.

Angelou lit her wings.
Scripture thundered through veins.

Speech contests became arenas.
Her voice tightened rooms.
Silence gathered.
Power arrived with one truth.

Her words could bend a room.

Shame fought back.
She tore it loose.
Mockery tried again.
She grew taller under it.

Scars stopped hiding.
Damage became fuel.
She learned a brutal rule.

Wounds power the climb.

Emotion moved into daylight.
Tears flowed without apology.
She spoke blood and truth.
Audiences leaned forward.

Strangers became kin.

Faith stayed like rope over floodwater.
Ritual did not save her.
Conviction did.

Journals filled.
Declarations sharpened thought.

I am chosen.
Pain refines me.

Imagination ignited next.
She rehearsed futures nightly.
Mocked dreams hardened into inevitability.

Alignment locked step by step.
As within, so without.
Reality obeyed.

Early Career Resistance

At nineteen, Nashville crowned her youngest anchor.
Lights flared.
Knives followed.

Too emotional.
Too heavy.
Too much.

A live broadcast turned cruel.
One colleague mocked her stumble.
Laughter cracked.
Doubt returned home with her.

Baltimore arrived as exile.
A dying morning show waited.

Exile became initiation.

She leaned forward.
She listened.
Presence replaced performance.

Ratings surged.
Emotion revealed gravity.

Humiliation returned.
She refused collapse.
Honesty hardened into armor.

Networks circled.
Contracts glittered like chains.
She refused silence.

Harpo rose brick by brick.
Sovereignty sealed her name.

The Color Purple Furnace

Hollywood tested her next.

Sofia required fire.
She recognized the woman instantly.

The audition scorched air.
Rage spoke.
Scars answered.

Silence swallowed the room.

Waiting crushed her chest.
Tabloids carved her body.
Shame hunted again.

She surrendered clean.

If it is not mine, I release it.

The phone rang.
Spielberg's voice cut sharp.

Lose one pound or lose the role.

Surrender broke the seal.
Fire surged.

The Role as Resurrection

Sofia demanded exorcism.
Buried wounds met flame.

When she roared,
"All my life I had to fight,"
history leaned in.

The sack girl refused to kneel.

Acclaim followed.
Awards answered.

But the deeper victory burned beneath.

Pain never disqualified her.
It armed her.

Potato sacks became armor.
Silence became signal.
Exile forged empire.

Wounds entered the furnace.
Steel emerged.

The sack girl crowned herself sovereign.
The silenced child became a global voice.
The wounded girl designed destiny.

One law ruled it all.

Change the inside, and the outside cannot resist.

Oprah did not chase empire.
Alignment summoned it.

Inner architecture locked tight.
Outer fortresses followed.

Universal Law: Correspondence

Reshape your inner code, and the outer world has no choice but to reflect it.

Core Lesson

Oprah's story is a full-system reconstruction from fracture to coherence. Her collapse did not take fame or status. It destroyed foundation. Poverty crushed her Mind. Abuse ruptured her Body. Shame drowned her Emotions. Doubt strangled her Spirit. Darkness dimmed her Imagination. The five energetic domains shattered early. Yet inside that void she made the first resilient declaration: *If the outer world will not change, I will rebuild the one within.* That vow became ignition.

She rebuilt each energy with intent. Mind rose through books and language. Body stood tall through humiliation and scrutiny. Emotions opened through honesty and shared wounds. Spirit anchored through prayer and meaning. Imagination caught fire and projected futures that pulled her forward. As her inner system rose, coherence stabilized. The Law of Correspondence activated. Her exterior world reorganized around the architecture forming inside her.

Setbacks became furnaces. Baltimore exile refined her voice. Public ridicule hardened her truth. Hollywood uncertainty sharpened surrender. *The Color Purple* resurrected her identity by forging her pain into power. Harpo Studios established sovereignty. Every fracture became fuel. Every humiliation became leverage. Every collapse became a load-bearing beam.

Her Resilience Architecture proves this principle:
When you redesign the inner structure, the outer world has no choice but to mirror the alignment.
What once mocked her bowed. What once caged her opened. What once shattered her built her throne.
Oprah did not rise from circumstance. She rose from system coherence created through relentless alignment across the five energies.

She is the living equation: inner architecture first, outer empire second.

Client Story: From Rubble to Blueprint

Erika lived like she had already won.
Her job gave her power.
Her days followed her rules.
Her kids did well.
Her house looked perfect.
Pictures showed a good life.
Cracks hid under the shine.

The break came fast.
Her phone buzzed on the counter.
A strange name filled the screen.
The words told the truth.
Her hands shook.
Betrayal hit hard.

Work grew heavier.
Her team split apart.
Goals rose higher each week.
She smiled for others.
At night, fear took over.
Sleep would not come.

Everything inside her started to fail.
Her thoughts went in circles.
Her body felt tired and heavy.
Anger came, then nothing at all.
Faith felt far away.
Ideas disappeared.

The outside showed the damage.
Her shoulders dropped.

Her voice lost strength.
She snapped at her kids.
She worked on habit alone.
Every day felt hard.

One morning, she sat in her car.
Tears marked her face.
Her hands gripped the wheel.
The air smelled old.
She saw herself in the mirror.
And did not know that woman.

A thought broke the silence.
This cannot be my life.
This cannot be the end.
She cried again.
Then something changed.
She refused to quit.

Coaching did not save her.
She spoke without hiding.
Named her fear.
Her need to be seen.
No one fixed it for her.
She faced the truth herself.

Pain became a teacher.
The mess showed what failed.
Collapse was not the end.
It showed what to build.
A plan appeared.
She started climbing.

She began each morning with order.
One sentence came first.
The words helped her breathe.
Soon they showed direction.
Her mind grew calm again.

She moved her body each day.
She drank water.
She stretched.
She breathed.
Her strength came back.
Her body woke up.

Her feelings changed.
Anger taught lessons.
She asked better questions.
She chose calm actions.
Feelings became guides.
Control returned.

Small acts rebuilt her spirit.
She lit a candle.
She wrote one thankful line.
Warmth came slowly.
Light grew inside her.
She felt connected again.

Her ideas came back last.
She wrote plans on blank pages.
A new business took shape.
Weekends felt joyful.
Peace replaced stress.
Hope felt real.

Daily systems held her steady.
She did not rely on force.
Truth guided her choices.
Life gained rhythm.
The plan worked.

Two years later, she saw change.
Her eyes looked bright.
She felt strong.
Finally left a harmful marriage.
Her home felt safe.
She chose peace.

Her work matched her life.
Her business grew bigger than before.
She slept well.
Moved with ease.
Her kids laughed freely.
Life felt whole.

Betrayal tried to break her.
Pressure reshaped her instead.
Success followed inner order.
Survival did not build her future.
Alignment did.

She did not stay in the rubble.
She used it.
Built something new.
Her life made sense again.

The Five Pillars Blueprint

Picture your life as an operating system under load. One corrupted file slows everything. A fractured core collapses the engine. Resilience obeys the same law. You do not operate in pieces. You function as a system anchored by five connected pillars.

Mental Precision

Focus cuts through chaos without apology. Clarity steadies the mind while others drown in noise. Crisis sharpens the question of priority. A calm voice answers what matters now. Lose that voice and panic takes command.

Physical Mastery

The body fuels every decision and every climb. Energy generation determines endurance under pressure. Strength, sleep, nutrition, and movement turn into lifelines during collapse. Neglect invites fatigue and decay. Discipline builds a fortress that holds.

Emotional Power

Emotion surges fast and carries force. Command converts feeling into courage and connection. Neglect allows hijack and reaction. Crisis tests whether emotion freezes or drives action. Mastery turns volatility into propulsion.

Spiritual Alignment

This compass holds when all other signals spin. Meaning roots you when wounds run deep. Crisis asks whether purpose still speaks. Ignorance invites despair and paralysis. Attention steadies the climb through faith.

Imaginative Strategy

Vision opens paths through rubble. Imagination sketches futures across broken ground. Crisis plants the seed of reinvention. Starvation repeats old patterns without mercy. Nourishment builds ladders where walls once trapped you.

When these five pillars lock together, the system hums with life. Storms still strike. Pressure still claws. Architecture holds.

Adjustment replaces collapse. Movement replaces fear. Elevation replaces survival.

When the storm clears, ruins lose authority. Design takes command.

Tools & Tactics: The Pillar Integrity Audit™

Step One: Score the System

Assess each pillar with ruthless honesty.
Use a scale from one to ten.
No averages.
No excuses.
No rounding.

- Mental Precision
- Physical Mastery
- Emotional Power
- Spiritual Alignment
- Imaginative Strategy

Numbers cut through self-deception.
They expose reality faster than stories.

Step Two: Identify the Anchor

Circle the highest score.
This pillar holds when pressure rises.
It stabilizes the system in chaos.
It becomes leverage when conditions turn hostile.

Strength reveals what already works.

Step Three: Expose the Fracture Line

Mark the lowest score without hesitation.
This pillar fails first under stress.
Collapse enters here before anywhere else.

Weakness always announces itself.
Now it has a name.

Step Four: Name the Truth

Write one clean sentence.

How does this weakness show up under pressure?

Be exact.
No disguise.
No spin.
No mercy.

Clarity cuts deeper than denial.

Step Five: Forge the Repair

Choose one small action for this week.
Strengthen only the fracture.

One action.
One reinforcement.

Consistency rebuilds the pillar.
Repetition seals the crack.
Force multiplies through precision.

This audit functions like an X-ray.
Structure appears without argument.
Strength shows itself without ego.
Failure stands exposed without shame.

This is not judgment.
This is diagnosis.

Diagnosis marks the start of reinvention.

You now know where to build.

Algorithm: The Pillar Activation Planner

The Daily Operating Code

Treat this like ignition, not reflection.
Engines start with command, not hesitation.
Each morning sets the system tone.
You decide how power flows.

Step One: Summon the Pillar

Ask one question before noise arrives.
Which pillar must I command today?
Do not negotiate with comfort.
Select the pillar that demands authority.

Choice creates direction.

Step Two: Ignite the Action

Choose one move that activates the pillar with force.
Action matters more than duration.
Precision beats volume every time.

For Mental Precision, write for ten minutes without
pause.
Carve one full page of clarity into ink.
Let the mind settle into command.

For Physical Mastery, train the body deliberately.
Drink water.
Take a ten minute walk that resets breath and posture.
Movement restores power faster than thought.

For Emotional Power, call one ally.
Speak truth until static breaks.
Connection converts pressure into strength.

For Spiritual Alignment, enter stillness.
Pray.
Meditate.
Read words that restore meaning and scale.
Purpose steadies the climb.

For Imaginative Strategy, sketch vision on blank ground.
List one new possibility.
Plant the seed of reinvention.
Imagination builds exits where none appear.

Step Three: Record the Shift

Close the day with one sentence.
How did this pillar change how I showed up today?
Write clean.
One line seals the signal.

Awareness locks in learning.

Step Four: Rotate the Charge

Tomorrow choose a different pillar.
Move through all five without skipping.
Rotation builds balance.
Balance builds rhythm.

Alignment arrives through repetition.

Commit to thirty days.
Watch collapse lose leverage.
Watch resistance thin.
Watch the system snap into coherence.

What once felt fragile now holds.
What once scattered now moves as one.

Reflection Questions

- Which pillar anchors you strongest right now? How do you know?
- Which pillar fractures under pressure? How does it crack open your life?
- How would your outer world bend if all five pillars moved in harmony?
- What one daily action this week will begin sealing the fracture in your weakest pillar?

Pillar Activation: Alignment Under Pressure

Game Plan
This chapter proves one hard truth. Pressure does not destroy you. It reveals whether your system stands aligned or fractured. When the five pillars move together, collapse loses authority.

Pillar Activation

- Mental Precision (Head): Oprah chose clarity over chaos. Books, language, and disciplined thought rebuilt command when confusion threatened to win.

- Physical Mastery (Body): She stood taller under scrutiny. Posture, presence, and endurance carried her through humiliation without breaking form.
- Emotional Power (Heart): Pain stopped hiding. She turned wounds into connection, truth into gravity, and emotion into fuel that pulled others close.
- Spiritual Alignment (Soul): Meaning held when comfort vanished. Conviction anchored her identity when circumstances tried to erase it.
- Imaginative Strategy (Vision): She rehearsed futures before they existed. Vision pulled her forward when reality offered no exits.

Alignment rebuilt her from the inside. The outer world had no choice but to follow.

Coach J's Challenge
When life hits hard, stop asking what broke. Ask what fell out of alignment. Pick one pillar today. Train it with intention. One action. One reinforcement. That is how systems stabilize under pressure.

Locker-Room Reflection

Which pillar in your life needs command right now: mind, body, heart, spirit, or vision?

Chapter 5: The Business of Being Unbreakable

"I never lose. I either win or learn."

~ Nelson Mandela

The world tests you without warning. Pressure strips away status and comfort. Crisis tears through every false layer until only one question stands clear. What remains when everything else falls? Money burns. Titles fade. Comfort disappears. Loyalty splits under heat. The collapse exposes your truth.

Strength rises from the code you choose in those moments. Unbreakable never arrives as a gift. You build it through daily choices. You carve it into your thoughts. You live it when the world closes in. Mandela endured twenty seven years in a cell because he shaped a code stronger than steel. He repeated it each day until the prison bent before his discipline.

The client in this chapter rose from the edge of bankruptcy through the same approach. He wrote rules inside himself. He trained those rules until doubt lost its hold. He treated crisis as a forge rather than an end. Discipline became his shelter. Action became his signal. His code carried him forward.

Unbreakable belongs to those who prepare before the flames rise. It belongs to those who design systems that hold under strain. It belongs to those who stand firm when the world demands surrender. You build it by writing a code that outlasts fear. You prove it when collapse arrives. That code becomes your anchor, your structure, your path through fire.

This chapter shows how leaders create that code. It shows how Mandela shaped freedom inside confinement. It shows how a business leader shaped renewal inside crisis. It invites you to build a code that no storm can break.

Nelson Mandela: The Furnace of Freedom

Nelson Mandela entered life in the Transkei, where wind pressed low roofs and red dust clung like inheritance. Smoke burned eyes before comfort learned its name. Bare feet chased cattle across cracked earth. Firelight nights carved warrior memory into bone. Every story honored land, blood, and refusal.

That fire struck early and stayed lit.

Mission bells carried him away from soil into stone halls. Polished grammar erased centuries without apology. History vanished mid-sentence. His jaw locked against the insult. Resistance learned patience.

Books became oxygen under pressure. Pages wore thin from return. Thought sharpened into weaponry. No chain could hold a trained mind. Knowledge outlasted muscle and survived every cell.

The Young Fighter

Johannesburg met Mandela with thunder. Mines roared. Smoke choked breath. Signs screamed *Whites Only* while dignity bent under force. The city demanded submission. He refused.

Candlelight burned through law books. Hunger learned structure. Offices opened for voices erased by power. Courtrooms turned into battlegrounds where silence lost ground. Justice stood upright.

Pressure intensified. Strategy adapted. The African National Congress widened the frame. Crowds shook streets. Police lines answered with batons. Repression forced descent underground. Networks formed. Messages moved like fire beneath ice. Locked doors taught hands to carve walls.

The Furnace of Exile and Arrest

The state named him terrorist and released hunters. Safe houses absorbed footsteps. Disguises erased faces. Borders cracked. The press crowned the chase and named him the Black Pimpernel. Freedom narrowed fast.

Police closed the distance on a quiet road. Steel and dust swallowed him. Chains struck earth. Courtrooms filled with hostile eyes. Judgment landed like a coffin lid.

Mandela did not fold. Iron set his spine. Silence carried one clean sentence. Preparedness for death defeated fear.

Robben Island: The Resilience Operating System

The cell cut tight and narrow. Mildew soaked blankets. A waste bucket poisoned air. Guards laughed. Men collapsed.

Mandela built a system.

Morning discipline folded blankets into sharp lines. Cold water shocked breath awake. Spit met squared shoulders. Fists split lips without stealing calm. Dignity held ground. Guards hesitated. Prisoners rose.

The quarry burned eyes white. Hammers tore skin. Each strike landed in rhythm. Labor carved code into muscle. Work did not break him. Work built him.

Letters delivered grief. A mother gone. A son gone. Rage demanded command. He refused it. Vision replaced emotion. Mastery ruled where chaos sought power.

Books returned. Lessons whispered. Minds sharpened. Roots drove deeper with every attempt to bury him. Discipline compounded. Patience bloomed.

The Release

Years crushed calendars into dust. Mandela emerged intact. Gates opened in 1990. He did not crawl. Daylight met command. A raised fist lifted the world.

The nation burned. Fear split white from Black. Civil war waited close. Anger was insufficient. Leadership required restraint.

Mandela stepped into the storm calm. Words lowered voices. A steady smile met hatred. Reconciliation answered blood.

A Springbok jersey crossed his shoulders. Sport became unity. Forgiveness hardened into law. A nation followed a man who mastered himself first.

The Legacy

Mandela left after one term. Principle beat power. Keys passed forward. Villages opened. Children ran into his arms. Former guards met his handshake.

Fire tested the system. Peace proved it.

That system belongs to you.

A folded blanket becomes ritual. Quarry strikes become the work you avoid. Patience learned through grief becomes breath under betrayal. Forgiveness guards when rage demands control.

Dreams do not rescue collapse. Codes decide outcomes. Mandela fell into his code. The code lifted him. A nation rose because discipline held.

Ritual replaces excuse. Collapse arrives without warning. Systems transmit strength. Transformation follows preparation.

Twenty-seven years forged command. Loss stripped everything extra. Discipline sowed destiny. The prisoner became president through patience. The chained man designed a nation through code.

Freedom followed structure.

Universal Law: Compensation

Crisis strips illusion and reveals the law that never bends: what you sow becomes what you rise into, and when you sow discipline in the ashes, destiny climbs unshakable from the fire.

Core Lesson

Mandela built a system of strength while the world tried to break him. Early trials cut deep. Poverty pushed his mind to the edge. Cultural assault tested his identity. Apartheid locked down his movement. Loss opened his chest to grief. Prison forced a reckoning of spirit. Each fracture demanded a rebuild. Each rebuild formed a new layer of power. Truth rose inside pressure.

Study shaped his mind into a sharp blade. Books fed thought like air. Law turned into a disciplined force that no cell could seize. Rage knocked hard. He mastered it before it claimed him. Ritual shaped his body inside a narrow cell and a white quarry that blinded many men. Purpose steadied his spirit when nights turned cold. Creative fire lived in quiet corners. He taught men to think. He turned whispers into plans for freedom. A prison hardened into a school for leaders.

Robben Island formed his Resilience Operating System. Ritual set the frame. Emotional control guarded dignity. Strategic patience shaped vision. Mastery of inner terrain held his world intact against steel and stone. His coherence grew inside confinement. Apartheid tried to splinter him. Alignment rose instead. Gates opened to a man who carried all five energies in balance.

No collapse returned him to former ground. Forward construction defined him. The code inside him held shape under pressure that crushed others. Depth took root when the world pushed him down. Structure lifted him when hope bent thin. His rise followed one law. Crisis strips dreams. Crisis reveals code. Mandela fell to his code. The code carried him out. The code rebuilt a nation.

Client Story: Building the Code in Collapse

The Illusion of Permanence

James ruled the sales floor with tailored certainty and relentless forward motion. Sharp suits cut authority through marble corridors echoing ambition and controlled hunger. City glass glittered outside his window, reflecting a belief that empires endure. Records shattered as voices followed his lead and contracts bent under pressure. Boardrooms quieted when he spoke because confidence carried the weight of law. Collapse never entered his calculations, not even as a distant possibility.

Pandemic Impact

COVID arrived without warning and rewrote the rules overnight. Phones stopped ringing mid-breath as deals evaporated into empty air. Creditors circled fast, scenting exposure where certainty once stood. The company folded hard, dragging identity down with the balance sheet. A repo truck hauled away status while metal chains scraped finality. Locks turned cold, sealing doors that once opened on command.

Exile in Plain Sight

Night found him curled inside a sedan with duffel bags and a thinning notebook. Million dollar signatures shrank into ink stains trembling under dashboard light. Shame pressed his chest until breath shortened and vision narrowed. A whisper repeated one sentence with surgical cruelty. You are finished. That moment forced a single choice between disappearance and reconstruction.

The Call for Structure

He called me without apology, desperation, or request for comfort. No speech interested him, and rescue held no value. He asked for a system that could hold under pressure. Together we began constructing one rule at a time, brick by brick, without sentiment.

Dignity Reboot

Rule One demanded waking before dawn without negotiation or excuse. I told him to seize morning darkness and declare unfinished intent aloud before the world stirred. Resistance surfaced immediately through shivering mornings and bitter muttering inside the car. Repetition drilled resolve deeper than comfort ever allowed. Shame lost its grip as posture straightened with returning authority.

Installed Command: Command the morning. Command the day. Command your worth.

The Discipline Hammer

Rule Two required fifty calls daily without exception or emotional debate. James pushed back, questioning silence and rejection before results appeared. I cut him clean and reminded him that effort mattered before response. Silence arrived first, followed by slammed lines and open hostility. Persistence fractured resistance until conversations emerged from the noise and meetings followed. Contracts arrived exactly as mathematics predicts.

Installed Command: Discipline compounds. Numbers bend before persistence.

The Compensation Engine

Rule Three banned spoken complaint in any form or tone. Every word programs direction, either toward collapse or controlled ascent. Doubt slipped once, and correction landed immediately with force. Language shifted from limitation toward deliberate solution framing. Results followed obediently because systems answer clarity.

Installed Command: Speak strength. Strength multiplies.

The Emotional Firewall

Rule Four required one act of generosity every single day. Loss tightened his grip until generosity felt irrational and dangerous. I reminded him that scarcity dies when generosity detonates its narrative. Small acts followed, coffee shared, résumés polished, gratitude spoken nightly until voices softened. Wealth returned slowly while abundance flooded his internal terrain.

Installed Command: Give daily. Reset your emotional code to abundance.

The Integrity Anchor

Rule Five closed each day with written evidence and honest accounting. Failures bled onto pages beside victories carved in permanent ink. Promises recorded held him accountable beyond memory or mood. When shame crept back, proof stared him down with facts. The page spoke one truth without negotiation. I am building.

Installed Command: Close each day coded. Integrity anchors your climb forward.

Tools & Tactics: The Five-Rule Daily Code

1. Morning Rule
Wake early. Stand tall.
Write one true line:
I build today. Collapse bends to me.
Say it once. Breathe slow.
Command: Own the morning. Win the day.

2. One Daily Discipline
Choose one action. Never miss it.
Fifty calls.
Fifty messages.
Fifty steps.
Count every rep. Effort compounds.
Command: Act daily. Consistency wins.

3. Word Control
Words steer outcomes.
Cut complaints.
Change *I can't* to *I will*.
Correct slips fast.
Strong words create strong action.
Command: Speak strength.

4. Daily Give
Give once each day.
Buy coffee.
Make the call.

Share something useful.
Giving destroys scarcity.
Command: Give daily. Create abundance.

5. Night Close
End the day on paper.
Write one loss.
Write one win.
Write one promise kept.
Proof silences doubt.
Command: Close clean. Move forward.

How This Works
Use all five.
Repeat every day.
Thirty days build habits.
Sixty days build identity.
Collapse will come.
Luck will not save you.
Your code will.

Algorithm: The Five-Pillar Daily Activation

Use this every morning. Total time: 12–15 minutes.

Step 1: Wake the Mind (3 minutes)

Sit or stand still.
Write one clear line:
"Today I build, not break."

Circle one task that matters most.
This sharpens focus.

Pillar: Mental Precision

Step 2: Wake the Body (4 minutes)

Move your body fast.
Push. Squat. Walk. Breathe hard.
Stop only when warm.
Strong body sends a strong signal.

Pillar: Physical Mastery

Step 3: Name the Feeling (2 minutes)

Ask one question:
"What do I feel right now?"
Write one word only.
Do not explain it.
Naming feeling removes its control.

Pillar: Emotional Power

Step 4: Choose the Meaning (2 minutes)

Place a hand on your chest.
Take one slow breath.
Say this line once:
"This day has purpose."
Stand tall after you say it.

Pillar: Spiritual Alignment

Step 5: Aim the Imagination (3 minutes)

Picture tonight.
See one win completed.
See yourself calm and steady.
Write one action that makes it real.

Pillar: Imaginative Strategy

Seal the System (1 minute)

Read this aloud:
"All parts of me move together."
Close the notebook.
Begin the day.

Why This Works

Mind chooses.
Body confirms.
Emotion clears.
Spirit anchors.
Imagination directs.

When all five move together,
collapse loses leverage.

Reflection Questions

1. When things fell apart, what habit saved you and what habit failed?
2. What one daily action, done every day, would change your future?

3. If comfort disappeared, what routine would still hold?

Pillar Activation: The Code of Fire

Game Plan
This chapter shows what holds when everything else burns. Collapse strips illusion and reveals the code you live by. Mandela and a modern business leader prove that unbreakable strength is built, not hoped for.

Pillar Activation

Mental Precision (Head)
Mandela trained his mind like a blade. Books sharpened focus. Clear rules cut through fear. The client did the same by choosing structure over panic.

Physical Mastery (Body)
A folded blanket. Quarry labor. Daily movement. Discipline in the body steadied the mind when chaos pressed in.

Emotional Power (Heart)
Rage knocked hard. Both men refused to let it drive. Naming emotion and choosing restraint turned pressure into fuel.

Spiritual Alignment (Soul)
Purpose outlasted walls and loss. Meaning anchored every day. Freedom formed inside before it appeared outside.

Imaginative Strategy (Vision)
Mandela taught, planned, and envisioned a nation while confined. The client rebuilt identity by seeing forward, not backward.

Coach J's Challenge
Write your code before crisis writes it for you. Choose one rule you will not break. Train it daily. When collapse hits, your system will answer before fear speaks.

Locker-Room Reflection
If comfort vanished tomorrow, which daily rule would still hold you upright?

Part 1 Summary

The First Five Leaders: A Unified Guide to Building Resilience Architecture Within Yourself

Nelson Mandela built strength inside confinement. Early wounds struck every domain. Poverty pressed his Mind. Erasure attacked his Creative identity. Apartheid crushed his Body. Loss shook his Emotions. Prison forced his Spirit to rise. Study sharpened his Mind into a blade. Discipline forged his Body inside a narrow cell. Purpose anchored his Spirit above suffering. Stories and teaching expanded his Creative reach across Robben Island. Mandela proved that crisis clears the ground for a new internal world. You rebuild until the inner structure can shape the outer one.

Oprah Winfrey rose from fracture to coherence. Poverty bent her Mind. Abuse tore her Body. Shame drowned her Emotions. Doubt thinned her Spirit. Darkness smothered her Imagination. She chose reconstruction. Books rebuilt her Mind. Presence restored her Body. Honesty opened her Emotions. Meaning strengthened her Spirit. Vision reignited her Imagination. Her inner order lifted her outer world. Setbacks refined her system. Oprah showed that resilience begins when you rebuild the person before you rebuild the life.

Howard Schultz returned to truth when drift hollowed the company he shaped. Rapid growth cut craft. Culture thinned. Noise replaced care. He closed stores to reclaim clarity, identity, and connection. Mental focus snapped back into place. Emotional warmth rose across teams. Physical operations tightened into discipline. Spiritual alignment returned when he named Starbucks a people company serving coffee. Creative energy rose through innovation guided by humanity. Schultz demonstrated that resilience starts when leaders cut rot and restore purpose.

Steve Jobs rewired himself through exile. Early success masked imbalance. Vision surged. Mind raced. Creativity sparked. Emotion faltered. Spirit drifted. The board removed him in a single vote. Collapse stripped ego and forced silence. Exile sharpened his Mind through NeXT. Pixar taught Emotional discipline and humility. Time reshaped his Spirit around purpose. Creativity matured into clarity. He returned with coherence and rebuilt Apple with simplicity and force. Jobs revealed that failure can redesign identity when you let the fire teach you.

Theodore Roosevelt forged strength through repeated furnaces. Asthma carved grit. Grief deepened his Emotions. The Badlands hardened his Body. San Juan Hill tested command. The presidency strained his Spirit. The River of Doubt demanded Creative adaptation at the edge of survival. Crisis knocked him down and he engineered the rebuild. He chose hardship when ease tempted him. He rebuilt structure through discipline, exposure, and decisive action. Roosevelt proved that resilience evolves through deliberate self-construction.

Unified Insight: The First Five Leaders Reveal the Blueprint Within You

One truth sits beneath every arc. Collapse can start coherence when you rebuild from within. Mandela modeled disciplined reconstruction under pressure. Oprah restored internal order after early fracture. Schultz returned to purpose to save culture. Jobs redesigned identity through exile. Roosevelt engineered strength through chosen hardship. Their collective message speaks directly to you. Resilience means redesign. You advance by crafting the structure of the person capable of carrying your destiny. You rise when Mental, Emotional, Physical, Spiritual, and Creative energy align. You move with coherence. You shape your future with intention.

Part II

Daily Dominance: The Win Your Day Method

Coding Resilience Into Ritual

Chapter 6: Wake Up Earlier Than You Want To

"Early to bed and early to rise makes a man healthy, wealthy, and wise."

~ Benjamin Franklin

Comfort coils near your mind with soft promise. It strokes your thoughts and urges delay. Its voice slides into your ear and tells you the world will wait.

Destiny rejects delay. Dawn knocks with force and demands discipline. You choose gravel when you trade the morning for another breath in bed. You choose a hollow day when you sink deeper into the warmth that dulls your edge. Comfort lulls you. Comfort drains you. Comfort ends you.

The first battle starts before your feet hit the floor. The alarm cuts the dark and tests your will. You rise, and the world leans toward your aim. You move, and the current of the day charges through you. You claim the morning, and openings appear that vanish for those who fall back into the sheets.

You fall when comfort wins. You stumble through hours already stolen. The day slips past you while you chase pieces of momentum you surrendered at dawn.

Benjamin Franklin: The Furnace of First Light

Philadelphia, 1730.

The city sleeps under frost and rot.
Alleys breathe ash. Windows stare blind.
One flame refuses surrender.

Inside a narrow brick house, a candle stands guard.

Benjamin Franklin bends over a desk scarred by ink and will.
The quill bites parchment. Thought spills fast.
Outside, silence presses inward.
Inside, a furnace answers.

Before war. Before revolution. Before empire.
His first battlefield lived before sunrise.
The enemy never changed. Drift.
The weapon stayed constant. Discipline.

Each morning began with a question carved in ink.
Simple. Merciless.
"What good shall I do this day?"

The words cracked the dark.
They demanded action.

The Boy Who Refused to Stay Small

Boston cast him poor and crowded.
Fifteenth of seventeen. Smoke-filled rooms. Empty plates.
At ten, school ended. Labor replaced hope.

He boiled tallow.
Dipped wicks.
Watched weak flames die young.

Franklin wanted more than candles.
He wanted fire.

At twelve, his brother's print shop closed around him.
Ink stained skin. Presses slammed judgment.
Mockery came free. Whips followed. Silence ruled.

So rebellion learned patience.

At night, he stole paper scraps.
Forged essays by candlelight.
Slipped them beneath doors under a borrowed name.

Silence Dogood spoke when Franklin could not.

The city laughed.
Then listened.
And learned his voice without knowing his face.

Resilience formed there.
Not through applause.
Through repetition.
Failure stacked on failure until strength learned shape.

The Code of Dawn

At seventeen, he left Boston with nothing intact but
intent.
Philadelphia met him hungry.
Bread filled both hands. No bag.
Benches served as beds.
Rain and ash greeted mornings.

Yet dawn met order.

Cold water shocked the body awake.
One question set direction.
Reading sharpened the mind.
The press hardened muscle and resolve.

Thirteen virtues rose as scaffolding.
He tracked failure in ink.
Faced weakness without flinch.
Returned sharper the next morning.

Each dawn reforged him.
Every ritual added steel.

The Fire That Built a Nation

Those mornings birthed more than habits.
They ignited invention.

The Franklin stove.
Bifocals.
The lightning rod.

Discipline widened thought.
Influence followed alignment.

He wrote treaties in silence.
Bent empires without noise.
Forged alliances with words trained before sunrise.

Storms still struck.

Businesses collapsed.

Politics betrayed.
Family fractured.

His own son chose the crown while Franklin chose liberty.
Each blow cut deep.
Every morning restored him.

Resilience replenished quietly.
Ink stroke by ink stroke.

When lightning struck, he harnessed it.
As tyranny rose, he negotiated it.
A man rehearsed by thousands of silent dawns does not panic.

The Closing Furnace

Franklin's genius never lived in office or invention.
It lived in habit fused to purpose.

He captured mornings.
Everything else followed.

When collapse loomed, he did not search for strength.
He withdrew it.
From a reservoir built before sunrise.

Every empire begins unseen.
Franklin's began with cold water, a candle, and a question.

That question still hangs, unchanged and unforgiving:
"What good shall I do this day?"
Resilience does not begin on battlefields.
It begins in bedrooms before dawn.
In ink-stained fingers gripping a quill.
With those who rise while the world still sleeps.

Universal Law Integration: Rhythm

The Law of Rhythm declares that life moves in cycles, and when you rise in harmony with those cycles through steady habits, you stay balanced when chaos strikes.

Core Lesson

Benjamin Franklin's life demonstrates resilience as a discipline-built architecture forged long before fame, invention, or nationhood. His resilience did not erupt in crisis. It was engineered in silence. Franklin grew through early fractures across every energetic domain. Mental energy sharpened in the print shop as he wrote in secret. Emotional energy strengthened as he endured poverty, ridicule, and exile. Physical energy rose through harsh labor, cold-water rituals, and the grind of manual printing work. Spiritual energy aligned through his vow to do good each day. Creative energy ignited in the essays he hid under doors, the inventions born from dawn discipline, and the civic systems he later shaped. The equilibrium between these energies created strong coherence. His daily system became the engine of resilience. The question, What good shall I do today, became his anchor. Through this structure he completed daily cycles of effort. He recovered through ritual reflection in his virtue journal. He heightened awareness through continuous self-observation and recalibration. His output rose because he built the muscle of coherence before crisis ever arrived. Franklin proves that resilience is constructed through habit, intention, and the mastery of dawn. He rose from poverty to shape a nation because he first shaped himself in the unseen hours before sunrise.

Client Story: Sunrise Resurrection

The Hollow Stare

Death met Erika eye to eye.
Cancer etched scars across skin and split fault lines through resolve.
Remission offered no victory parade, only a narrow hallway of waiting.
Limbo pressed harder than diagnosis.
Survival felt unfinished.

The Betrayal of Morning

Morning turned traitor.
A phone glowed against her face while minutes drained without resistance.
Numbness thickened as scrolling replaced breath.
Children learned silence in the hallway.
Work moved on without her voice.
Life hovered between pulse and pause.

The Strike of Command

A coach cut through the fog.
Wake earlier than comfort allows. Claim the first hour.
Laughter broke sharp and bitter.
Exhaustion already dragged behind her like iron.
Question followed fast and raw.
How does a body rise after war?

Law Over Feeling

Belief never entered the order.
Rhythm demanded action before faith arrived.
Discipline answered only repetition.
Ease offered nothing.
The strike mattered.

The Shredding Week

Darkness still held the street when she rolled upright.
Hands shook around cold water.
One pushup tore free and dropped her flat.
Sweat pooled as if a summit fell beneath her.
A mirror returned a stranger with hollow eyes.
Still, the rhythm stood.

Five Minutes of Law

Five minutes shaped the hour.
Wake.
Hydrate.
Move.
Reflect.

Anchor.
Silence received each act without applause.

Carving the Ritual

Quills once dipped before dawn.
Ritual cut into quiet with the same resolve.
Each motion struck steady and plain.
Drumbeats teach the body before the mind listens.
Law settles through repetition.

The Body Learns Music

Weeks stacked into months.
Breath arrived without protest.
Groans faded into motion.
Morning walks carried children toward school.
Sunlight warmed her face.
Laughter filled the space she reclaimed.

Return of Command

Work felt different under her feet.
Words landed clean and firm.
Decisions sharpened.
Evenings loosened their grip.
Fatigue no longer crushed.
Time opened.

Carrying the Rhythm Forward

One morning followed her into a hospital ward.
Women sat tethered to machines and quiet fear.
Scars shone fresh.

Voices thinned.
She spoke without ceremony.
The sun still rises. So can you.

Weight of Earned Words

Those words held mass.
Mornings forged that gravity.
Routine hardened into authority.
Presence replaced sympathy.
Truth traveled without force.

Victory Redefined

Cancer fell once.
Drift fell daily.
Silence lost its grip.
Morning after morning lifted her upright.
Survival turned active.

The Light Established

Rhythm remade her role.
Survivor shifted into lighthouse.
Children straightened inside her beam.
A team felt steadiness spread.
Community leaned closer.
Dawn now burns because she lights it.

Tools & Tactics: The Rhythm Operating Kit

These tools do one thing:
Make execution automatic when willpower fails.

1. The Compass Page

Purpose: Direction without debate

Tool:
 One notebook.
 First page labeled DAILY COMPASS.

Tactic:

- Never write more than one sentence.
- Never revise.
- Never skip the question.

If the sentence feels weak, that is the signal.
Weak clarity equals weak action.

Rule:
One sentence decides the day.

2. The Water Lock

Purpose: End sleep. Start command.

Tool:
 One glass. Filled before sleep. Placed where your feet land.

Tactic:

- Drink it before standing.
- No exceptions.
- Miss once, pay with 20 bodyweight squats.

Cold water is not comfort.
It is a switch.

3. The Movement Minimum

Purpose: Energy before thought

Tool:
 A fixed list of five movements you rotate.

Example:

- Pushups
- Squats
- Plank
- Arm circles
- Forward folds

Tactic:

- Five minutes total.
- No counting reps.
- Stop only when the timer ends.

This is not training.
This is ignition.

4. The Ledger Rule

Purpose: Truth without emotion

Tool:
Two-column page titled RHYTHM CHECK.

Tactic:

- One win only.
- One break only.
- No explanations.

If you write stories, you are avoiding truth.
Truth sharpens rhythm.

5. The First Strike Task

Purpose: Daily leverage

Tool:
One index card labeled FIRST STRIKE.

Tactic:

- Write one task the night before.
- If you hesitate in the morning, start anyway.
- Stop only when time ends, not when comfort appears.

This task carries the day.
Everything else is noise.

6. The Noise Gate

Purpose: Protect the rhythm

Tool:
Phone stays face down.
Notifications off.
Browser tabs closed.

Tactic:

- No screens until after the Rhythm Block.
- If broken, restart the timer.

Attention is fuel.
Guard it like oxygen.

7. The Evening Seal

Purpose: Close the loop

Tool:
Same notebook. Same pen. Same place.

Tactic:

- Answer the night question in one line.
- Do not judge the answer.
- Close the book immediately.

Open loops drain energy.
Closed loops restore it.

Failure Protocol (Non-Negotiable)

If you miss a step:

1. Do not restart the whole system.
2. Resume at the next step immediately.
3. Write one line:
   "I returned to rhythm."

Recovery speed matters more than perfection.

Core Truth

This system does not motivate you.
It conditions you.

Rhythm beats intensity.
Daily order beats chaos.
Executed long enough, this becomes identity.

Algorithm: The Dawn Rhythm

1. Ask the Compass Question

Write one line: "What good shall I do this day?"
Set intention before motion.

2. Strike the Water

Drink a full glass of cold water.
Signal the shift from sleep to action.

3. Move for Five Minutes

Pushups. Squats. Stretching.
Let your body play the first beat of the day.

4. Anchor the First Work Block

Protect 20 to 30 minutes.
Attack your most important task in silence.

5. Run the Reflection Ledger

Two columns.
Left: yesterday's wins.
Right: yesterday's breaks in rhythm.
Adjust your cycle with truth, not wishful thinking.

6. Close the Loop

Ask at night: "What good have I done today?"
Lock the day. Prime the next rhythm.

Reflection Questions

1. When the alarm hits, do I rise with intention or fall into drift?
2. Which single act today will anchor me when chaos strikes?
3. Tonight, when I ask "What good have I done?", will I offer truth or excuse?

Pillar Activation: The Furnace of First Light

Game Plan
This chapter tells the hard truth. Comfort steals futures. Discipline at dawn builds them. Franklin proves resilience starts before the world wakes, not when crisis arrives.

Pillar Activation

- Mental Precision (Head): Franklin began every day with one ruthless question. Clarity cut through drift. Focus replaced delay.
- Physical Mastery (Body): Cold water, labor, movement. He shocked the body awake and trained it to obey command. Energy followed action.
- Emotional Power (Heart): Poverty, ridicule, exile never ruled him. He converted frustration into repetition. Repetition hardened resolve.
- Spiritual Alignment (Soul): "What good shall I do this day?" anchored his life. Purpose steadied him when storms hit family, politics, and loyalty.
- Imaginative Strategy (Vision): Essays written in secret became influence. Dawn discipline fueled inventions, diplomacy, and nation-shaping ideas.

Coach J's Challenge
Here's the line you cannot dodge.
If you lose the morning, you lose leverage.
Stop negotiating with comfort.

Claim one hour before the world touches you.
Ask one clear question.
Move your body.
Strike your most important task in silence.
Do it daily until rhythm becomes identity.

Locker-Room Reflection
When the alarm hits tomorrow, will you rise into discipline? Or sink back into drift?

Chapter 7: Establish Your Primary Mission

"One child, one teacher, one book, one pen can change the world."

~ Malala Yousafzai

Distraction hunts your destiny. Mission hunts it back.

Distraction shadows your life long before you notice its reach. It slips through cracked attention, pulls at loose thoughts, and feeds on moments you never guard. Nothing announces its attack. It arrives disguised as comfort, convenience, and curiosity. By the time you feel the drift, hours have vanished and purpose has dimmed.

Yet mission cuts through that slow death with one clean strike.

Every human being carries an internal code. Yours waits beneath the noise, ready to ignite the moment you choose direction. Without mission, that code sleeps. Your energy scatters. Days slide into repetition. You chase tasks that never build anything worth remembering. Motion replaces meaning. Survival pretends to be purpose.

Then mission arrives, and everything changes.

It does not whisper. It does not negotiate. Mission demands allegiance. It pulls your mind into clarity, hardens your emotions into resolve, steadies your spirit toward one horizon. Where drift dissolves you, mission concentrates you. Where distraction spreads you thin, mission gathers you whole.

A truth like this becomes undeniable in the furnace that forged Malala Yousafzai.

On a quiet bus rattling through Pakistan's Swat Valley, a masked man climbed aboard and spat a question that sliced the air: "Who is Malala?"
The bullet that followed aimed to end her name.
Instead, it awakened her mission.

Doctors fought for her life. Machines kept rhythm when breath could not. Weeks passed before her lips moved, but the first words she forced through pain carried more power than the bullet that tried to silence her: "I am Malala."

Identity reclaimed.
Direction chosen.
Mission born.

From a hospital bed in Birmingham to a podium at the United Nations, she rose with a steadiness that stunned the globe. No tremor touched her voice. No bitterness tangled her purpose. Instead of revenge, she spoke of education. Instead of fear, she offered vision. Her mission: a desk for every child, a book in every hand, ignited across nations because mission speaks in a frequency the world cannot ignore.

This chapter teaches that same law.

Purpose does not appear out of luck. You forge it. You declare it. You live inside it until distraction bows. Drift dies the moment you anchor your life to one clear aim. When mission burns in your chest, your decisions sharpen, your steps align, and your energy stops leaking into tasks that steal your strength.

Look at your own life.
How many mornings have dissolved before you took aim?
What conversations drained you because they held no meaning?
Which opportunities slipped because your focus scattered?

The pattern ends here.

Mission hunts your destiny back.
Mission gives your days a spine.
Mission builds the architecture your future stands on.

Choose it now.
Write it clean.
Hold it tight.
Let the world adjust to the force of your direction.

This is where your aim begins.

Malala Yousafzai: The Furnace of the Indestructible Voice

The Bullet

October 9, 2012. Swat Valley.

A school bus rattles along a narrow road. Girls laugh. Books press tight to chests. Futures feel close enough to touch.

Malala Yousafzai sits upright. Fifteen. Alert. Unafraid.

The bus jerks to a stop.

A man steps inside. His voice carries one demand. Flat. Final.

"Who is Malala?"

The air collapses. Breath vanishes. Time fractures.

The gun fires.

Metal tears through flesh. Blood blooms across her scarf. Screams rupture the bus. Malala falls forward into darkness.

The world believes the story has ended.

It has not.

The Bed of Silence

Weeks dissolve.

Birmingham, England.

White light burns through closed lids. Tubes crowd her throat. Machines keep count when breath cannot. Surgeons speak in numbers stripped of hope.

Odds thin. Silence thickens.

Then motion.

A twitch. A breath. A sound pulled from depth.

"I am Malala."

Three words survive a bullet.

No plea. No fear. No apology.

Identity stands upright before the body can.

The furnace ignites.

The Podium of Fire

July 12, 2013.

United Nations. New York City.

Her sixteenth birthday.

She walks forward wrapped in a pink shawl once worn by Benazir Bhutto. The cloth carries blood and inheritance. Power remembers power.

The room settles. Leaders still. Cameras tighten.

She grips the lectern.

Her voice returns without tremor.

"They thought the bullets would silence us. But they failed."

The sentence lands. Clean. Unavoidable.

Fear shifts seats.

The Cadence of Defiance

"The terrorists thought they would change my aims and stop my ambitions."

Pause.

"But nothing changed."

Another pause.

"Except this."

The room leans in.

"Weakness died. Fear died. Hopelessness died."

Silence bears the weight.

"Strength was born. Courage was born. Power was born."

A translator freezes mid-motion.

Language cannot outrun truth.

The Turn

She does not attack.

She ascends.

"I am not here to speak against the Taliban."

Expectation breaks.

"I am here to speak up for the right of education for every child."

Revenge dissolves. Mission replaces it.

This is not resistance.

This is architecture.

The Declaration

"One child. One teacher. One book. One pen."

Each word steps forward alone.

"Can change the world."

The room rises before permission arrives. Applause swells. Leaders stand. Some weep. All listen.

She does not bow.

Does not flinch.

The bullet failed.

The Lock

"Let us pick up our books and our pens. They are our most powerful weapons."

When she stops, silence holds.

Then thunder.

From bus to bed to podium, collapse becomes compass.
Wound becomes weapon.
Silence becomes signal.

Malala Yousafzai did not survive the furnace.

She became it.

Universal Law: Divine Oneness

When you declare your mission with full truth, your energy joins the larger field and the universe moves in rhythm with you.

Core Lesson

Malala's story shows resilience as the alchemy of collapse into mission. A bullet shatters her body, yet awakens a deeper identity that refuses extinction. She rises from coma with clarity, steps onto the global stage with courage, and converts personal tragedy into universal advocacy. Her energies align in near-perfect coherence as Mental focus, Emotional courage, Spiritual purpose, and Creative expression surge toward a singular aim: education for every child. Her awareness transforms wound into weapon and trauma into trajectory. She does not return to who she was. She becomes who the world needs.

Client Story: Mission in the Pandemic

The Shattered Office

Before collapse, Daniel lived inside rhythm, morning light sliding across marble as glass doors opened wide and suits cut clean lines through the halls. Coffee clinked, phones rang sharp, screens glowed green with climbing metrics, and momentum answered every step he took. Presence powered his leadership because energy traveled fastest through crowded rooms where hands met, backs were clapped, and deals sealed face to face. Growth defined the mission then, and prestige followed without resistance. That world felt permanent until it vanished.

Silence After March

March arrived without warning and stripped the building bare. One Friday the office hummed with motion, and by Monday empty chairs faced dark screens while the city outside froze in place. Fear moved unseen yet filled every corner, pressing against walls and settling into breath. Zoom replaced the office floor as faces appeared from bedrooms, kitchens, and basements pushed into service. Wrinkled sheets, stacked mugs, sagging shoulders, and muted voices revealed erosion before anyone spoke.

Twenty five professionals stared back at their leader through glass rectangles. Fire once answered his command, and now only shadows returned, thin and uncertain. Recognition landed hard as he felt the same erosion moving through his own chest. Authority thinned in silence, and the mirror showed truth without mercy.

The Weight of the Head

Weeks blurred into a long drain where revenue slipped, clients vanished, and projects stalled under quiet dread. Meetings thickened with hollow stares as exhaustion hunted him through daylight hours and news fed fear late into the night. Anger surfaced fast, patience vanished, and sharp words replaced guidance while silence followed retreat. Leadership cracked under pressure, and the system reflected its source.

Our first conversation carried collapse in his voice. Complaints poured about weakness, lost drive, and divided attention pulled toward families and stress. Language fractured as truth pushed through, and I waited until the moment opened. Then I cut clean.

"The fish stinks from the head down."

The words landed and held the room still as breath caught short and reflection began without defense. Ignition sparked in that pause.

Ignition of Truth

Mission does not disappear on its own. Loss begins at the top and spreads fast because teams mirror posture, tone, and courage under pressure. Fire demands a match, resilience demands demonstration, and unity demands example before belief follows. Purpose outlasts fear when leaders carry it first. The bullet found its mark.

Mission Before Metrics

Night brought a notebook and long silence as ink crossed pages, returned, and crossed again. Lines died under his pen until one remained, cutting through noise with clean force.

"I lead people to health, clarity, and purpose no matter the chaos."

That sentence shifted the ground beneath him as profit released its grip and protection replaced pursuit. Mission claimed command. The line echoed until his voice steadied, planning followed with calm precision, and leadership prepared to stand exposed.

The Address

Morning screens flickered alive with dull eyes and flat voices framed by homes turned into quiet cages. He faced the lens and held steady as resolve locked in place. Memory flashed of a young girl standing firm after violence, refusing silence before the world. Breath slowed, courage aligned, and truth led.

"I see your fear and your children behind you."
Stress showed itself and he named it aloud, replacing isolation with shared weight.
"Our mission stands larger than this virus."

Health moved first, clarity followed, and purpose anchored everything else as fear lost ground. Permission came for rest and help, strength redefined itself through care, and forward motion demanded unity. Silence held, then broke, and applause filled the gaps.

Reawakening

Faces lifted across the grid as tears surfaced without shame and jaws set with new resolve. Energy crossed distance again, not through numbers but through meaning. The team returned because mission restored identity first.

The Compass Installed

Every meeting opened with the mission spoken clear. Health showed through boundaries and shared movement, clarity arrived through written priorities named aloud, and resilience stood visible against despairing headlines. The team mirrored what they saw. Revenue stabilized, clients returned, and homes transformed into command centers as purpose bled into families and friendships.

No lead carried this bullet. A pandemic forged the impact. Mission traveled outward through example, collapse delivered direction, and legacy took root.

Tools & Tactics: The Mission Command System™

Tool 1: Mission Statement Forge

Formula (Upgraded):
"I [verb] [specific result] so that [people] can [measurable change]."

Rules

- Use an action verb that costs energy.
- Name a real result, not a feeling.
- The outcome must change behavior or capacity.

Example
"I build disciplined systems so leaders can win their days without burning out."

Why it works
 Clarity sharpens aim. Vague missions produce vague days.

Tool 2: The Daily Mission Compass (Non-Negotiable)

This is not journaling. This is command and control.

Morning: Identity Lock (2 minutes)

- Write your mission once by hand.
- Under it, finish this sentence:
  "Today I prove this mission by doing _____."
- Only one proof allowed.

This locks identity to action.

Day: Mission Filter (5 minutes total)

Before starting work, ask one ruthless question for each task:

"Does this move my mission forward today?"

- Choose 3 tasks only.
- Each task must:

    - Create leverage
    - Remove friction
    - Or compound results

Busy work is mission theft.

Night: Mission Audit (3 minutes)

Score using criteria, not emotion.

Scorecard

- 10 = I executed the proof without hesitation.
- 7 = I executed late or with resistance.
- 4 = I avoided the proof.
- 1 = I betrayed the mission.

Then write one sentence only:
"What blocked execution today?"

No storytelling. No excuses. Data only.

Tool 3: Weekly Mission Calibration (10 minutes, once per week)

- Review 7 scores.
- If the average is under 7:
    - Your mission is either unclear or dishonest.

- Rewrite the mission only if behavior refuses to follow it.

Truth follows behavior, not intention.

Why This System Wins

- Neuroscience: Writing + decision framing strengthens prefrontal control.
- Performance science: Fewer priorities increase execution speed.
- Behavioral economics: Scoring with consequence reduces self-deception.
- Leadership reality: Identity is proven daily or it decays.

This is not inspiration.
This is operational identity.

Use it for 14 days.
Your calendar will expose who you really are.
Then you get to decide who you become.

Algorithm: The Mission Compass

1. Write one sentence: your mission.
2. Read it aloud every dawn.
3. Align three daily actions with it.
4. Reflect nightly: Did I live it?

Five minutes. Compass installed. Drift demolished.

Reflection Questions

1. What desire stalks you relentlessly?
2. What would a focused version of you build in 90 days?
3. What has drift already stolen from you?

Pillar Activation: Mission Over Distraction

Game Plan
This chapter draws a hard line between drift and destiny. Distraction steals your days quietly. Mission takes them back with force. When you choose a clear aim, your life stops leaking energy and starts building momentum.

Pillar Activation

- Mental Precision (Head)
  Mission sharpens focus. Malala's clarity cut through chaos. One identity. One direction. No wasted thought.
- Physical Mastery (Body)
  Her body took the hit. Recovery became discipline. Breath, rest, and resilience carried her forward. The body served the mission.
- Emotional Power (Heart)
  Fear never led. Anger never drove. Courage replaced both. Emotion turned into fuel instead of noise.
- Spiritual Alignment (Soul)
  Purpose anchored everything. Education became

her north star. Meaning steadied her when pain tried to scatter her.

- Imaginative Strategy (Vision)
  She transformed a wound into a worldwide movement. Words replaced weapons. Vision opened doors bullets could not close.

Coach J's Challenge
Drift ends the moment you declare your mission. Write one sentence that tells the truth about why you lead. Prove it today. One hard action. No negotiation. No delay. Mission demands allegiance. Clarity follows commitment.

Locker-Room Reflection
Where has distraction been stealing your energy? And what mission will you lock in to take it back today?

Chapter 8: Get G.A.S.

(Gratitude, Affirmation, Structure)

"Nothing can dim the light which shines from within."

~ Maya Angelou

First light pushes across the sky and the house stays still while your mind leaps ahead of the sun. An alarm cuts the dark as a phone flashes with demands. Children shout from distant rooms and bills glare like quiet threats from the counter. Breath rushes fast and pressure forms the first note of the day. Many people begin here in combat rather than calm and chaos sets the rhythm while the body scrambles to match its frantic beat.

Another path waits with clarity and truth. Three words shape that path: Gratitude, Affirmation, Structure. Gratitude lowers the storm inside before it grows. Affirmation shapes identity before the world pushes a false one. Structure gives the day a spine before fear bends it. These forces ignite rather than soothe and they convert chaos into power. Panic shifts into presence and noise sharpens into direction. Collapse lifts into a steady climb as order replaces overwhelm and command replaces survival.

Maya Angelou proved this with her rise. She moved through childhood shadows that tried to silence her. Violence shattered safety and stole her voice as silence closed around her for years. Shame stalked her steps and the world turned into a cage. Gratitude cut the first crack of light through that cage. A sunrise offered warmth. A page carried escape. A breath arrived that did not break her. Small sparks formed her first truth and gratitude shifted her frequency long before sound returned.

Affirmation rebuilt her sense of worth. Stories filled the space where words once lived. Lines shaped her strength in the dark and identity formed without witnesses. Structure held the pieces with steady discipline. Daily reading shaped her mind. Daily imagining shaped her spirit. Daily rebuilding shaped her future. She anchored herself in ritual while the world tried to erase her.

Her voice returned with thunder rather than tremor. It rose steady and warm and reached nations. It carried truth strong enough to free others. She mastered the path before she named it. Gratitude. Affirmation. Structure. A girl who feared her voice could kill became a woman whose voice saved millions.

Your morning holds the same threshold. G.A.S. offers your way through it. This is the morning you were meant to build.

Maya Angelou: The Furnace of Gratitude

Before the world knew her as Maya Angelou, she was Marguerite Johnson.
A child of the segregated South.
Passed between homes.
Stability never stayed long enough to learn her name.

Red clay dust clung to her shoes.
Pine needles cracked beneath thin soles.

Kitchen smoke carried cornbread and heat into narrow rooms.
She moved quietly through it all, tall and awkward, eyes holding questions too heavy for a child to carry.

She was not a symbol yet.
She was a girl learning how to disappear.

The Collapse

At seven, violence shattered her world.
Her mother's boyfriend violated her.
Pain entered without permission and refused to leave.

When she spoke the truth, the man went to prison.
Days later, others killed him.

A child drew a fatal conclusion.
My voice kills.

She stopped speaking.

Five years passed in silence.
No answers in school.
No hymns in church.
No reply at home.

Sound died in her throat before it reached air.
Her body lived.
Her spirit hid.

Silence became a furnace.

Shame fed it.
Isolation sealed it.

The Ignition

Silence removed her voice.
It sharpened her attention.

She read everything.
Dickens. Shakespeare. Poe.
Black writers hidden from classrooms but alive on
pages.

She memorized language.
Stored rhythm.
Collected meaning.

Books became breath.
Imagination became speech.

Gratitude entered quietly.
Not politeness.
Survival.

She thanked the morning for arrival.
The air for permission to breathe.
Words for giving her a world untouched by violence.

Gratitude hummed beneath her silence.
Low.
Steady.
Alive.

The Reframe

Her life revealed a law before she could name it.
Frequency shapes form.

Her world pressed down with racism and loss.
She tuned upward anyway.

Not through denial.
Through attention.

Gratitude shifted her internal signal.
The signal reshaped her path.

Circumstance did not rescue her.
Alignment did.

The Transformation

When Maya spoke again, she did not whisper.
She arrived.

Years of silence compressed grief into power.
Gratitude gave it structure.

Her voice carried velvet and thunder.
Honey and iron.

She did not perform language.
She transmitted it.

Each poem carried charge.
Every sentence carried survival refined into art.

I Know Why the Caged Bird Sings did not explain pain.
It transmuted it.

The cage remained.
The song changed everything.

The Legacy

Her voice multiplied.

Language became architecture.
Rhythm became refuge.
Discipline became transmission.

When she stood at the presidential inauguration,
millions felt their own cages weaken.
As she said, "Still, I rise," she spoke biology, not bravado.

Her life proved the law without teaching it.

Gratitude changes frequency.
Frequency changes form.
Form becomes destiny.

She did not escape the fire.
She turned it into light.

Universal Law: Vibration

Shift your frequency with intention and your entire
reality moves to meet you.

Core Lesson

Maya Angelou demonstrates resilience as the alchemy of gratitude turned into creative power. Maya survives a childhood collapse that steals her voice, yet inside that silence she forges the inner architecture that will later move nations. She absorbs books, cultivates gratitude, and aligns with the Law of Vibration until her internal frequency rises beyond trauma's reach. When she finally speaks again, her voice carries the force of transmuted pain shaped into art. Through poetry, memoir, activism, and her commanding presence, she converts suffering into structure and silence into song. Her resilience proves that the highest transformation occurs not by escaping trauma, but by elevating its frequency until it becomes destiny.

Client Story: The Executive Who Found His Fuel

Armor and Pressure

At forty two, Jonas wore power like armor and trusted it to protect him. Crisp suits cut sharp lines. Polished shoes struck marble with command. Glass walls framed a skyline that promised permanence and rewarded obedience. From the outside, invincibility radiated confidence and order. Inside, collapse ticked quietly like a hidden charge wired to his chest.

Morning arrived with mechanical cruelty and never varied its attack. An alarm screamed at five thirty before his feet touched the floor. The phone vibrated with urgent messages flashing danger in capital letters. Children shouted down the hall as milk splashed across tile. Silence followed from his wife, heavier than any argument. Pressure passed for success in his mind, but the body kept better records. Shoulders locked into stone knots. A heart hammered like a drum signaling combat without end. Acid burned through each meal as stress consumed digestion. The system warned him long before language caught up.

The Collapse

One morning, restraint finally failed and spilled across the table. Blue light from the laptop burned tired eyes without mercy. Unread messages stacked like bricks dropping toward his head. Noise rose as milk spilled, a daughter shouted, and the dog barked. Control snapped without a sound.

A fist crashed into oak and sent the mug sliding sideways. Scalding coffee raced across unpaid bills and soaked ambition in brown stains. Children froze as if danger learned their names. His wife stared, pale and unmoving, as truth entered the room. Hands pressed against temples while a whisper escaped through clenched teeth. I cannot keep this up.

Breath shortened. Tears sharpened vision instead of blurring it. Millions in contracts collapsed into a narrow tunnel of panic. Decades of ambition shrank into exhaustion. The identity of high performer closed tight around him. Success suddenly felt like a coffin built with his own hands.

The Ignition

That afternoon, Jonas reached out before pride could intervene. The first word cracked and exposed strain beneath control. Composure tried to stand, but desperation leaked through every syllable. A simple confession landed heavy and honest. Every day feels like war before I leave the house.

Truth required no comfort, only precision. You do not need more hours, I told him. Fuel runs this engine, not willpower or punishment. A Ferrari dies fast on an empty tank. Gratitude, affirmation, and structure create ignition. Without fuel, burnout wins. With it, combustion begins.

Silence followed and carried more weight than resistance. A long exhale emptied years of held breath. Something shifted without argument or defense. That quiet moment marked the turn. Ignition never announces itself with noise.

The Choice

Night brought paper, ink, and shaking hands to the table. A notebook opened like a door left unlocked too long. Three lines appeared, simple and unprotected. Gratitude named his children's laughter. Affirmation claimed calm and power together. A clear goal promised closure and family celebration by week's end.

The notebook closed with finality. Words spoken aloud anchored intention in the room. Breath deepened as tension loosened. A shift occurred without fireworks. Choice replaced reaction for the first time in years.

The Transformation

Morning returned but failed to ambush him. Panic slept while he claimed the kitchen table first. Three minutes passed with discipline instead of dread. Gratitude filled one minute with a son's laughter. Affirmation steadied his voice through repetition. A goal formed clearly behind closed eyes.

Children thundered down the stairs and met a different presence. The chest stayed open. The jaw relaxed. A smile reached his wife without effort. Calm entered the house and stayed.

Later, the first call revealed change without explanation. Words landed with clarity. Authority held steady without force. A message appeared in the chat window. You seem different today. Good different.

Days stacked into weeks through repetition. Three minutes anchored each morning without exception. Fuel came first. Conflict waited. Mornings transformed from battlefields into launch pads. Calm spread outward and multiplied quietly.

The Legacy

Understanding arrived without ceremony. This practice never aimed at productivity alone. Transmission mattered more than output. Energy carried forward into every room he entered. Others rose because his frequency changed first.

Gratitude lifted the household into rhythm. Affirmation stabilized a team under pressure. Structure restored coherence across the company. Leadership replaced survival without announcement. Collapse transformed into controlled combustion.

Jonas learned the law beneath performance and peace. Fuel shapes frequency. Frequency shapes destiny.

Tools & Tactics: The G.A.S. Ignition Protocol™

Tools & Tactics for Daily State, Identity, and Execution Control

1. G.A.S. Command Journal (90–180 seconds)

Setup
 Draw three columns. Write one line per column. No more.

Column 1: Gratitude (Stability)

- Write one thing that proves life is working *right now*.

- No abstractions. Real, present, specific.

Example:

> I express gratitude for my ability to greet
> this new day with love in my heart.

Rule: If it doesn't calm your breath, rewrite it.

Column 2: Affirmation (Identity)

- Write one identity statement in present tense.
- Start with "I am".
- Then write "I affirm my _____.
- Tie it to behavior, not hope.

Example:

> I am the person who executes before doubt
> speaks. I affirm my execution over any
> spoken doubts.

Rule: If it feels soft, it's wrong.

Column 3: Outcome Target (Impact)

- Write one executable result for today.
- Observable. Finishable. Binary.

Example:

> Complete the proposal draft and send it to
> my boss by 3:00 PM today so my desk is
> clear.

Rule: If someone else couldn't verify it, it's not a real target.

Why this works

- Gratitude stabilizes the nervous system.
- Identity directs behavior.
- Outcome forces movement.
  This is state → self → execution.

2. 3-Minute Frequency Lock Protocol

This replaces "visualization" with neurological anchoring.

Minute 1: Ground the System (Breath + Proof)

- Inhale through the nose for 4.
- Exhale through the mouth for 6.
- On each exhale, whisper one real win from your life.
  Not fantasy. Evidence.

Purpose: Signals safety and capability to the brain.

Minute 2: Declare Identity (Voice + Posture)

- Stand up.
- Feet planted. Chest open.
- Speak your affirmation out loud, once, slowly.

Example:

I execute under pressure. I finish what I
start.

Purpose: Voice + posture hard-wire identity faster than
thought.

Minute 3: Seal the Result (Mental Rehearsal)

- See the exact moment today's target is complete.
- Not the work. The finish.
- See the send button pressed.
- Feel the relief and control.

End with one internal command:

Do it now.

Purpose: The brain moves toward completed pictures.

Optional (But Lethal) Add-On: The Evening Echo (60
seconds)

At night, answer one line:

Did my actions match my morning identity?
yes or no

No journaling. No stories. Just truth.

This closes the feedback loop and sharpens tomorrow.

Bottom Line

- This is no longer a mindset tool.

- It's a daily alignment weapon.
- Three minutes to set state.
- One clear target to bend the day.
- One identity reinforced through action.

Use it daily for 30 days and behavior changes.
Use it for 90 days and identity locks.

Algorithm

The G.A.S. Algorithm (3 Minutes to Fuel Your Day):

1. Minute 1: Gratitude: Write one. Whisper it.
2. Minute 2: Affirmation: Write one. Speak it.
3. Minute 3: Goal: Write one SMART goal. Visualize it done.

Fuel secured. Day ignited.

Reflection Questions

1. What am I currently vibrating into my environment?
2. Which gratitude shifts my inner state fastest?
3. What goal excites my nervous system into forward motion?

Pillar Activation: Gratitude as Alchemy (G.A.S. Ignition)

Game Plan
This chapter proves one truth without apology: collapse does not end you. It fuels you, if you ignite it correctly. Gratitude stabilizes your state, affirmation forges identity, and structure drives execution.

Pillar Activation

- Mental Precision (Head): Maya Angelou trained her mind inside silence. Books replaced chaos. Focus replaced fear. Jonas reclaimed clarity by naming one outcome each morning.
- Physical Mastery (Body): Breath slowed the storm. Posture and voice anchored control. Calm entered the body before performance followed.
- Emotional Power (Heart): Gratitude softened trauma's grip. Emotion stopped driving behavior and started fueling direction.
- Spiritual Alignment (Soul): Purpose rose before comfort returned. Maya aligned with meaning beyond pain. Jonas chose presence over pressure.
- Imaginative Strategy (Vision): Silence became a forge for story. A three-minute ritual became a launchpad. Creativity turned confinement into motion.

Coach J's Challenge
Stop waking up to combat. Fuel comes first. Tomorrow morning, take three minutes. Write one gratitude that

calms your breath. Speak one affirmation that feels uncomfortably strong. Lock one outcome you will finish today. Then move. No debate.

Locker-Room Reflection
What frequency are you transmitting before the day ever touches you?

Chapter 9: Meditate with Warrior Stillness

"The strength of the team is each individual member. The strength of each member is the team."

~ Phil Jackson

Most mistake stillness for softness. The quiet man sits alone with slow breath and calm eyes. Crowds assume he stepped out of the fight. They judge silence as surrender. Truth hides beneath that false read.

Stillness builds strength through presence. Silence sharpens sight until noise loses its pull. Phil Jackson shaped eleven titles with that code. Turmoil rose around him as egos clashed and kingdoms strained. Chaos filled every room he entered.

Pressure tore the Bulls apart as ambition cracked the floor. Conflict pulled the Lakers into a cold war between giants. Reporters circled each practice while rumors stalked each flight. Most coaches would have hurled more fire across the blaze. Jackson chose a different strike.

Breath anchored his command. Meditation shaped his huddles. Players sat in circles and drew air through fear. They released ego on the exhale. They replaced panic with steady attention. They studied the moment instead of the storm.

A frantic mind loses the court. A centered mind sees the entire map. Jordan found fresh edge in the quiet. Pippen reclaimed confidence through calm work. Kobe stepped beyond talent into pure discipline. Shaq stopped wrestling the world and began to anchor it.

Crisis rose in many forms. Injuries strained rotations. Feuds split rooms. Executives pushed agendas that sliced trust. Cameras hunted weakness. Jackson met each test with stillness. Silence formed the shield that held each dynasty in place. Presence guided every decision.

He never tried to shout over turmoil. He refused to join the noise. He stood inside a calm no one could break. That calm shaped warriors capable of clarity under heat. That clarity forged seasons that still define greatness.

Warrior Stillness follows the same truth. Meditation does not signal escape. Meditation provides reconnaissance. It offers a high view of threat and opportunity. It builds ground no crisis can steal. It prepares you for conflict and choice.

A centered leader bends the field. A calm presence steadies the tribe. A single breath realigns a fractured group or a collapsing day. Stillness makes you unshakable. Silence keeps you unreachable. Master both and you become the axis that holds the room.

Warrior Stillness gives you the power to lead when others break. It lets you think when others panic. It lets you see when others distort truth. It lifts you when others collapse. Phil Jackson lived that secret in every season.

Champions rise from quiet. True power forms in rooms where noise cannot enter.

Phil Jackson: The Furnace of Stillness

Phil Jackson did not arrive in Chicago with glory.
He arrived with scars.

He played for the New York Knicks as a role player.
Defense. Hustle. The work nobody praised.
Injuries ended his career early and without ceremony.

Collapse came quietly.
No spotlight. No farewell tour.
Just the question that follows broken bodies.
Who am I now?

Most disappear there.
Phil did not.

He went where ambition rarely traveled.
Puerto Rico. Dirt courts. Rattling buses.
Basketball stripped to rhythm and breath.

He coached men clinging to last chances.
Learned patience before power.
Humility before authority.

He carried books instead of schemes.
Taoist texts. Native American mysticism.
Not theory. Survival tools.

While others shouted, Phil listened.

As controlled, he aligned.
Basketball became a practice of self-mastery.

By the time Chicago noticed him, his furnace was
already lit.
Obscurity had burned ego clean.
Silence had sharpened him.

Fire Meets Stillness

Michael Jordan tested every structure he entered.
Talent without limit.
Fire without pause.

"Why pass," Jordan asked,
"when no one else can do what I do?"

Phil did not argue.
He let silence answer first.

"If you want to be great," he said,
"make others great."

That was not strategy.
It was law.

Phil had already lost everything once.
A career. An identity. A future.
Jordan's fire could not intimidate him.

The Triangle was not an offense.
It was alignment.

Every cut mattered.
Each pass demanded trust.
Dominance without harmony collapsed the system.

Jordan resisted.
Fire always does.

But resilience is not submission.
It is adaptation under pressure.

A pass to Paxson.
The kick-out to Kerr.
Trust replaced control.

Fire learned restraint.
Stillness learned motion.

Three championships followed.
Then three more.

Not because Jordan softened.
Because he expanded.

Harnessing the Storm

Dennis Rodman arrived as chaos.
Noise. Color. Collapse waiting to happen.

Most would have crushed him.
Phil gave him space.

Freedom off the court.
Stillness on it.

Rodman learned to sit.
To breathe.
And stop spinning.

Chaos found rhythm.

Phil gave him purpose.
Rebound everything.
Defend relentlessly.
Sacrifice without applause.

Jordan resisted again.
Control wanted order.

Phil reminded him of the first furnace.
Greatness multiplies when shared.

Jordan trusted.
The storm obeyed structure.

Three more titles.
A dynasty doubled.

Stillness did not eliminate chaos.
It transmuted it.

Collapse, Again

Phil left Chicago discarded.
Six titles meant nothing to power.

Silence returned.
So did the furnace.

He did not cling.
Instead, he practiced.

Meditation.
Journaling.
Surrender.

Then Los Angeles called.

The Lakers were fractured royalty.
Shaq and Kobe shared a court, not a crown.

Phil brought no force.
Only alignment.

The Triangle returned.
Silence returned.
Ego resisted.

Then yielded.

Three championships followed.

Collapse refined him again.

Birth of the Black Mamba

When Shaq left, the league celebrated.
They saw an ending.

Kobe remained.
Brilliant. Isolated. Consumed.

His fire burned inward.
Obsessed with proof.

Phil recognized the pattern.
Jordan had walked it before.

This furnace demanded surrender.

Silence returned.
Meditation returned.
Breath replaced rage.

Kobe resisted.
Then listened.

The Black Mamba was born.
Cold. Precise. Lethal.

Not fury.
Mastery.

Two more titles followed.

Phil finished with eleven rings.
But trophies were not the triumph.

He proved the law.

Resilience transmutes ego into empire.
Stillness sharpens fire into destiny.

Universal Law: Correspondence

When you align your inner world with stillness and purpose, the outer world reorganizes into harmony and power.

Core Lesson

Phil Jackson learned resilience in the quiet after pain. Injuries ended a modest career and forced him into wilderness. Puerto Rico offered dirt courts and raw spirit. The CBA offered broken rosters and hungry men. Each stop shaped his patience, his vision, his inner code. He studied rhythm, culture, and breath. He built a calm center strong enough to survive noise. He forged a mind that saw patterns in chaos. He crafted an emotional steadiness born from years of being ignored. He formed a spiritual anchor through Zen and Native wisdom. He added creative force through ritual and the Triangle offense. He found humility in a body that betrayed him. He walked into Chicago with a furnace already lit. He knew how to hold fire without fear.

Chicago tested that fire. Jordan played with raw power. Jackson placed stillness around him. One man hunted greatness. The other built a frame for that hunt. Silence replaced command. Trust replaced force. The Triangle gave shape to instinct. Jordan learned to lift others. The team rose as one. Jackson watched ego bend under purpose. He saw dominance turn into orchestration. He taught that greatness grows when shared. His insight created a new kind of champion.

Rodman carried a storm into the room. Many coaches tried to cage it. Jackson gave it a path. He honored the wild spirit and shaped it with clarity. Chaos found a job in defense and rebounding. Disorder turned into advantage. Rodman trusted him because Jackson never sought control. He sought alignment. He turned noise into signal. He turned impulse into craft. He saw talent where others saw trouble. He saw possibility hiding under frenzy.

Collapse returned when Kraus dismantled the Bulls. Jackson walked out with no anger. He returned to meditation and wrote his truth. Ego dropped. Stillness rose. He rebuilt identity with quiet honesty. Loss shaped new insight. Collapse became kiln and not coffin. He stepped into the Lakers with a restored core. He entered a war between Shaq and Kobe. Fire met fire. Jackson offered structure. He offered breath. He offered one shared system. He turned fracture into a dynasty through presence and trust.

Kobe then stood alone. Talent burned fierce. Rage threatened to consume him. Jackson sat with him through the heat. He guided him toward discipline. Kobe shifted from fury to precision. He changed from validation to purpose. He sharpened craft until it cut through doubt. Jackson watched the Mamba form. He watched ego soften into mastery. He watched a young star accept the burden of leadership. He watched resilience take shape in real time.

Phil Jackson built no empire of ego. He built an architecture of stillness. He showed that storms reveal structure. He proved that talent needs truth. He proved that chaos bows to calm. Rings followed, yet rings never told the story. His true legacy lives in the repeatable system he forged: sit inside chaos, breathe, see the unseen pattern, guide the wild force, and rebuild after every fall. That path turns pressure into power. That path turns men into masters. That path forms the quiet spine of resilience.

Client Story: Panic Becomes a Throne

Ignition Under Glass

Adrian stood thirty four, a tech founder choking inside a burning machine. Millions sat raised while investors circled and his team waited for direction that never arrived. Calendars crushed daylight, thoughts sprinted unchecked, the body survived on caffeine and fear. Success tightened like wire around his chest and cut circulation to judgment.

The Stall Where Power Failed

Collapse arrived inside a boardroom thick with questions and sharp eyes. Pressure seized his chest, vision smeared, breath vanished mid sentence. He fled the hallway, locked a bathroom stall, and folded onto porcelain. Panic owned him there, stripped of titles, stripped of command.

The Stillness Prescription

Instruction followed with ruthless simplicity and no room for debate. Five minutes daily demanded stillness, posture grounded, breath four in and six out. An anchor phrase cut through noise and claimed territory inside the storm. Silence became the assignment, not escape but confrontation.

Training the Unruly Mind

Early sessions scraped nerves raw and made skin crawl. Thoughts screamed mutiny while muscles twitched for flight. Return followed return as discipline replaced impulse through repetition. Presence learned its weight the same way champions earned rings through boredom and grind.

The Room Turns

Weeks later another boardroom ignited with anger and impossible demands. Eyes darted toward him as panic climbed toward the throat. Breath entered on count four, exited on count six, words slowed. Shoulders dropped, voice steadied, gravity returned to the room.

Recognition Without Applause

Noise bent toward quiet authority and questions lost their barbs. An investor paused him near the door and spoke without flourish. Something changed when you enter now, the room listens. Power announced itself without volume or explanation.

The Throne Claimed

Command settled not as dominance but as coherence under fire. Stillness rippled outward and rewired trust across the team. Pressure still arrived yet no longer fractured his center. He conducted the storm instead of absorbing its damage.

The Law Revealed

Legacy coaches proved the pattern across dynasties and decades. Stillness never erases chaos but shapes it into usable order. From that seat Adrian learned the governing law of resilience. Panic transforms into presence, presence into harmony, harmony into command.

Tools & Tactics: The 5-Minute Warrior Stillness Protocol

Stillness as Dominance, Not Escape

Purpose

This drill is not for relaxation.
It is for commanding your internal battlefield when pressure rises.
Stillness here equals control. Control equals power.

Phase 1: Structural Command (30 seconds)

Sit upright. Spine tall. Chin level. Feet flat and grounded.

No slouching.
Posture signals authority to the nervous system.

Phase 2: Tactical Breath Control (3 minutes)

Close your eyes.

Inhale through the nose for 4.
Exhale through the mouth for 6.

Complete 15 slow cycles.

Longer exhales downshift cortisol, stabilize heart rate variability, and place the prefrontal cortex back in command. This is proven autonomic regulation, not mysticism.

Phase 3: Warrior Focus Lock (1 minute)

Bring attention to a single internal point.

Not relaxation.
Not drifting.

Focus like a sentry tracking movement in the dark.
Calm, alert, unblinking.

Stillness with awareness trains dominance under stress.

Anchor Phrase Forge

Identity, Not Affirmation

Rule

Your phrase must be:

- Short
- Declarative
- Non-emotional
- Absolute

Examples:

- "I remain unmoved."
- "I hold the line."
- "I decide the pace."
- "Stillness commands outcomes."

Avoid poetic softness.
This is a verbal trigger, not inspiration.

Phase 4: Identity Imprint (30 seconds)

Repeat the phrase slowly on each exhale.

Do not hype it.
Do not rush it.

Let repetition fuse state + meaning + breath into one signal.

This is classical conditioning applied to leadership performance.

Why This Works

- Controlled breathing regulates the vagus nerve.
- Posture shifts hormonal signaling.
- Focused attention reduces threat reactivity.
- Repetition under calm states encodes identity responses.

You are training how you respond before chaos arrives.

Execution Rule

- Use daily.
- Use before decisions.
- Use after emotional spikes.
- Use when silence is required to win.

Stillness is not passive.
Stillness is the throne from which action is chosen.

Algorithm: The Warrior Stillness Protocol (≤10 minutes)

Order: Sit → Breathe → Anchor → Command

1. Sit. Establish Authority (1 minute)

Sit upright. Spine tall. Feet planted. Hands still.

Posture first.
The body obeys structure.

2. Breathe. Take the Nervous System (4 minutes)

Close your eyes.

Inhale through the nose for 4.
Exhale through the mouth for 6.

Complete 15 steady cycles.

Long exhales cut noise.
Control returns

3. Anchor. Install the Signal (3 minutes)

Choose one short command phrase.

Examples:

- "I hold the line."

- "I remain unmoved."
- "Stillness commands."

Repeat it silently on every exhale.

Do not hype it.
Let it sink below thought into reflex.

4. Command. Identity Visualization (2 minutes)

See the day ahead.

Noise. Pressure. Conflict. Speed.

Now see yourself unchanged.
Breath slow. Eyes clear. Decisions precise.

You do not react.
You choose.

Execution Rule

- Use daily.
- Use before difficult conversations.
- Use when emotion rises.
- Use when silence is required to win.

Five to ten minutes builds internal sovereignty.
Chaos cannot shake what is seated on its own throne.

Reflection Questions

1. What thought or emotion takes control when I stop moving, and how has it been directing my actions?
2. Where does my attention leak the most right now, and what boundary will reclaim it today?
3. In my next moment of pressure, how would silence change my presence and my decision?

Pillar Activation: Warrior Stillness

Game Plan
This chapter proves a hard truth: stillness is not weakness. It is dominance under pressure. Phil Jackson showed the world that calm presence bends chaos, shapes egos, and builds dynasties.

Pillar Activation

- Mental Precision (Head)
  Phil trained clarity through silence. Breath replaced noise. Stillness widened perception until the whole court came into view.
- Physical Mastery (Body)
  Posture, breathing, and ritual grounded the nervous system. Calm bodies supported clear minds when stakes exploded.
- Emotional Power (Heart)
  Ego, anger, panic, and fear were not crushed. They were redirected. Fire became fuel instead of fracture.

- Spiritual Alignment (Soul)
  Zen, purpose, and meaning anchored leadership beyond wins. Phil led from principle, not volume.
- Imaginative Strategy (Vision)
  The Triangle Offense mirrored life. Every role mattered. Harmony created space. Creativity turned conflict into advantage.

Coach J's Challenge
When pressure spikes, stop adding noise. Sit tall. Breathe slow. Choose silence before reaction. Stillness is how you reclaim command. That is how leaders hold the room when others break.

Locker-Room Reflection
When chaos hits, will you react with noise, or respond with stillness?

Chapter 10: Listen Deeply

"More and more I've come to understand that listening is one of the most important things we can do for one another."

~ Fred Rogers

Static fills the world. Meetings collapse into noise. Notifications strike like drums. People trade arguments like arrows. Voices rise while truth fades. Connection breaks when no one listens.

Most hear nothing. They wait for their turn to fire. They hold silence only long enough to reload. They treat conversation like combat and lose what matters.

Another power rises beneath the noise. Stillness stands firm. Presence sharpens focus. Deep listening cuts through confusion and reveals the truth under fear.

Fred Rogers lived this art. He stepped into rooms filled with frantic children, tired parents, and anxious teams. He never met chaos with force. He met it with attention.

Rogers leaned into quiet and opened space for truth. He restored worth when he looked at someone with full presence. He healed shame when he listened without judgment. He made people feel human.

He spoke less so others could rise. He treated every person as someone with a story that deserved air. He honored grief. He honored fear. He honored hope.

Listening, in his hands, acted like precision. Silence steadied the body. Presence softened tension. Attention closed distance. Care shaped connection stronger than speech.

The world does not lack talkers. It lacks listeners who hear beyond words. It needs people who wait for truth.

It needs leaders who draw out the hidden parts of another soul.

Listening is not absence. Listening is power. Attention shapes meaning. Stillness reveals clarity. Presence builds trust that no argument can break.

This chapter teaches the discipline Rogers lived each day. You quiet the inner storm. You widen the space inside your chest. You hear the truth beneath the noise. You become a leader whose silence carries more strength than most speeches.

Connection forms here. Dignity returns here. Healing begins here. Listening becomes the force that turns noise into clarity and chaos into understanding.

This skill is not soft. This craft is strength. Listening becomes your superpower. You learn to wield it now.

Fred Rogers: The Furnace of Gentle Power

Washington, D.C., 1969.

The Senate chamber tightened like a clenched jaw.
Marble walls trapped smoke and impatience.
Pens scratched. Power vibrated, cold and amused.
Public Broadcasting waited for execution.

Twenty million dollars stood on the chopping block.
Not cartoons. Not spectacle.

The quiet refuge.
Mister Rogers' Neighborhood.

Then a man in a cardigan entered the lion's den.

Fred Rogers carried no armor.
No charts. No lobbyists.
Only breath and belief.
The chairman granted six minutes.

Six minutes before the machine closed its jaws.

Senator John Pastore presided.
Sharp eyes. Short temper.
He cut witnesses for sport.
His smirk promised dismissal.

Rogers felt the heat.
Sweat burned his palms.
Breath tightened.
Yet another rhythm steadied him.

Millions of children stood behind his ribs.
Their fear. Their anger.
Their unnamed storms.
He inhaled and began.

His voice stayed soft.
Not weak.
Precise.
Each word placed like stone.

He spoke of anger children could not name.
Fear that twisted them awake at night.
Violence born from silence.
He offered one truth.

If feelings stay unspoken, they explode.

Indifference met him first.
Pens moved.
A watch flashed.
The room buzzed flat.

Then Rogers stopped.

Silence filled the chamber.
Not absence.
Presence.
A tuning fork struck the nervous system.

Men shifted.
Breath slowed.
The room entrained to him.

He asked to sing.

Eyebrows rose.
A ripple of disbelief moved the benches.
A song before the Senate?
Rogers leaned forward.

He released the note.

What do you do with the mad that you feel,
When you feel so mad you could bite?

The melody carried no performance.
Only truth.
Anger held without harm.
Thunder wrapped in velvet.

The room changed temperature.

Pastore's jaw loosened.
Arms dropped.
Eyes softened.
Rogers held the frequency.

Each pause carried children unseen.
Each word modeled restraint.
Anger transformed into care.

When the song ended, silence returned.
This time it rang.

Pastore leaned forward.

"I think it's wonderful," he said.
"Looks like you just earned the twenty million dollars."

Power bent.

In six minutes, Fred Rogers rewired authority.
PBS survived.
Children kept their mirror.

Gentleness earned protection.

Noise never won that day.
Resonance did.

In the lion's den, silence sang.
And the quiet giant stood crowned.

Universal Law: Vibration

The Law of Vibration declares that your inner frequency
shapes your outer world, and in this story Fred Rogers'
calm, sincere resonance overpowered a hostile chamber
and transformed resistance into support.

Core Lesson

Fred Rogers embodies a form of resilience rarely
acknowledged: the power to bend hostile systems not
through force, but through frequency. He carried a quiet
force into a hostile room. Senators watched him with
cold eyes. Power pressed against him like heat from a
furnace. He breathed once and met the moment with
calm intent. His purpose shaped his focus. His clarity
shaped the room.

Stillness steadied his body. Breath anchored his
presence. Words moved with care and precision. The
chamber leaned forward without knowing why. His
inner structure stood firm while the system around him
tried to shake him. Coherence raised his strength above
the noise.

A simple song revealed his true weapon. He sang about anger and choice. He opened a path for truth to enter men who expected a fight. The melody softened the air. The meaning cut deeper than argument. Senators felt their walls shift.

The room changed first in breath, then in tone. Cynicism lost ground. Pastore lowered his guard. Rogers lifted the frequency. He turned skepticism into respect through patience, honesty, and control. Silence followed him like a second voice.

Resilience rose from discipline, not dominance. He regulated himself with mastery. He shaped the chamber by shaping his internal world. The moment ended with Pastore's surrender to coherence. The approval came from something deeper than policy. It came from resonance.

Client Story: The Frequency of Trust

The Charisma That Stalled

Samantha owned Manhattan rooms on contact. Charisma moved first. Vision followed fast. Stages ignited under her voice, yet sales calls collapsed the spell. Prospects nodded, smiled, vanished. Growth hit a ceiling and stayed there.

The Wrong Question

Frustration carried her into my office. Sharp words cut the air before she sat. Why did they not sign when everything sounded right. The answer landed clean. Listening never happened.

Battles Masquerading as Calls

Calls turned into contests. Replies loaded before clients finished. Pauses filled with pitch. Language pushed forward without landing. Clients felt chased, not understood. Silence never worked.

Rewiring the Signal

Change began with restraint. One question opened every call, then five beats of quiet. Fear climbed her throat. Pulse surged. She waited. No one hung up.

What Silence Draws Out

Something shifted across the line. Clients leaned into quiet. Truth spilled without polish. Stories arrived heavy and exposed. Needs showed themselves. Silence pulled honesty forward.

The Mirror Held Steady

Reflection replaced rebuttal. Scripts disappeared. Arguments stopped. She mirrored their words with care. Overwhelm surfaced. Fear named itself. Breath slowed. Shoulders dropped.

Pressure That Reveals

The close demanded patience. One question ended each call. What changes when this problem ends. Waiting followed. Ten seconds. Fifteen. More. Pressure built. Breakthrough came.

Conversion Without Force

Ninety days rewrote results. Conversions doubled. Numbers shifted, yet the deeper change held. Clients felt seen before they felt sold. Trust replaced tension. Presence closed.

The Quiet Advantage

She learned the oldest lesson. Stillness carries authority. Attention shifts rooms. Silence held with care multiplies power. In crowded markets, the listener wins.

Tools & Tactics: The 3-Level Listening Map

Most people listen to reply.
Leaders listen to *locate truth*.

Level 1: Surface Listening
Hear the words. Facts. Story. Claims.
This is data, not direction.

Level 2: Emotional Listening
Track tone, pace, pauses, tension.
Notice what spikes energy or drains it.
Emotion reveals pressure points.

Level 3: Essence Listening
Listen for the *need beneath the narrative.*
What are they protecting?
What are they afraid to lose?
What do they want but can't yet say?

Essence is where decisions are actually made.

The Silence-First Drill

This is how you access Level 3.

1. Ask one clean question.
   No framing. No advice. No stacking.
2. Breathe twice.
   Slow. Visible. Controlled.
   Your nervous system sets the room.
3. Hold silence until they finish.
   No interruptions.
   No rescues.
   No early conclusions.

When people talk past resistance, truth surfaces on its own.

Operational Reality

These are not soft skills.
They are leverage tools.

- Silence lowers defenses faster than persuasion.
- Deep listening creates trust without agreement.

- Essence-level insight collapses conflict and accelerates alignment.

Use them in coaching.
Use them in negotiations.
Use them in conflict.

Most conversations stay shallow and go nowhere.
This system turns conversation into conversion.

Algorithm: The Deep Listening Algorithm

Pause → Breathe → Mirror → Ask → Wait

This is not about being nice.
It is about controlling the field.

1. Pause: Claim the Space

Before you speak, stop.
Silence resets tempo and breaks reactivity.
Whoever controls the pause controls the frame.

2. Breathe: Stabilize the Signal

Inhale slowly through the nose.
Exhale longer through the mouth.
Your nervous system settles first.
A regulated body becomes the anchor in the room.

3. Mirror: Confirm Contact

Reflect only what was said. No edits. No spin.
"What I hear you saying is..."
Accuracy builds safety.
Safety unlocks honesty.

4. Ask: Cut Deeper, Not Wider

Ask one question that opens depth.
Not "Why?"
Use "What" or "Where."
The goal is insight, not explanation.

5. Wait: Let Truth Rise

Say nothing.
Hold eye contact.
Do not rescue the silence.
Silence applies pressure without force.

What emerges next is what matters most.

Application Protocol

Use this once per day:

- One conversation
- One meeting
- One coaching moment
- Or one journal entry with yourself

Five minutes is enough.
Reaction dissolves.
Presence takes over.

Others unconsciously sync to the calmest signal in the room.

This is not listening.
This is positional advantage.

Reflection Questions

1. Where today did I stop listening and start preparing my reply, and what did it cost the conversation?
2. When I held silence after asking a question, what truth surfaced only because I did not interrupt it?
3. When I listened to myself without judgment, what message repeated, and what need did it reveal?

Pillar Activation: The Quiet Giant in the Lion's Den

Game Plan
This chapter proves a hard truth: power does not always shout. It listens. Fred Rogers shows how stillness, presence, and disciplined attention can bend hostile systems and restore human dignity.

Pillar Activation

- Mental Precision (Head): Rogers entered chaos without reactivity. He chose clarity over defense. Focus replaced fear.

- Physical Mastery (Body): Breath steadied his nerves. Still posture regulated the room. His body set the tempo before words landed.

- Emotional Power (Heart): He honored anger without amplifying it. Empathy transformed volatility into connection.

- Spiritual Alignment (Soul): His purpose anchored him. Children mattered more than approval. That "why" held firm under pressure.

- Imaginative Strategy (Vision): A song cut deeper than argument. Creativity bypassed cynicism and reached truth directly.

Coach J's Challenge
When rooms heat up, slow down. Breathe first. Ask one clean question. Then wait. Let silence do the heavy lifting. That is how you lead without force and win without combat.

Locker-Room Reflection
Where today can you replace your next argument with presence and let listening change the outcome?

Chapter 11: Read to Refuel Your Edge

"When something is important enough, you do it even if the odds are not in your favor."

~ Elon Musk

Books hold ignition. Pages wait for a mind brave enough to strike fire. Sentences act as prototypes of the future self. Ideas carve new circuitry that lifts you beyond old limits. Knowledge becomes propulsion for a life built with intent.

Titans treat reading as design work. They build brilliance through deliberate study. Elon Musk read with the hunger of a man shaping entire worlds. Headlines never satisfied him. He reached for physics, engineering, economics, propulsion theory, and science fiction. Possibility expanded each time he fed his mind.

Reading fueled every venture he forged. A book sparked the vision for SpaceX. Another reshaped the path for Tesla. Others guided PayPal, Hyperloop, SolarCity, and the systems that orbit his imagination. He never sought comfort. He pursued capacity. He widened his map until the impossible shifted into the inevitable.

Purpose turns reading into acceleration. Your edge sharpens when you read with discipline. Your strategy strengthens when you meet ideas with action. Your future leaps forward when your mind evolves faster than your fear. Books burn away the ordinary and reveal the extraordinary.

Step into that furnace with courage. Feed it with consistency. Rise with the clarity that comes from a mind trained to grow. Leaders who stop reading halt their evolution. Leaders who read with intention shape the world that follows them.

Elon Musk: The Furnace of Applied Knowledge

Pretoria, South Africa.

A thin boy hides in a school library.
Blood drips from his nose onto an encyclopedia page.
Laughter and fists echo outside.
Inside, only silence and stars.

He reads to survive.
Reads to escape pain by understanding it.
If the world runs on rules, he wants the rules.

Science fiction becomes instruction.
The Hitchhiker's Guide to the Galaxy cracks his mind open.
"If the answer is forty-two," he thinks, "then I will find the question."

At twelve, he codes video games for cash.
By seventeen, he decides the universe is not a place.
It is a problem.

Reading becomes rebellion.
Knowledge becomes armor.

Collapse

Silicon Valley, 2002.

PayPal sells.

One hundred eighty million dollars lands in his account.
Freedom, they call it.

He feels nothing.

He scans the world instead.
Oil wars.
Climate collapse.
NASA shrinking into nostalgia.

Humanity stopped aiming forward.

He could retire.
Instead, he wagers everything on three impossible bets:
electric cars, solar power, and rockets to Mars.

Experts laugh.
Engineers quit.
Money evaporates.

Tesla misses payroll.
SolarCity stalls.
SpaceX rockets explode and fall into the Pacific like
burning confessions.

Christmas Eve, 2008.

One rocket remains.
If it fails, everything ends.

His marriage collapses.
Friends disappear.

Sleep vanishes.

He watches the countdown and whispers,
"Fly."

The engine ignites.
The rocket rises.
It keeps rising.

For the first time in six years, something he built
survives.

Ignition

He does not celebrate.

He drives back to the office.
Sits on the floor.
Opens a grease-stained textbook on orbital mechanics.

Newton.
Tsiolkovsky.
Propulsion ratios.

He traces equations like scripture.

Every book he ever consumed converges into one
moment.
Reading was never escape.

It was rehearsal.

When he looks up, he understands the truth:
Words become engines when applied under pressure.

Transformation

His life accelerates beyond normal human cadence.

At Tesla, factories bleed cash.
He studies battery chemistry and supply chains.
Sleeps on the floor.
Emails instructions at three in the morning.

Metal begins to obey.

At SpaceX, failure turns into data.
He reads until rocket design becomes instinct.
PhDs argue credentials.
He rewrites their models overnight.

At SolarCity, he studies energy economics.
"The sun," he says, "doesn't send invoices."

At Neuralink, he learns how neurons fire.
Thought becomes signal.
Signal becomes code.

At Starlink, he studies networks.
Five thousand satellites stitch the sky together.
Remote villages log into the future.

Different industries.
Same method.

Read.
Learn.
Apply.
Build.

Failure becomes feedback.
Information becomes leverage.

Reframe

A law hardens inside him:

Information is energy.
What you consume becomes what you create.

"The best minds already wrote it down," he tells an engineer.
"Why reinvent ignorance?"

He does not read to know.
But reads to compress time.

Books become portals.
Dead geniuses lend him decades.
The future arrives early.

Legacy

His systems hum now.
Cars without combustion.
Rockets that land themselves.
Internet without borders.

Machines that listen to thought.

None of it is magic.

It is literacy under extreme pressure.

The boy bleeding onto an encyclopedia never stopped reading.
He just changed libraries.

From paper to planets.

And when the first human steps onto Martian soil,
it will not only mark a technological triumph.

It will confirm a quieter truth:

The future does not belong to the strongest.
It belongs to those who read it carefully enough to build it.

Universal Law: Perpetual Transmutation of Energy

When you feed your mind higher knowledge and act on it with relentless courage, you activate the Law of Perpetual Transmutation of Energy and turn information into invention, curiosity into power, and impossible dreams into reality.

Core Lesson

Elon Musk built a resilience architecture shaped by fear, pain, and a fierce hunger for knowledge. A small boy took beatings he could not stop. A thin body bent under fists and insults. A library offered shelter. Books opened maps of new worlds. Knowledge filled the gaps where safety failed. He learned to turn information into fuel. He treated reading as oxygen and imagination as escape. He formed an inner structure long before he entered his first boardroom. He believed humanity should rise above misery.

Silicon Valley confronted him with a new fracture. PayPal sold. Money filled his accounts. Purpose did not. He sensed drift. He studied threats to the planet. He tracked every headline on war and decline. He refused comfort. He pushed his chips toward three dying industries. He bet on rockets, electric cars, and solar fields. His body cracked under long nights. His marriage fell apart. Crowds mocked him. Investors fled. Workers quit. He kept reading. He kept building. He kept turning collapse into ignition. SpaceX reached orbit in 2008. That moment rebuilt him. He rose from failure with proof that learning could outlast ruin.

A new cohesion formed inside him. Mental energy sharpened into fierce study. Emotional energy steadied around mission. Physical energy endured through brutal schedules. Spiritual energy locked onto the belief that human life needed new frontiers. Creative energy fired across every domain he touched. Factories changed shape. Rockets grew smarter. Cars learned to think. Satellites formed constellations. Tunnels cut under cities. Neural links hinted at new futures. He read with intent. He built with speed. He corrected with force. He rebuilt faster than the world could break him.

His architecture followed a simple path. Absorb information with intensity. Apply learning with bold action. Rebuild without delay. Collapse did not stop him. Collapse shaped him. He forged a future drawn from pages he once read as a frightened boy. He did not predict the future. He read it into existence.

Client Story: Twenty-Minute Rebuild

Before the Fall

Ethan led rooms and owned attention wherever ambition gathered. At thirty four, charisma carried him through conferences and investor dinners as millions followed his startup in year one. Calendars throbbed, phones vibrated, applause tracked every move, and opportunity arrived in waves. Behind the glow, hunger grew quiet and sharp. Focus thinned, thoughts filled with static, and books vanished as feeds replaced pages. Stoplights hosted skimmed headlines and half read opinions. He called it staying informed. The truth cut deeper. He starved his mind.

The Night the Light Went Out

Failure arrived without mercy and stayed. The launch collapsed, reviews shredded credibility, capital fled, and the CTO left with a clean verdict. Vision disappeared. Darkness swallowed the office except for blue monitor glare. Graphs plunged like falling stars, keystrokes ticked like a clock, and a whisper named the fracture. Dawn found him empty, unslept, unfed. Oxygen drained from the career he chased. Dreams of building futures trapped him inside machines.

The Sentence That Sparked a Soul

Static cracked through his voice when he called. Loss filled every word. Correction came fast. A starved mind cannot build rockets or futures. Twenty quiet minutes, pages, silence. Laughter surfaced and fell hollow. Doubt questioned repair. Certainty answered. That night he opened a forgotten gift, dust lifting from Meditations. A single line struck clean and hard. Power lives within the mind. Ink underlined truth, breath slowed, and a whisper named the real enemy. Ignition arrived without noise.

From Noise to Knowledge

Morning light framed a ritual. Coffee, sunrise, twenty minutes before screens. Pages replaced feeds and focus settled. Stoics led, rebuilt leaders followed, notes filled with lightning sentences. Failure arrived and panic did not. Breath slowed, one call followed, and infrastructure formed where reaction once ruled. Pages turned into scaffolding.

From Collapse to Creation

Six weeks crowned mornings with reverence. Study replaced scrolling, depth replaced noise, margins moved into meetings. Iterative scaling rebuilt workflows. Ship, test, refine. Velocity over vanity burned red on a whiteboard. Momentum returned, trust followed, and emails sharpened. Ninety days brought profit and purpose together. Headlines lost pull. Mastery took command.

The Man Who Reads to Lead

A year later the office hums. Keyboards chatter, laughter travels, pages open first. Meetings begin with one shared line. Fuel drops set direction. New hires hear a law. Factories fail without stocked shelves. Shelves fill through reading. A long bookshelf anchors the wall, each title scarred by use. Speed once ruled his plans. Depth now drives every decision. He rebuilt the business after rebuilding the mind. He read himself back to life.

Tools & Tactics: The Identity Engineering Arsenal

1. Legacy Reading List Builder

Most people read to feel smart. You read to become someone else.

Curate ten books that aim directly at your *next identity*, not your current comfort. Read with intent, not curiosity.

Balance the list across five arenas:

- Resilience: pressure, recovery, endurance
- Leadership: decision, authority, influence
- Innovation: first principles, reinvention, leverage
- Health: energy, longevity, physical command
- Legacy: meaning, stewardship, long-term impact

Before starting any book, answer one question in writing:
Does this build me, or numb me?
If it numbs, it's entertainment. Cut it.

2. Knowledge-to-Action Flow

Reading without execution is intellectual hoarding.

Every page must convert into movement. No exceptions.

Read → Highlight → Apply → Share

- Read with a pen in hand. Passive reading is wasted time.
- Highlight only what changes behavior, not what sounds smart.
- Apply within hours, not weeks. Delay kills insight.
- Share one takeaway. Teaching locks learning into muscle memory.

Information unused is noise.
Applied information becomes power.

Algorithm: The 10-1-1 Protocol

10 Minutes: Read for Future Identity
Read only material that supports who you are becoming next, not who you were.

1 Insight: Capture the Strike
Underline one idea that creates friction or clarity. If nothing strikes you, the book is wrong, or you are distracted.

1 Action: Move Before Sunset
Apply the insight the same day. One email. One decision. One behavior shift. Action is the proof of learning.

Repeat daily.

By year's end:

- ~30 books digested with purpose
- 365 insights converted into behavior
- A fundamentally new operating system installed

This is not a reading habit.
It is identity engineering.

Reflection Questions

1. Which book forged your current edge? And which book could forge your next one?
2. What subject, if mastered this month, would neutralize your greatest fear?

3. How would your world change if you treated every page as a prototype for action instead of escape?

Pillar Activation: Reading the Future Into Existence

Game Plan
This chapter proves one thing. Reading is not escape. Reading is engineering. When pressure hits, the mind you've built decides whether you collapse or create.

Pillar Activation

Mental Precision (Head)
Musk trained his mind on first principles. He read to understand reality, not opinions. Physics over headlines. Clarity replaced confusion. Decisions sharpened under pressure.

Physical Mastery (Body)
He endured brutal schedules and long nights. He slept on factory floors. Energy followed mission. The body became a tool, not an excuse.

Emotional Power (Heart)
Fear showed up. Failure hit hard. He did not numb it. He directed it. Emotion fueled persistence instead of panic.

Spiritual Alignment (Soul)
Purpose anchored everything. He believed humanity needed new frontiers. That "why" carried him through ridicule, loss, and near ruin.

Imaginative Strategy (Vision)
Books fed imagination with structure. Science fiction met engineering. Ideas turned into rockets, cars, satellites, and systems that changed civilization.

Coach J's Challenge
You don't need more motivation. You need better input. Read for who you are becoming, not who you've been. Take one idea. Apply it today. That's how identity changes.

Locker-Room Reflection
Which pillar strengthens when you read with intention, and which one weakens when you don't?

Chapter 12: Move for Playlife

"Never underestimate the power of dreams and the influence of the human spirit."

~ Wilma Rudolph

The human body never waits behind bars. It rises as a promise ready to return. Muscles store truth the mind forgets. Bones call for rhythm. Motion summons you back to the self you left behind. Childhood knew this truth and lived it.

Wind met your open stride. Bare feet chased the horizon. Jumps cracked puddles into laughter. Branches bent under small hands that reached for sky. Joy moved through you without effort or fear. Life then pressed you into chairs and called it maturity. Stillness replaced wonder. Motion faded into memory and felt distant.

Play never vanished. You pushed it aside. Adults exile the very force that keeps them alive. Wilma Rudolph rejected that exile. Poverty closed around her. Doctors named her broken. Polio bent her leg. Braces locked her in place. The world wrote a story of limits around her young body.

She tore that story apart. Steps replaced stillness. Stride replaced struggle. Speed replaced doubt. She reclaimed the truth hidden inside her bones. Movement turned into power. Play rose from the ashes of pain. She outran predictions and became the fastest woman alive.

Her victory carved a law into the world. Freedom begins in motion. Reclamation starts with a step. Resilience forms when joy returns. Play lifts the weight that fear builds. You carry that same spark beneath years of noise.

Your body does not hold you back. Motion never punishes you. Strength waits for permission. Freedom rises when you move for joy. Play brings you home to yourself. Fire returns when you stop taming your own power.

This is the Freedom Code. This is the path back to the life you abandoned. This is your return.

Wilma Rudolph: The Furnace of Defiance

The Girl in the Brace

Tennessee, 1943.
The morning sun drips like honey across red dirt roads. Chickens scatter as a thin girl limps down the porch steps.
Metal braces cling to her legs. Two cages of cold steel that bite with every step.

Wilma Rudolph is four years old.
Polio has locked her left leg in a vise of pain.

Her mother, Blanche, kneels beside her on the splintered floor, hands slick with oil. Eleven brothers and sisters gather in a half-circle, each taking turns rubbing warmth into the leg that doctors called hopeless.
"Again," Blanche says. "Keep the blood moving."
The room smells of liniment and grit. Outside, the world runs; inside, Wilma learns stillness.

Each night she whispers the same vow into her pillow:
One day, I'll run so fast the wind won't catch me.

The Furnace of Limitation

Years fold like paper.
Sunday church. Schoolhouse steps. Long stares.
Children tease. "Hey, metal legs!"
Wilma lowers her head and keeps moving.

Pain becomes rhythm.
Click. Step. Click. Step.
Each sound says *try again.*

At twelve, she removes the brace and stands under the oak behind her house. Her mother watches from the porch, silent.
Wilma breathes once, twice, and runs.

The brace clatters to the ground.
Her bare feet slap the dirt, sending up a storm of red dust.
Wind tears through her braids; sunlight hits her face like applause.

Her mother shouts her name.
But Wilma is already gone. Laughing. Crying. Flying.

The Spark of Resilience

High school track.
The air tastes like metal and rain. She lines up against girls taller, stronger, whole.

A whistle slices the air.
She launches forward, knees pumping, lungs burning,
legs screaming.
Every stride defies prophecy.

By sixteen, she's in the Olympics.
By twenty, Rome 1960.

Cameras flash.
Crowds chant her name in dozens of languages.
Gunshot start. Silence breaks into thunder.

Wilma blurs past the pack. Gold once. Twice. Thrice.
Three medals, one truth: the universe moves for those
who move first.

The Transmission

When she returns home, she refuses to enter through a
segregated parade line. "If the town wants to celebrate
me," she says, "they celebrate *everyone*."

Movement, again, becomes rebellion.
She coaches girls who believe their scars disqualify
them. She tells them, "Play isn't a luxury, it's liberation."

Wilma's body no longer runs, but her story runs
through generations.
Every girl who ties her shoes and believes she can
outrun her past hears her whisper:
Move. The world will catch up.

Universal Law: Inspired Action

The universe advances only when you move first, and Wilma Rudolph proved that inspired action turns the impossible into momentum.

Core Lesson

Wilma Rudolph's story rises from fracture to flight. Polio pinned her legs. Poverty pressed her family. Segregated clinics blocked treatment. Doctors predicted a life without motion. Her body failed, yet her will surged. A child with braces built strength from ritual touch and quiet vows. Pain shaped focus. Repetition shaped belief. Defiance shaped identity. She forged an inner frame long before her stride met daylight.

Morning heat wrapped her feet when she stepped free of the brace. Bare skin met dirt. Muscles burned. Faith lifted her frame. Movement carried her toward destiny. Each run sharpened her mind. Each race steadied her heart. Each stride reclaimed her body. She outran fear. She outran doubt. She outran every voice that named her broken.

Rome tested her. The track glowed under fierce sun. Runners shadowed her lane. She held her breath, held her form, held her truth. Speed answered. Power climbed through her legs. Purpose guided her steps. Three gold medals marked her rise. She left the stadium with a new name. The world called her the fastest woman alive.

Her impact stretched far beyond the lines of a track. Victory gave her leverage. She demanded integrated processions in towns that denied her dignity. Girls lined fields to learn her craft. She taught discipline. She taught belief. She taught liberation through motion. She moved first. The world shifted next. Her life proved one law. Limitations turn into momentum when you refuse to stand still.

Client Story: Dance with Burnout

The Collapse
Brooklyn, winter grips 2023 with gray teeth. A neon screen washes blue across Sofia L.'s drained face. Three empty cups crowd the desk while six tabs blink without mercy.

Joy never arrives.
Her heart flutters, clamps, then sends heat climbing her neck. Hands claw wood as breath stalls and pride shatters.

An EMT later names it stress.
Sofia names it collapse dressed in heels. Night ends with her perched on the bed, laptop humming alone.

The Call for Rebellion
Our first call carries a voice split between sarcasm and surrender. Work never stops, she says, because stopping feels like erasure. One question cuts through the noise. When did your body last move for joy rather than obligation?

Silence fills the line like a career dying mid sentence.
A laugh breaks through, cracked and hollow, then folds
into tears.

The Ignition
The following afternoon my phone lights with three
words.
I did it.

Bare feet press into cool wood as daylight slices the
blinds. Queen thunders through a cheap speaker and
rattles the room awake. Movement starts stiff, then
loosens, then remembers itself.

Laughter bursts, tears follow, spinning steals balance
and returns breath. When sound fades, her chest rises
steady like tide. A final text lands.
I feel human again.

The Reframe
The next morning she blocks three p.m. with blunt ink.
Dance Break claims the square. Privacy holds at first, a
quiet mutiny between spreadsheets. A designer
stumbles into a spin during Zoom and freezes.
What are you doing?
Saving the company answers back, twirl intact. Within
days the team joins. Socks slide, dogs bark, laughter
ricochets. Output climbs. Burnout retreats.
Joy takes root.

The Transformation
Three months pass before music pauses in a crowded
room. Sofia scans flushed faces and loose shoulders.

Eyes shine with something long missing. She asks if anyone remembers believing success required suffering. Recognition hums without words.
Her finger hits play.

Bass drops.
Fifty bodies move for life rather than metrics.

The Legacy
Every meeting now closes with one question. Did you move today?
Paint curls across the wall in bright loops. Move. Laugh. Build. Repeat.

Clients sense the charge through screens. Investors feel it before numbers load.
Motion hardens into culture. Play steps forward as leadership.

Tools & Tactics: The Playlife Method

Tool 1: The Playlife Movement Map

Tool:
 Keep a dedicated note titled Joy in Motion. Paper or phone. No apps. No metrics.

Daily Entry (30 seconds):

- Write how you moved today.
   Walked. Danced. Stretched. Wrestled with my kid. Shook it out at a red light.
- Add one word only for how it felt.
   Free. Fierce. Light. Alive. Grounded. Wild.

Rule:
No explanations. No analysis. One line. One word.

Why it works:
Emotional states change faster than body composition.
Track emotion through motion, and physical change
follows without force.

Over time, patterns emerge.
You don't guess what restores you.
You *see* it.

Tool 2: The Micro-Movement Menu

Choose based on energy, not time availability.

3 Minutes: Reset

- Stand tall.
- Roll shoulders back.
- Inhale deep through the nose.
- Exhale slow through the mouth.
- Smile on purpose.

Effect: Interrupts stress chemistry. Reclaims posture
and presence.

5 Minutes: Rhythm

- Step outside.
- Walk without destination.
- Match breath to footsteps.
- No phone. No podcast.

Effect: Re-syncs nervous system. Clears mental static.

15 Minutes: Liberation

- Play music that erases thought.
- Move without choreography.
- No mirrors. No rules.
- Stop only when sweat or laughter shows up.

Effect: Restores agency, creativity, and emotional power.

Algorithm: The Playlife Protocol

1. Choose
   Pick one movement that feels exciting *right now*.
   Excitement beats discipline every time.
2. Set
   Start a timer. Short is fine. Consistency is king.
3. Move
   Move until breathing deepens and your face softens.
   Thinking fades. Feeling takes over.
4. Name
   Whisper one word you choose to become today.
   Power. Peace. Joy. Calm. Fire.
5. Seal
   Smile. Nod. Say, "Done."
   Celebration locks the pattern.

Core Truth (Don't Skip This)

Motion is identity rehearsal.
Every time you move on purpose, you remind your nervous system who's in charge.

You're not exercising.
You're training your emotional operating system.

Reflection Questions

1. What movement brings you back to life?
2. Where does your body crave freedom your mind denies?
3. How would your energy change if movement became celebration, not correction?

Pillar Activation: The Freedom Code

Game Plan
This chapter proves one truth. Motion restores identity. When the body moves with joy, resilience ignites and life accelerates.

Pillar Activation

• Mental Precision (Head): Wilma rejected the verdict of limitation. She chose belief over prediction. Focus sharpened with every step forward.
• Physical Mastery (Body): Braces fell. Feet hit dirt. Movement rebuilt strength before strength existed. The body remembered its purpose through rhythm.
• Emotional Power (Heart): Pain transformed into resolve. Joy replaced fear as fuel. Emotion stopped collapsing her and started carrying her.

• Spiritual Alignment (Soul): Purpose anchored her through doubt. She ran toward freedom, not applause. Meaning held when the world resisted her rise.
• Imaginative Strategy (Vision): She pictured motion before motion arrived. Play reopened a future others denied. Imagination cleared the lane reality followed.

Coach J's Challenge
You don't think your way back to power. You move your way there. Today, choose motion for joy. Dance. Walk. Stretch. Play. Start small. Start free. That single act trains every pillar at once.

Locker-Room Reflection
Where has your body been craving movement your mind keeps denying?bStand up. Move first. The world will follow. I am here. I am free. I am moving forward.

Chapter 13: Install Your Recovery Protocol

"I've grown most not from victories, but setbacks. If winning is God's reward, then losing is how he teaches us."

~ Serena Williams

Burnout hides no glory. The body revolts when pressure crushes balance. The nervous system fires warnings that demand respect. Recovery answers with power that rises clean and true. Champions rise when they restore the ground beneath their feet.

Grind culture sells a lie. It crowns exhaustion as virtue and calls collapse a trophy. Serena Williams rejected that lie and rewrote the law. She uncovered strength in restoration. She found balance in contrast. She held fire in one hand and calm in the other. Greatness grew from that polarity.

Serena built her reign through mastery of the pause. She guarded sleep and treated ritual like oxygen. She listened to her body before the world caught the signal. She reinforced her foundation each time pressure tried to crack it. The calm she built shaped the force she unleashed.

Crisis struck without mercy. Injury carved doubt across her path. Surgery stripped her strength. Childbirth nearly killed her. Public voices questioned her rise. She answered each blow with careful recovery. She rebuilt her frame with patience and grit. She returned as a sharper version of herself.

Her comebacks arrived like tides that refused retreat. One at 33. Another at 35. Another after she fought for her life in the delivery room. No athlete controlled recovery with equal precision. Her path proved a simple truth. Resilience grows in the quiet hours.

You grow when you step back from noise. You grow when you let the system restore its charge. You grow when you prepare a version that walks back into the world with new strength. Recovery becomes a strategy rather than a pause. It becomes a ritual rather than a reward. It becomes discipline rather than escape.

Serena lived that code with clarity and force. You now hold that same code in your hands.

Serena Williams: The Furnace of Reset

Picture a teenage Serena Williams on cracked courts in Compton.
Asphalt blisters under the sun.
The ground gives nothing back.

Sweat hangs thick. Rubber burns the air.
Hope smells metallic.

Her father's voice cuts through the heat.
Sharp. Unyielding. Precise.
Venus waits across the baseline. Shadow stretched long.

Two sisters. Two rackets. One future.

Sirens cry beyond chain-link fences.
Dogs bark.
None of it matters.

The ball answers instead.
Pop. Pop. Pop.
Heartbeats refusing surrender.

Serena's palms split.
Her lungs burn.
Pain negotiates nothing.

She swings anyway.
Greatness is carved, not granted.

She enters the pro circuit like weather.
Seventeen. Unapologetic. Explosive.
Beads snap beneath stadium lights.

Veterans retreat.
History blinks.

At the 1999 U.S. Open, she lifts more than a trophy.
She destroys the myth of permission.

The world names her unstoppable.
Her body keeps score.

By her twenties, warnings arrive.
Knees ache. Ankles twist. Shoulders scream.
Every match becomes a bargain with anatomy.

Doctors advise restraint.
Champions rarely listen.

Indian Wells, 2001.
The crowd turns hostile.
Boos cut deeper than losses.

Racial venom poisons the air.
She wins anyway.
Victory tastes like ash.

That day teaches her the truth.
Sometimes the enemy is noise.

2003.

Her body yields before her will.

Surgery replaces competition.
The U.S. Open fades without her.
Critics sharpen their knives.

They call her finished.
They confuse sleep with death.

Fire rests.
Fire waits.

2011 ends everything.
A hospital room in Los Angeles.

Machines beep.
Antiseptic stings.
Fear occupies the lungs.

Blood clots choke her breath.
Each inhale questions survival.

Doctors whisper the unspeakable.
You may never play again.

The scoreboard disappears.
The battlefield moves inside.

Recovery becomes the opponent.
Stillness becomes the method.

Therapy replaces drills.
Meditation replaces fury.
Sleep becomes law.

Nutrition turns strategic.
Rest becomes resistance.

She learns the paradox.
Reloading beats retreat.

Wimbledon, 2012.
Grass whispers beneath her feet.

Center Court holds its breath.
Scars still speak.

First serve detonates.
The power remains.
It has been refined.

Each match resurrects her.
Every step rewrites possibility.

She lifts the trophy with tears.
Not for victory.
For survival.

The streak follows.

U.S. Open nights burn electric.
Exhaustion hunts her late.
Recovery answers louder.

She wins through patience earned in stillness.
The scream releases transcendence.

2013 bends history again.
Clay yields.
Grass obeys.
Hard courts surrender.

Four majors.
One reign.

Then Australia, 2017.
Eight weeks pregnant. Unknown to the world.

She does not drop a set.
Claims twenty-three.

The number stands as proof.
Not of force.
Of wisdom.

She outlasts systems designed to break her.
Wins with strategy born of surrender.

By the end, the record is clear.

Twenty-three Grand Slams.
The greatest serve ever struck.
A reign spanning surgery, scrutiny, and motherhood.

But numbers miss the lesson.

Polarity builds power.
Stillness fuels speed.
Recovery leads.

Serena Williams did not master tennis.
She mastered the human system.

Resilience is not relentless pressure.
It is intelligent pause.

And that is how legends endure.

Universal Law: The Law of Rhythm

Mastery comes from honoring the rhythm of rise and rest, because every season of stillness reloads the power that domination requires.

Core Lesson

Serena Williams grew through polarity. She learned to generate force and then create more through stillness. Compton built her first furnace. Heat pressed her skin. Sirens cut the air. Asphalt cracked under her feet. Her father pushed her mind and body past fear. She rose inside that pressure. She shaped Creative energy through unorthodox movement. She forged Emotional strength through ridicule. She built Spiritual belief through a vision that lifted two Black girls beyond a hostile world. She carried that belief like armor.

Injury struck next. Racism hit her on the court at Indian Wells. Expectations crushed her breath. The weight split her system. A pulmonary embolism nearly ended her life. Her Physical energy collapsed. Her Emotional balance shook. Critics wrote her story for her. She refused their script. She stopped. She breathed. She rested with intent. Nutrition rebuilt her core. Meditation steadied her nerves. She treated silence like medicine. She rebuilt her system from the inside out.

Clarity returned first. Focus cut through noise. Strength rose with patience. Her Spirit anchored each step. Her Emotions sharpened into discipline. Her Mind locked onto purpose. Her Body followed with calm power. Coherence formed inside her like a new frame. She rose again with quiet certainty.

Her return carried force. Wimbledon fell. The U.S. Open followed. She swept the Serena Slam. She dominated across surfaces. She won Australia while pregnant. Each victory proved a deeper law. Recovery does not pause greatness. Recovery generates greatness. Power grows when renewal grounds it.

Her legacy extends beyond twenty three major titles. Her life proves that resilience moves through polarity. Fire needs stillness. Drive needs surrender. Strength needs restoration. She rewrote the human code. True power rises when the inner engine rebuilds itself with intent.

Client Story: Return to Breath

Before collapse, Jordan lived on caffeine and conquest. At thirty-nine, the fast-rising founder treated sleep like theft and meals like meetings. Red-eye flights stacked into weeks as twelve-hour slogs erased daylight and screens burned past midnight. He named it drive and praised the grind. The body kept a different ledger and prepared its bill.

By spring, wrists tingled from strain, the back locked hard, the chest turned to stone. Sweat soaked sheets before sunrise while the pulse raced ahead of thought. During a quarterly investor call, panic seized the throat mid-sentence. Autopilot finished the deck with the camera dark and hands shaking below frame. A hotel mirror later caught a man whispering truth through fear.

"I built this company to live free, and now I cannot breathe."

The Warning Light

Two weeks later, emergency room lights burned white into his eyes. Doctors spoke of extreme fatigue, cortisol flooding the system, early cardiac danger. A nurse urged rest with quiet certainty. Jordan laughed, brittle and hollow, time cracking inside the sound. He carried the warning home and ignored it.

That refusal lasted one call.

The Call

Exhaustion rasped through his voice when he reached me. Fear hid behind resolve as speed and collapse tangled in every sentence. "If I slow down, everything falls apart," he said. I answered with the law Serena learned on Wimbledon grass. "If you never stop, you never rise again. Recovery trains immortality." Belief did not arrive that day.

The Furnace Reset

Work began with The Furnace Reset.

Day One

Dawn met him without mercy. Five minutes on the assault bike drove lungs to fire. I stopped the clock and cut the noise. "Drop. Breathe." Confusion blinked back at me. "We are not done." "Exactly," I said. "You never learned stopping as a skill."

Day Seven

Cold claimed him next. Two minutes in ice stripped resistance down to breath alone. Air came ragged and shallow. "Control the exhale," I said. "Stillness builds strength." When he surfaced shaking, hunger dimmed and humility flickered for the first time.

Week Three

Training shifted to trust. Mobility drills flowed into yoga while contrast therapy followed iron pushes. Weighted sleds surrendered to twenty-minute recovery naps. Heartbeats slowed from panic to purpose. Exertion finally bowed to restoration, the same sacred cycle Serena mastered. Every pause earned its place.

The Reframe

One morning, teeth chattering in a cold tub, clarity cut through noise. "The win comes from cleaner work," he said. That sentence rewired everything.

A new calendar rose like a training plan. Morning held strength and sweat. Midday opened recovery windows with walks, breathwork, fuel. Evening closed with a digital sunset and gratitude ink. Results followed discipline. Blood pressure normalized within two months. Sleep returned by the fourth. By the sixth, the team met a calmer leader, sharper and contagious.

The Legacy

Last winter, Jordan finished his first triathlon for rhythm, not speed. At the line, arms stayed low as hands folded over heart. Breath slowed into sovereignty.

Now fatigue whispers and memory answers with law. "Rest is not retreat. It recalibrates." Recovery no longer waits for permission. He installs it daily, faithfully, in rhythm. Company, marriage, and body rise together. The crown never belonged to endless grind. Mastery lives in the pause between strikes.

Tools & Tactics: The Furnace Reset™ Protocol

Recovery is not rest. It is strategic regeneration.

Elite performers don't recover to relax.
They recover to reload.

From Serena Williams to Michael Jordan, the pattern is identical:
Breakthrough follows recovery precision, not effort volume.

The Furnace Reset™ Protocol is a full-spectrum recovery operating system designed to restore body capacity, nervous system control, and mission clarity, fast.

The Five Tools of the Furnace Reset™

1. The Duality Calendar

Schedule recovery with the same discipline as competition.

Principle: Polarity drives performance. Every push requires a pull.

Practice

- For every 90 minutes of deep work or training, schedule 15–20 minutes of active recovery (walk, mobility, hydration, breath).

Weekly Rhythm

- 3 Fire Days (high output)
- 3 Flow Days (active recovery)
- 1 Restoration Day (full system reset)

Why it works

Tension without release creates breakdown.
Release without tension creates stagnation.
Polarity creates momentum.

2. Red-Zone Tracker

Detect failure before it announces itself.

Red-Zone Signals

- Irritability
- Shallow breathing
- Delayed recovery
- Insomnia
- Creativity drop

Method

- Each morning, score Body | Mind | Emotion from 1–10.

Action Rule

- If any score < 6 → activate Light Mode:

  - Reduce output
  - Increase recovery by 25%

Elite Parallel
Serena treated recovery as data.
Her edge wasn't toughness. It was self-awareness under pressure.

3. Contrast Therapy Flow

Fire and ice to reprogram resilience.

Step 1: Cold (3–5 min)
Cold shower or immersion
→ constrict vessels
→ reset inflammation
→ sharpen alertness

Step 2: Heat (10 min)
Infrared sauna, light cardio, or sun exposure
→ re-oxygenate tissue
→ restore circulation

Step 3: Breath Seal (2 min)

- Inhale 4
- Hold 4
- Exhale 6
- Pause 2

Benefit
Trains the nervous system to find calm inside stress, not after it.
That is the Furnace Reset.

4. Breath Recovery Ladder

The fastest reset you own.

Protocol

- Inhale 4 sec (expand)
- Hold 4 sec (stabilize)
- Exhale 6 sec (release)
- Pause 2 sec (stillness)

Repeat 10 rounds.

Outcome

- Cortisol drops
- HRV rises
- Mental clarity returns

Coach Cue
"Your exhale is your recovery rep.

5. Furnace Journal

Turn recovery into intelligence.

Morning Prompt

"What do I need to release before I rise?"

Evening Prompt

"Which recovery act earned me energy tomorrow?"

Purpose
Moves recovery from random to ritual.

Emotion becomes metric.
Awareness compounds into mastery.

Algorithm: The Daily Furnace Reset

Time: 15 minutes minimum (scales to 45)
Objective: Train the nervous system to return to neutral faster than stress can hijack it.

Step 1: Notice Awareness

- Pause midday.
- Scan body and mind.
- Ask: *Where am I tight, tired, or reactive?*
- Identify one red-zone signal.

Step 2: Breathe Regulation

- Perform the Breath Recovery Ladder (4-4-6-2 × 10).
- Pulse slows.
- Perspective widens.
- Control returns

Step 3: Reset Recalibration

Choose one:

- 3 minutes cold shower
- 5 minute walk
- 10 minute mobility flow

Then:

- Drink 16 oz water with electrolytes or trace minerals.

Step 4: Refuel Replenishment

- Eat clean fuel: protein + greens + healthy fats.
- Add 90 seconds of gratitude reflection.
  Gratitude discharges tension faster than force.

Step 5: Record Reinforcement

In the Furnace Journal:

- Score Body | Mind | Spirit (1–10).
- Write one line: *What energy did recovery return today?*
- Circle one adjustment for tomorrow.

Weekly Rhythm: The Recovery Arc

Day	Focus	Duration	Key Re
Mon–Wed	Fire (Performance)	15 min	Contrast + Bre
Thu	Release (Mobility)	30 min	Yoga + Hydrat
Fri	Flow (Creative Recovery)	20 min	Walk + Gratitu
Sat	Recharge (Full Reset)	45 min	Sauna + Cold + Meditation
Sun	Reflect (Stillness)	30 min	Journal + Weel

Final Truth

Burnout is not caused by effort.
It's caused by slow recovery latency.

Master the Furnace Reset™
and stress stops being a threat.
It becomes fuel.

Reflection Questions

1. Where have I mistaken exhaustion for success, and what has it cost me?
2. What is my red-zone warning, and why do I ignore it?
3. If winning meant sustaining energy, how would I recover differently?

Pillar Activation: The Furnace and the Rebirth

Game Plan
This chapter tells the truth grind culture hides. Power does not come from endless push. It comes from mastering rhythm. Serena Williams proves recovery is not weakness. It is the source of dominance.

Pillar Activation

- Mental Precision (Head): Serena chose clarity over noise. She listened before the world screamed. She treated recovery as data, not doubt.

- Physical Mastery (Body): Sleep became strategy. Nutrition became armor. Stillness rebuilt her body stronger than force ever could.
- Emotional Power (Heart): Injury, racism, and criticism hit hard. She refused collapse. She turned pain into discipline and patience into fuel.
- Spiritual Alignment (Soul): Purpose anchored her through fear and motherhood. Survival deepened belief. Meaning steadied every return.
- Imaginative Strategy (Vision): She rewrote the athlete code. Pause became power. Recovery became leadership. Rhythm became law.

Coach J's Challenge
Listen closely. Your body is talking. If you feel fried, you are out of rhythm. Schedule recovery like it matters, because it does. Protect sleep. Guard breath. Install stillness with the same discipline you bring to the fight. Recovery is not retreat. It is reload.

Locker-Room Reflection
Where are you pushing harder when you should be restoring smarter?

Chapter 14: Force Someone to Smile

"I used to think that the worst thing in life was to end up alone. It's not. The worst thing in life is to end up with people who make you feel alone."

~ Robin Williams

Laughter speaks in a code that darkness cannot read. Heat rises in rooms fear once ruled. Light cuts through grief with clean force. Sound lifts the spirit before thought can resist. Truth rides inside that burst.

Joy never plays decoration. Strength forms inside its pulse. Calm returns when breath widens. Crisis weakens when the face softens. A smile shifts the field.

Robin Williams lived inside that shift. Rooms bent when he entered. Grief cracked when he spoke. Humor erupted like fire from a man carved by pain. His gift rose from wounds, not ease.

Watch him move and you feel it. His eyes flicker. His voice jumps. His body creates worlds from thin air. Soldiers remember hope. Children forget fear. Strangers rise from despair. He turns anguish into warmth.

True joy grows from scars. Power gathers in those who choose light after nights that hollow the chest. A single laugh becomes a beacon. A single spark turns the room.

Crisis asks for silence. Joy refuses the order. Crisis pushes collapse. Joy stands and lifts someone else first. Service becomes rescue. Rescue becomes strength.

The one who laughs in the storm meets fire with a weapon crisis cannot blunt. Pressure builds. Heat climbs. Yet joy rises faster. The choice transforms the battle.

Laugh inside the fire. Offer the spark. Watch the world rise with you.

Robin Williams: The Furnace of Laughter

The Quiet Forge

Before the laughter, there was absence.

Robin Williams grew up in rooms too large to hold warmth.
His father brought authority home, not tenderness.
His mother brought light that never landed.

Silence ruled the house.

So the boy populated it.

Toy soldiers spoke. Cars argued. Accents multiplied.
The living room became a stage because it had to.

Imagination did not entertain him.
It kept him intact.

Every voice said what he could not: Notice me.
Each character crossed distance love refused to travel.

At school, intelligence made him strange.
Loneliness made him funny.

Laughter worked faster than truth.
It closed gaps.
Earned entry.

He did not seek applause.
His soul sought permission to belong.

Stardom's Gravity

Fame arrived without brakes.

Mork & Mindy erupted in 1978.
Robin did not deliver jokes.
He overwhelmed rooms with velocity.

Scripts failed. Cameras chased. America laughed.

Then the laughter stopped.

Dressing rooms cooled. Sweat dried. Silence pressed
inward.
The quiet hurt more than rejection ever had.

So he outran it.

Alcohol softened edges. Cocaine erased stillness.
Not indulgence.
Containment.

He feared the pause.
Because the pause remembered everything.

March 5, 1982.

John Belushi lay dead.
Robin had been there the night before.

He studied his reflection.
Saw the trajectory.
And did not negotiate.

Drugs flushed. Bottles poured. Help called.

He chose survival.
The war simply changed terrain.

Ignition

A realization settled hard.

Laughter was not escape.
It was intervention.

Robin walked into children's hospitals unannounced.
Rubber gloves became balloons.
Machines lost command.

Pain loosened.

Parents breathed. Children rose above fear.
Minutes mattered.

Then came the desert.

USO stages. Folding chairs.
Soldiers hollowed by heat and memory.

Robin stepped forward.
The microphone screamed.
"Helloooooo!"

Silence cracked.
Laughter followed.

For ten minutes, war released its grip.

Afterward, a Marine spoke quietly.
"I was going to end it tonight."

Robin listened.
Held him.
Understood.

Laughter did not distract pain.
It delayed death.

Purpose locked in.

The Law Reveals Itself

Pain was never fixed.

Context governed everything.

A joke in a hospital restored scale.

The laugh in combat restored humanity.

Joy did not eliminate suffering.
It resized it.

Robin learned the law.

Depression compresses reality.
Laughter expands it.

On screen, he transmitted without instruction.

"Good morning, Vietnam!"
Not humor.
Defiance.

"Carpe diem."
Not romance.
Urgency.

"You're not perfect."
Not comfort.
Truth.

He was not performing.
But confessing.

Comedy became architecture.

Discipline Under Strain

When darkness returned, he moved outward.

He served.

Dropped into clubs.
Lifted young comics.
Sat with veterans.
Entered burn wards.

Giving steadied the noise.

Still, the illness advanced.

Depression carved grooves.
Medication dulled velocity.
Then Parkinson's.
Then Lewy body dementia.

The improviser slowed.
Words hid.
The mind fractured itself.

Cruel symmetry.

He joked anyway.
Called it timing.

Some days he forgot why he arrived.
Then laughter reminded him.

For moments, spirit outran biology.

Each laugh resisted decay.

The Signal That Remains
August 11, 2014.

The world stalled.

The man who carried joy could no longer carry pain.

Grief moved fast.
Then something else followed.

Quotes resurfaced.
Scenes replayed.
Desks were stood upon.

Laughter returned through tears.

Soldiers remembered survival.
Children remembered relief.
Comedians remembered permission.

His voice did not end.
It dispersed.

Laughter became inheritance.

Robin Williams proved the truth.

Joy is not denial.
It is resistance.

Resilience is not endurance.
It is radiant rebellion.

And every time laughter interrupts despair,
his signal still travels.

Universal Law: Relativity

Pain shrinks or expands according to the meaning you give it, and Robin Williams proved that joy becomes a weapon when you choose to reframe your suffering into service.

Core Lesson

Robin Williams carried a resilience shaped by transmutation. Loneliness pressed into his childhood and carved deep hollows. A cold father and a restless mother left him with silence that gnawed at his heart. Voices rose inside him and filled the empty rooms. Humor shielded his wounds. Imagination turned his private ache into living worlds. His first act of resilience grew from that alchemy.

Fame arrived and cracked him again. Applause roared while isolation tightened around him. Substances filled spaces no crowd could touch. Belushi's death cut through the haze and forced a reckoning. Service replaced escape. Children in hospitals felt his spark.

Soldiers in war zones felt his warmth. Humor shifted from armor to medicine. A new coherence rose inside him and shaped his purpose.

The Law of Relativity reframed his life. Pain changed when measured against perspective. Laughter shrank darkness to size. His roles carried that truth. Good Morning, Vietnam fired rebellion. Dead Poets Society lifted courage. Good Will Hunting revealed compassion as strength. His characters taught people to breathe, forgive, and widen the frame. His art mirrored his fight and offered a path through it.

Illness formed his final furnace. Parkinson's advanced. Lewy body dementia crept through his mind and clouded his brilliance. Physical strength fell. Mental clarity thinned. Creative sparks still pushed through the fog. Spiritual fire held steady. He gave whatever he could with fierce devotion. Biology weakened him. Frequency outlived him.

His legacy burns with simple truth. Joy rises from suffering when shaped with intention. Laughter breaks open heavy rooms. Hope returns when humor lights the way. Millions carry his echo each time they reach for light inside their own pain. Radiant defiance defined his resilience. His laughter still heals what he never healed himself.

Client Story: The Smile That Saved a Day

Elena entered coaching already half gone.

The job that once defined her had cut her hours until her calendar looked like a blank stare. The partner she had built her future around packed their life into boxes and left without ceremony. Friends spoke softly around her, as if grief were contagious. Bills stacked. Silence grew loud. Her reflection hardened. Bitterness became armor. It kept her upright. It also kept her alone.

She did not come looking for hope. She came because there was nothing left to lose.

When I gave her the assignment, she laughed without humor.

"The Smile Challenge," I said. "Smile at yourself in the mirror. Smile at a stranger. Smile with intention at someone you know. Three a day."

She looked at me like I had insulted her intelligence. Her world was on fire, and I was handing her a matchstick.

But the next morning, she stood in her bathroom anyway. Pale light. Unmade bed behind her. She lifted the corners of her mouth and watched the face in the mirror resist. The smile felt foreign. Her eyes stayed tired. She dropped it quickly, embarrassed, even though no one was watching.

The second smile came on the street. She passed a man walking his dog and forced the expression again. He didn't notice. Didn't care. Kept walking. The rejection landed harder than she expected. It confirmed the story she had been telling herself for weeks. No one sees me. No one responds. Nothing changes.

That night, she almost quit.

The third smile came by accident.

At work the following afternoon, she crossed paths with a colleague who had always seemed cold. Closed. Someone she had silently resented for years. As they passed, Elena caught her reflection in a glass wall. She remembered the rule. Three smiles. No excuses.

She looked up. Smiled. Not wide. Not cheerful. Just present.

The colleague stopped.

Then she smiled back.

It was small. Human. Real.

They spoke. Nothing profound. A comment about the weather. A shared complaint about the coffee. But something loosened in Elena's chest. A laugh escaped her before she could stop it. The sound startled her. It had been weeks since she heard it.

That night, she slept deeper.

She kept going.

Three smiles a day. At first it was work. Then it became routine. Then it became law.

She noticed how people softened when she entered a room. Conversations stretched instead of ending early. A friend she had not heard from in months reached out. A manager asked her opinion again. The world did not change all at once, but the air around her did.

What Elena was really doing was not smiling.

She was changing her signal.

Each smile interrupted the story of rejection running in her mind. Each smile forced her body to practice openness before her thoughts caught up. Neuroscience would later explain what she lived. Facial feedback loops alter emotional state. Social mirroring rewires trust. Micro-actions compound into identity shifts.

But Elena didn't need the science.

She felt it.

Her shoulders dropped. Her breath slowed. The bitterness thinned. The armor cracked.

Weeks passed. Then months.

Her hours increased. Not dramatically, but steadily. A conversation with that once-distant colleague led to a collaboration. The collaboration led to visibility. The visibility led to opportunity. She did not chase it. She met it halfway.

At home, she began catching herself in the mirror and smiling without instruction. Not because she was happy. Because she was alive again.

She still had hard days. She still grieved the relationship that ended. She still worried about money. This was not a fairy tale. It was better than that.

It was real.

A year later, Elena volunteers to mentor new hires. She is known as steady. Warm. Grounding. People seek her out when the room feels tense. When conflict needs softening. When morale slips.

She teaches the Smile Challenge without calling it that.

"Change your signal," she tells them. "Before you try to change your life."

Her legacy is not perfection. It is transmission.

Elena did not rebuild her world by force. She did not positive-think her way out of collapse. She rewired her relationship to it. Smile by smile. Signal by signal.

And in doing so, she proved a quiet truth most people miss.

You do not wait for life to smile at you.

You smile first.

That is how the world learns who you are becoming.

Tools & Tactics: The Smile Challenge

Purpose:
Train emotional leadership, social influence, and internal state control in under two minutes a day.

1. Prime the System (30 seconds)
Stand in front of the mirror.
Lift your posture.
Smile fully—not politely.
Hold for 30 seconds.
This is not vanity. It's nervous-system calibration.

2. Disrupt the Field (1 interaction)
Offer one unearned smile to someone outside your circle.
No explanation. No follow-up.
You are practicing presence without agenda.

3. Direct the Signal (1 person)
Choose one person to brighten intentionally.
A smile plus eye contact.
Hold it long enough to be felt.

4. Lock the Learning (1 line at night)
Write one sentence:
"Today, my smile changed ___."
Name the ripple. Train awareness.

Algorithm: Daily Smile Ritual (under 5 minutes)

1. Mirror → Smile at yourself.
2. World → Smile at a stranger.
3. Circle → Smile with intention.
4. Journal → Capture the ripple.

Reflection Questions

1. When did a smile rescue me from despair?
2. Who in my world needs my smile today?
3. What shifts inside me when I choose joy in crisis?

Pillar Activation: The Furnace of Laughter

Game Plan
This chapter shows how pain can become power when you change its meaning. Robin Williams proves that joy is not denial. Joy is disciplined defiance.

Pillar Activation

- Mental Precision (Head):
  Robin learned early to reframe pain. He used humor to widen perspective and shrink despair. Clarity arrived when he chose service over escape.
- Physical Mastery (Body):
  His energy came from output, not rest alone. Performing, visiting hospitals, and showing up

for soldiers regulated his nervous system through action.

- Emotional Power (Heart):
  Loneliness turned into connection. Sadness became empathy. Laughter transformed emotion into medicine instead of poison.
- Spiritual Alignment (Soul):
  Purpose grounded him. Humor became service. Healing others gave his suffering meaning when relief never fully came.
- Imaginative Strategy (Vision):
  Voices, characters, and stories opened paths where silence once lived. Creativity built bridges where words failed.

Coach J's Challenge
When darkness tightens the frame, you do not argue with it. You change the signal. One smile. One act of service. One moment of shared humanity. That is how pain loses authority and purpose takes command.

Locker-Room Reflection
Where in your life can you reframe pain into service today?

Chapter 15: Finish Strong

"I am a slow walker, but I never walk back."

~ **Abraham Lincoln**

Endings do not finish a life. They forge it. Night drops like molten iron into the mold of tomorrow. The glow fades. The heat endures. It presses into your spirit and shapes your rise. A careless close burns the next dawn. A deliberate one builds steel in your spine.

History favors the few who command the end of each day. Drift never touched them. Intent guided their final acts. Strength gathered in the quiet.

Picture a small room in Springfield. A candle flickers against worn walls. A tall man bends over a scarred desk. His sleeves cling to a tired frame. His pen moves through another hard night. The nation trembles toward war. Letters from grieving mothers sit in a heavy stack. Arguments from Congress claw at his skull. The weight of a fractured country rests on his back.

Lincoln writes. He reshapes each line. He measures each decision with a slow breath. His signature lands with purpose. Night becomes his anvil. Setbacks strike like hammers. He rises through the fire.

Truth reached him early in life. A leader does not climb on morning optimism. A leader climbs on evening discipline. Lincoln treated each night as judgment. He met each close with clear eyes and honest thought. He promised himself a stronger stand with every dawn. Hard days tested him. Hard endings strengthened him.

Finish well and the future bends. Finish poorly and collapse stalks you at first light. Lincoln proved this with each sunset he survived. He forged resolve while others hid from their despair. He built courage in the hour most men avoid.

Endings do not mark closure. Endings cast prophecy. They decide who steps through fire and who fades in its smoke. Tonight that choice waits in your hands.

Abraham Lincoln: The Furnace and the Finish

The Making of the Underdog

Abraham Lincoln came from dust.
He was born in a one-room cabin where survival outranked comfort.
Rails cut his hands before books ever touched them.

His father chased work.
His mother carried wisdom, then died early.
Loss arrived before language learned mercy.

Lincoln worked fields by day.
He read by candlelight at night.
Words became leverage against gravity.

Jefferson taught him structure.
Paine taught him courage.
Hunger taught him endurance.

He owned nothing but reach.

His belief that language could lift people.
That belief struck the first spark.

The Fall and the Fracture

Failure followed him without apology.
He ran for office and lost.
Borrowed money and failed.

Debt wrapped tight around his future.
Ann Rutledge died suddenly.
Grief hollowed his chest.

Darkness pressed close.
Friends feared the edge.
Lincoln felt it too.

Elections rejected him again.
Poverty mocked persistence.
Depression stalked his steps.

Each fall rehearsed him for weight.
Each scar thickened resolve.
He learned how not to shatter.

The Fire of Resolve

War split the nation open.
Cannons rewrote American silence.
Brothers turned weapons inward.

Lincoln carried grief through marble halls.
Telegrams stacked like tombstones.

Loss became daily language.

Critics sharpened their knives.
Newspapers called him weak.
Cabinets whispered betrayal.

Lincoln refused collapse.
He chose presence over poison.
He chose prayer over panic.

He walked among the wounded.
He listened without defense.
Resolve replaced hope.

Hope waits.
Resolve moves.
Lincoln began to act.

The Birth of Meaning

Gettysburg changed the signal.
Forty thousand bodies fed the soil.
The nation stood stunned.

Lincoln spoke briefly.
Two minutes.
Two hundred seventy-two words.

He consecrated purpose.
Redirected grief.
Rewrote the war's meaning.

A new birth of freedom entered language.
Death gained instruction.
Sacrifice gained direction.

Lincoln understood the law.
Meaning is forged, not granted.
Endurance decides outcome.

The Finish and the Freedom

April 9, 1865.
The Union held.
The war ended.

Lincoln bowed his head.
Victory demanded humility.
Freedom required reverence.

In Richmond, freed men knelt.
Lincoln stopped his horse.
He redirected the praise upward.

Five days later, a bullet struck.
The body fell.
The finish held.

His ending sealed the law.
Collapse can become calling.
How you finish creates what follows.

Universal Law: Perpetual Transmutation of Energy

Every lower condition becomes fuel for a higher purpose the moment you rise above it, and Lincoln proved that any collapse: poverty, grief, failure, or war, can be transformed into the strength that shapes destiny.

Core Lesson

Abraham Lincoln built resilience through collapse and conviction. Poverty carved endurance into his frame. Loss carved depth into his heart. Books carved fire into his mind. Each hardship widened the space inside him. Identity rose from scarcity and pain.

Early defeats struck hard. A failed store crushed his finances. Debt chased him for years. Heartbreak cut deep. Election losses hit again. Darkness closed in. He met each fracture with study, reflection, and quiet resolve. Expansion followed pain every time.

Ignition arrived when the country cracked. War loomed. Grief surrounded him. Critics circled him. Rivals plotted against him. He steadied his breath. Duty replaced comfort. Conviction replaced ease. He carried the weight of a nation with slow steps and clear purpose.

Nightly vigils shaped him. Hospital visits softened him. Battlefield dust humbled him. Service replaced ambition. His energies gathered into one force guided by truth. He chose presence over fear and clarity over noise.

The Gettysburg Address sealed his reframe. He took a national wound and shaped meaning from it. He lifted sacrifice into honor. He lifted pain into renewal. He lifted death into a vision of freedom reborn. Every word pressed coherence into the nation. Every line fixed purpose into history.

Legacy defined his finish. He fell to a bullet five days after victory. The cost of his duty became his final act. Integrity stayed intact. Purpose stayed intact. His transmission stayed intact. A nation stood taller because he carried its fire.

Lincoln did not escape the furnace. He became the furnace. His life taught the country how to rise from its own ashes.

Client Story: The Finish That Freed Her

The Unfinished Life

Maria built her life on effort and momentum. Days filled with managing a marketing team, nights consumed by caring for two children, every spare minute swallowed by motion. From the outside, success held its shape through answered emails, met deadlines, practiced smiles. Inside, an ache lingered that never resolved. Each night replayed a loop of what remained undone, what went unsaid, who felt disappointed. Sleep came beside the blue glow of a phone offering one more check, one more comparison, one more reminder of falling behind. Morning arrived heavy because night never truly closed. Somewhere along the way, she lost the art of finishing.

The Breaking Point

The call landed at 11:37 p.m. Her mother collapsed. Days dissolved into hospital lights, guilt, deadlines, fear. Maria pushed forward until the body revolted through panic, migraines, breath that refused to arrive. Work placed her on leave. Silence greeted her one morning as she stared at lists stripped of meaning. The identity built on achievement split open. That was when she called me. Her voice held no edge. She said she did not know how to stop. She said she did not know how to finish. I asked what it might look like to close a day instead of collapsing into it. She blinked and said nothing. The silence marked the beginning.

The Turning Point

Lincoln entered the room through story. A man who failed in business, lost elections, buried love, wrestled darkness, yet finished his life sealing freedom for millions. I told her effort was not the issue. Closure was. The way a day ends programs who wakes tomorrow. Together we built a simple algorithm called the End of Day Review. Three victories written no matter how small. One lesson pulled from failure. One strong action defined for tomorrow. One breath to seal it by drawing strength in and releasing weight out. Ten minutes each night became the practice. Resistance screamed about wasted time. Persistence answered quietly. Thought slowed. Breath deepened. Ignition took hold.

The Return of Meaning

Three weeks passed before the journal spoke clearly. She wrote that finishing strong did not mean doing more but closing what she started with grace. Desks emptied on time. Wins appeared on paper before sleep. Phones rested elsewhere. Evenings shifted toward listening instead of multitasking through stories. When setbacks arrived, spirals stopped short. Cause met effect and rhythm replaced chaos. Each completed day became proof. Each night cast a vote for the woman forming. Coworkers noticed the change and called it calm. Control told the truer story. Time no longer chased her. She defined the line herself.

The Woman Who Finished Strong

Months later recovery came for her mother. Results followed for her team. Promotion arrived without harder hours because work now finished clean. The ritual stayed unchanged. She taught it forward. Friday afternoons gained a name called the Lincoln Close. Teams stood together to answer three questions aloud about wins, lessons, and what carried into tomorrow. One shared breath ended the week. She told me exhaustion once closed her days. Evolution closes them now. Collapse turned into cause. Cause hardened into code. Finishing became freedom.

Tools & Tactics: The Daily Finish Kit

Tool 1 — The Win Ledger (Confidence Builder)
Write 3 wins from today.
Rules: one must be *small*, one must be *hard*, one must be *human* (relationship, kindness, leadership).

Tool 2 — The Lesson Extractor (Failure Converter)
Write 1 lesson from today's friction.
Prompt: "This happened. It taught me ____."

Tool 3 — The Next-Step Script (Momentum Engine)
Write 1 next step for tomorrow that takes 15 minutes or less.
Make it specific: "At ___ time, I will ___ for 15 minutes."

Tool 4 — The Gratitude Breath (Nervous System Reset)
One slow inhale.
On the exhale, whisper: "Thank you."
That's the seal. You close the day instead of dragging it into sleep.

Algorithm: The Daily Finish Ritual (10 Minutes)

1) List: 3 Wins (3 minutes)
Write three wins: small, hard, human.
Feel the proof. Confidence is evidence.

2) Name: 1 Lesson (2 minutes)
Write one lesson from the day's stress.
Turn pain into a coach.

3) Script: 1 Next Step (4 minutes)
Write one clear action for tomorrow (15 minutes max).
Add: time + place + first move.
Example: "7:10 AM at desk: open doc and write 150 words."

4) Seal: Gratitude Breath (1 minute)
Inhale slow. Exhale longer. Whisper: "Thank you."
Then stop. No extra planning. No doom scroll. Day closed.

Rule: If you skip everything, do Tool 3. Momentum beats mood.

Reflection Questions

1. Where in my life do I leave the day unfinished?
2. What would closing my day with power look like?
3. What truth am I avoiding that finishing strong would free me from?

Pillar Activation: The Furnace of Finish

Game Plan
This chapter is about endings. Not quitting. Not collapsing. Finishing with command. Lincoln shows that how you close the day shapes who you become tomorrow.

Pillar Activation

- Mental Precision (Head):
  Lincoln trained his mind at night. He reviewed decisions. He chose clarity over chaos. Each ending sharpened his thinking.
- Physical Mastery (Body):
  Long walks. Hospital visits. Sleepless nights managed with discipline. He respected fatigue without surrendering to it.
- Emotional Power (Heart):
  Grief stayed present, not dominant. He felt deeply without losing direction. Pain informed him. It never ruled him.
- Spiritual Alignment (Soul):
  Purpose anchored every close. He answered to duty, not comfort. Faith turned despair into resolve.
- Imaginative Strategy (Vision):
  Lincoln reframed loss into meaning. Gettysburg proved vision can outlive violence. Words became architecture for a future.

Coach J's Challenge
Do not let your days collapse into sleep. Close them with intent. Write three wins. Pull one lesson. Script one next move. Take one breath of gratitude. Ten minutes trains leadership faster than motivation ever will.

Locker-Room Reflection
When tonight ends, will it weaken tomorrow, or forge it?

Part II Summary

The Architecture of Habit

Resilience never appears by chance.
It emerges through structure, repetition, and deliberate practice.
Across centuries, cultures, and crises, ten lives reveal one law.
Strength follows ritual.

Franklin forged dawn into discipline.
Cold water shocked his body awake.
One question anchored his mind.
Virtue charts trained behavior.
Books widened vision.
Order unlocked creation.
Morning shaped the man.

Malala rebuilt herself through vow and repetition.
A bullet tried to end her voice.
She spoke anyway.
Mission hardened identity.
Purpose stabilized courage.
Ritual protected truth.

Angelou transmuted pain through expression.
Silence sharpened perception.
Books deepened thought.
Gratitude steadied emotion.
Writing reclaimed power.
Habit lifted her beyond trauma.

Jackson met chaos with stillness.
Meditation cleared vision.
Journaling ordered thought.
Breath steadied emotion.
Ritual created calm inside pressure.
Presence changed the room.

Rogers shaped presence into practice.
He slowed his voice.
He chose words with care.
Breath guided rhythm.
Attention softened fear.
Ritual shaped resonance.

Musk learned faster than collapse.
Books fed models.
Curiosity fueled experiments.
Engineering followed insight.
Study became systems.
Action became industries.
Ritual stayed ahead of failure.

Rudolph moved through pain.
Polio restrained her body.
She walked anyway.
Touch rewired muscle.
Practice restored motion.
Ritual carried her to victory.

Serena rebuilt strength through recovery.
Breath reset focus.
Nutrition restored clarity.
Sleep repaired power.

Phased training rebuilt fire.
Rest became discipline.

Robin Williams served through laughter.
Clubs revived spark.
Hospitals opened heart.
Soldiers felt care.
Giving stabilized pain.
Service became shield.

Lincoln reframed suffering into purpose.
Long walks cleared thought.
Letters refined truth.
Prayer steadied resolve.
Reflection shaped judgment.
Ritual forged leadership.

Different rituals.
One mechanism.

Each habit loop aligned mind, body, emotion, spirit, and
imagination into one system.
When crisis struck, structure held.
When collapse threatened, repetition converted
pressure into power.
These leaders did not rise through talent or luck.
They rose by practicing who they chose to become.

Resilience follows ritual.
Habit shapes identity.
Identity directs action.
Action builds destiny.

Part III

BUILDING THE UNBREAKABLE VERSION OF YOU

Chapter 16: Futurecasting Your Identity

*"If you can dream it, you can do it.
Remember, this all started with a little mouse."*

~ Walt Disney

The life you crave breathes behind your eyes. A quiet field opens there. Imagination moves before thought can touch it. Chance plays no part. Luck never enters. The future hums inside the frame you build in silence. You shape that hum with intent.

Close your eyes and a world ahead sparks like a struck match. Your mind does not chase that world. Memory lifts it. Color rises in sharp lines only you can see. Vision settles. Your body follows. Discipline repeats the pattern until the outer world mirrors the inner command. Creation answers clarity.

Imagination stands as foresight. It draws blueprints before hands lift stone. It speaks in dark hours when the present feels tight around your ribs. It sends a whisper toward the figure waiting in the distance. That figure forms through action. That figure waits for you to meet it.

Words raise scaffolding. Habits swing hammers. Courage paints the next section of a life already sketched inside you. The future never appears. You build it piece by piece. You build it with the force of repeated truth.

Walt Disney lived that truth. A young artist stepped into rooms filled with debt and cold air. Frost clung to windows. Hunger pressed close. Studios collapsed from under him. Characters slipped from his grasp. Floors became beds. Candlelight became his only witness. Still he imagined new colors. Still he shaped lines no one else could see. Still he dreamed past bare evidence. His mind held worlds that refused to die.

A narrow space opened between vision and proof. Between dream and dirt. Between hunger and creation. That space became his kingdom. A small mouse rose from it and changed the globe. A studio grew from it and redefined childhood. Magic Kingdoms lifted from it and turned continents bright. Imagination took command. Reality followed.

Disney proved that silent pictures can rise and sing in light. Identity forms in vision long before it takes flesh. The future never waits to be found. A future waits to be summoned. This chapter shows you how to summon yours with precision and courage.

Walt Disney: The Furnace of Imagination

Walt Disney lived inside a furnace most people never named.
It burned with disbelief.

He was born in Chicago in 1901, fourth of five children, into a house that honored labor and distrusted dreams. His father demanded obedience. Imagination earned no wages. Walt delivered newspapers through winter darkness, pedaling before dawn as snow split his hands open. While other boys slept, he bled into the cold and learned endurance early.

Most children saw chores. Walt saw stories.
Horses became knights. Dogs became heroes. Barn
doors became canvases.
Reality pressed hard. He refused to surrender the
unseen.

The First Collapse: Laugh-O-Gram Studios

In his twenties, Walt built Laugh-O-Gram Studios in
Kansas City. He hired friends. He chased vision. He
burned cash faster than it arrived. The studio starved
before it stabilized. His team went hungry. Walt ate cold
beans from a tin and slept on the office floor.

Mice shared the room.
One stayed.

When creditors closed in, the company collapsed.
Kansas City expelled him. The dream should have
ended there. Instead, the furnace intensified. Walt
boarded a train to Hollywood with forty dollars and
reels no one wanted.

Loss did not stop him.
It clarified him.

The Theft: Oswald the Lucky Rabbit

Hollywood offered momentum. Oswald the Lucky
Rabbit succeeded fast. For a moment, victory
shimmered.

Then betrayal landed clean.
The distributor seized Oswald. He took the character, the staff, and the future. Walt lost everything again, this time in daylight.

On the train ride home, despair pressed heavy. The industry declared him finished. Inside that collapse, Walt returned to instinct. He sketched a mouse with round ears and stubborn joy. He gave it courage. He gave it a whistle.

Mickey Mouse was born in loss, not triumph.
Imagination survived theft.

Universal Law of Imagination

Imagination precedes form.
The unseen builds the seen.
Those who envision clearly command creation.

Walt obeyed the law before he could name it. He trusted what others mocked. He drew tomorrow until tomorrow arrived.

The Folly: Snow White

In the 1930s, Walt announced his next vision. A full-length animated film. Investors laughed. Critics mocked. Friends warned him.

They called it *Disney's Folly.*

Walt mortgaged his home. He pawned possessions. He bet everything on belief. He did not see sketches. He saw breath, music, fear, and love moving across a screen.

When *Snow White* premiered in 1937, the audience gasped. Then they wept. Then they stood. Records shattered. Oscars followed. Mockery collapsed into myth.

The folly was never the dream.
It was the failure to imagine it.

The Impossible Park: Disneyland

After cinema, Walt dreamed of space. Not screens. A world people could enter.

Banks refused him. Executives scoffed. Even his brother doubted. Reporters sneered at the idea of a cartoonist building a park.

Walt saw the castle anyway.

Opening Day, 1955. Heat scorched. Asphalt melted. Water failed. Rides broke. Headlines called it a disaster.

Walt walked the park smiling. He listened. He adjusted. He refined. Day by day, chaos became magic. Magic became ritual. Disneyland became legend.

Imagination does not launch perfect.
It refines relentlessly.

The Final Vision: Walt Disney World

Success never satisfied him. Walt envisioned something larger. Florida. A kingdom. A city of the future.

Cancer arrived before completion. In the hospital, he studied ceiling tiles like maps. His fingers traced roads, rivers, and monorails through the air. He designed from memory.

He died in 1966.
The vision did not.

His team built exactly what he described. His body left. His frequency remained—encoded in castles, laughter, and light.

Walt Disney is not a memory.
He is imagination still transmitting.

Universal Law: Correspondence

As within, so without, Disney showed that the reality you construct in your imagination becomes the reality the world eventually walks inside.

Core Lesson

Walt Disney proves that resilience rises when imagination refuses to yield. A boy sketches hope on barn doors while cold winds cut his hands. A young artist builds studios that fall apart around him yet fuels new visions with hunger and belief. A builder watches ideas collapse, then lifts fresh worlds from rubble. Each setback sharpens his mind, steadies his emotions, brightens his spirit, and ignites his creative fire. He trusts the unseen world more than the visible one, and that trust becomes his engine. Imagination becomes design. Design becomes destiny. His inner world grows stronger than the furnace outside, and resilience takes form as creation without fear.

Client Story: From Paycheck to Purpose

The Gray War

Burnt coffee clung to the air every morning as screens glowed in endless rows and gray walls swallowed light. Lauren stepped inside like a soldier reporting for duty while the building repeated itself without mercy. I asked her once what she noticed first when she walked in and she said her shoulders rose before the doors closed. The body always tells the truth.

Once, the work fueled her and the title meant something. Director of Strategic Initiatives impressed strangers who never paid the cost. Quarterly reports tightened into silent nooses as emails multiplied without restraint. An elevator mirror returned a stranger dressed for a life she no longer recognized. I told her this feeling had a name. Erosion.

Praise landed like salt in an open wound while sleep disappeared quietly, then laughter, then the dreams she once guarded. She nodded when I said success can still kill you. Friday proved it.

A spreadsheet blurred into rain as fingers froze above obedient keys and a question escaped before permission arrived. What am I doing here. Her heart answered first, then the walls leaned inward. Someone called her name as darkness closed the file.

The Collapse

Hospital light cut her awake without apology as a nurse spoke calmly about anxiety masquerading as a heart attack. Lauren laughed and sobbed in the same breath. Later she repeated the words to me. A job almost killed me.

Machines marked time through the night while the city stared back cold and bright. Something broke open where fear had lived. I told her collapse never arrives as punishment. It arrives as instruction. The voice she buried returned clear and sharp. This is not your life.

The Ignition

We met with exhaustion still clinging to her voice as words came out sharp and brittle from holding too long. I leaned forward and told her the truth. If you feel lost, the old identity already died. That is good news.

I handed her a blank notebook and gave one rule. Three years forward. Write it as memory. No wishing allowed. She hesitated, then let the pen move.

Ink scratched at first, unsure and tight, then breath slowed and shoulders dropped. Sunrise runs appeared along the ocean. Women gathered in retreat circles. Mornings carried laughter instead of screens. When tears came, I did not interrupt.

She said it felt impossible. I smiled and told her fear always guards the door to power. Magic never announces itself politely.

The Reframe

Ritual replaced reaction one morning at a time as a candle lit before dawn marked the shift. Her future voice spoke aloud like prayer and I had her repeat it until the room changed. Peace enters through repetition.

Movement followed belief. Ten minutes reminded her she lived inside a body, not a calendar. One aligned action closed each morning. One email. One call. One brick laid forward.

Doubt returned often and the old world pulled hard. I reminded her of Disney eating cold beans after collapse. Imagination outlasts circumstance when discipline protects it. She stayed.

The Transformation

A year erased the gray building entirely as whiteboard walls bloomed with color and intention. The Lighthouse Initiative took its first breath. Clients spoke gratitude without scripts or slogans. Recognition finally felt clean.

Espresso replaced alarms as bare feet touched warm floors and sunlight filled working hours without apology. Laughter returned deep and unrestrained. Life answered presence.

She faced her team one afternoon, six women forged by their own furnaces. Lauren spoke without shaking. Collapse stripped the false. Truth survived.

The Legacy

I watched her claim authorship of her world as dreams returned through remembrance, not pursuit. Imagination proved itself practical engineering. The future responded because action stayed aligned long enough.

Collapse cleared ground for construction. Kingdoms rise only after demolition. Purpose always waits beneath fear. She remembered. The world followed.

Tools & Tactics: The Futurecast Framework™

Identity precedes behavior. Behavior compounds destiny.

You are not "visualizing."
You are pre-installing an operating system.

You are the studio.
Imagination is the camera.
Habits are the animators.

This framework turns intention into repeatable identity expression, the same way Disney turned pencil marks into a permanent myth.

1. The Future Self Script (Identity Encoding)

Tool
Write your life three years ahead in the past tense, as if it already happened.

Begin every paragraph with:
"I am so grateful now that..."

Cover five domains only:

- Morning rhythm
- Work and contribution
- Relationships
- Health and energy
- Impact and legacy

Write with sensory precision:
What you hear.
What your body feels like.
What the room smells like.
What pace your life moves at.

Read it out loud every morning.
Voice activates belief faster than thought.

Purpose
Imagination becomes identity only when it carries emotion.

Emotion changes chemistry.
Chemistry drives behavior.

This is not fantasy.
This is memory creation for the nervous system.

2. The One Aligned Action Rule (Behavioral Proof)

Tool
Every day, execute one action your future self would consider normal.

Not ten.
Not someday.
One.

Send the message.
Make the call.
Train like the person you wrote.
Dress like the person you described.

Fear is not a stop sign.
It is confirmation you are on the correct path.

Purpose
Belief without action decays.
Action without identity collapses.

This rule keeps imagination and execution locked together.

3. The Frequency Filter (Environmental Control)

Tool
Audit your inputs weekly:

- Music
- Language
- Screens
- Rooms
- People

If it drains, remove it.
If it expands, amplify it.

Your environment is not neutral.
It is programming you whether you consent or not.

Purpose
Your future does not arrive through effort alone.
It arrives through what you allow around you.

4. The Mirror Moment (Neural Lock-In)

Tool
Each night, stand in front of a mirror.
Look directly into your eyes and ask out loud:

"Did I act in harmony with my future today?"

Then say:
"Thank you for showing up."

No judgment.
No negotiation.

Purpose
Self-recognition completes the loop.
This seals behavior into identity instead of leaving it as effort.

Algorithm: The 15-Minute Futurecast Ritual

Objective: Install tomorrow's identity into today's behavior.

Step 1: Project the Scene (2 minutes)

Sit upright.
Breathe slow until the body settles.

Visualize one ordinary day three years ahead.
See the pace.
Feel the energy.
Hear the sounds.

Not dramatic.
Normal.
Stable.

This is the storyboard.

Step 2: Script the Line (3 minutes)

Write one sentence in your journal:

"Today, I move like the person who _____."

Use one verb only:

- Leads
- Builds
- Creates
- Heals
- Commands

Underline it.
Read it out loud.

This is identity declaration, not motivation.

Step 3: Act the Scene (7 minutes)

Five minutes of physical effort.
Two minutes of controlled breathing.

Move until warmth rises.
Breathe until clarity sharpens.

The body believes first.
The mind follows.

This is embodiment.

Step 4: Cut to Action (2 minutes)

Choose one concrete task that aligns with your script.
Execute it before noon.

No delay.
No optimization.
No overthinking.

Momentum responds to speed.

Step 5: Credits Roll (1 minute)

At night, whisper:

"I lived closer to my future today."

Exhale.
Sleep.

This closes the loop and primes continuity.

Final Truth

You don't rise to the level of your goals.
You fall to the level of your installed identity.

This framework installs it daily, quietly, relentlessly.

Reflection Questions

1. What future scene feels so real it already breathes inside you?
2. When doubt spoke, did you answer as your present self or your future self?
3. If imagination is your blueprint, what construction begins tomorrow?

Pillar Activation: The Furnace of Imagination

Game Plan
This chapter proves one hard truth. The future gets built inside you before it ever shows up outside. Imagination is not fantasy. It is precision design under pressure.

Pillar Activation

- Mental Precision (Head): Disney refused consensus thinking. He trusted inner clarity over external proof. Focus stayed locked on what did not yet exist.
- Physical Mastery (Body): Hunger, cold, exhaustion never stopped the work. He kept showing up. Energy followed commitment, not comfort.
- Emotional Power (Heart): Betrayal, ridicule, and loss hit hard. He used them as fuel, not excuses. Emotion sharpened resolve instead of breaking it.
- Spiritual Alignment (Soul): His why stayed bigger than setbacks. Joy, wonder, and belief anchored him when money and validation vanished.
- Imaginative Strategy (Vision): He saw finished worlds while others saw ruins. Vision acted as blueprint. Discipline turned sketches into kingdoms.

Coach J's Challenge
Stop waiting for certainty. It never comes first. Write your future like it already happened. Then act once a day as if that identity is normal. Imagination without action stays weak. Action without vision collapses. Lock them together.

Locker–Room Reflection
If your future already lives inside you, what construction begins tomorrow? Step into your studio tomorrow at dawn. Call, *Action.*
The world is waiting for the premiere.

Chapter 17: Design Your Deathline

"You can't connect the dots looking forward; you can only connect them looking backward."

~ Steve Jobs

Most people drift as if tomorrow waits forever. Others cling to the dream of easier days ahead. Someday becomes an escape. Someday becomes a trap. Someday becomes a grave.

Time cuts without mercy. Another sunrise pulls a day from your account. Each breath shortens the road toward the finish line you pretend not to see. Acceptance arrives only when you stop running from the truth.

Few refuse the lie. One glance at mortality clears the fog. A stripped life reveals its core. Purpose sharpens when nothing extra survives. Freedom grows in that clean space.

Steve Jobs worked inside that pressure. Mortality hunted him, yet he moved toward it. Waste fell first. Noise vanished next. He shaped every choice with the focus of a man who sensed the clock closing. Design turned pure. Attention locked tight. Illusion broke under the weight of honest vision.

Death never crushed him. Mortality forged him. Truth pressed him toward essence. Focus lifted him beyond fear. Work hardened into legacy. His deadline formed the frame that held his greatest creations.

Deathline never marks the end. It draws the blueprint. It strips false wants. It reveals the few things worthy of your time. It shows the life you must build before the final page turns.

Your Deathline stands here now.

Steve Jobs: The Furnace of Finality

Apple was dying when Steve Jobs came home.

The company that once bent culture now suffocated in
fluorescent silence.
Outdated prototypes gathered dust.
Engineers moved without conviction.
The logo flickered like a memory losing oxygen.

Ninety days from bankruptcy.
Ninety days from erasure.

Jobs entered without ceremony.
Black turtleneck. No smile.
Armor, not fashion.

He walked the halls like a coroner.
Beige machines squatted lifeless on tables.
Slogans peeled from walls like abandoned prayers.

"This isn't Apple," he said.
"This is noise."

He drew a cross on the whiteboard.

Consumer.
Pro.
Desktop.
Laptop.

"That's it."

Everything else died.

Markers slashed through divisions, products, careers.
Each stroke landed clean.
Fear filled the room.

Then electricity followed.

Simplicity wasn't design.
It was survival.

Jobs believed complexity was decay.
Clarity carried voltage.
Beauty was integrity made visible.

He learned that in exile.
NeXT. Pixar.
Two laboratories of essence.

Now he returned to resurrect a soul.

Meetings became confessions.
Design reviews became trials.
He interrogated silence itself.

The click of a mouse.
Curve of glass.
Pause before a boot tone.

Nothing escaped intention.

One year later, resurrection stood under blue light.

The iMac appeared—curved, translucent, alive.
Not a computer.
A declaration.

Sales surged.
Belief returned.

Jobs didn't save Apple with code.
He saved it with feeling.

But the furnace kept burning.

The Friction

Success amplified strain.

Midnight erased mornings.
Laughter vanished.
Innovation hissed under pressure.

"Show me," became a threat.

Two seconds.
"Wrong."
"Start over."

He wanted inevitability.
Beauty you felt in your bones.

Some engineers broke.
Others fled.
The rest stayed because they couldn't imagine creating
without him.

"He's killing us," they said.
And no one argued.

Then his body joined the revolt.

Pain arrived.
He ignored it.

Cancer followed.
He dismissed it.

"I don't have time."

He returned to work the next morning.

Mortality sharpened him.
Perfection became urgent.
Every flaw insulted time itself.

He wasn't designing products anymore.
He was designing what would survive him.

The Deathline Plan

Finality stripped illusion.

Jobs marked time differently now.
Not by quarters.
By meaning.

Each day carried one question:

If this were my last, what would still matter?

Volume vanished.
Refinement ruled.

He delegated power.
Transferred DNA.
Architected continuity.

Tim Cook learned restraint.
Jony Ive guarded essence.

Then came the ring.

Glass. Light. Silence.
A structure meant to outlive its maker.

His final brief followed.

The Post-PC era has begun.

iCloud.
iPad.
Ecosystem as memory.

He wasn't building market share.
He was designing permanence.

Departure

Jobs planned his exit like everything else.

Minimal.
Private.
Exact.

Succession secured.
Roadmaps sealed.
Family protected.

Mortality became the final prototype.

And like every prototype, it demanded refinement.

October 5, 2011.

Jobs died.

Apple didn't.

Products launched.
Signals pulsed.
Glass remembered his hands.

The Deathline Plan worked.

Not because he defeated death.

But because he designed around it.

Energy does not end.
It changes form.

As for simplicity:
Simplicity is the shape of eternity.

Universal Law: Vibration

Energy shapes reality, and Steve Jobs proved that when you raise your frequency with clarity, purpose, and conviction, everything around you rises with it, even after you're gone.

Core Lesson

Steve Jobs demonstrates resilience as the act of transmuting crisis into coherence. Crisis struck and his mind sharpened. Noise filled the room and he cut through it. Mortality pressed close and he steadied his breath. Fear rose and he turned it into purpose. The furnace shaped his awareness into clear truth.

Pain hit his heart and he refined it into direction. Anger tried to scatter him and he centered his focus. Weakness crept into his body and he lifted his spirit. Loss closed around him and he built new meaning. Everything he touched carried the imprint of this shift.

Tools filled his hands and he shaped systems that carried his vision. People doubted and he designed culture that outlasted their doubts. Time thinned and he raised his creativity to full force. Ideas sparked and he carved them into form. Each act extended his reach beyond the clock.

Mortality moved closer and he faced it without retreat. Meaning became his final craft and he shaped it with clean intent. Vision anchored him and he built with steady hands. Light faded and he kept building. Eternity grew from that resolve.

Client Story: The Deathline Within

The Diagnosis

When Samantha came to see me, success no longer mattered because breath had taken its place. Forty years at full speed had carved a cost into her body. Agency founder. Mother of two. Emails answered from hospital chairs while life waited. Symptoms passed as stress until truth arrived with force and refused negotiation.

A rare autoimmune disorder had turned on her heart and the doctor spoke without softness. Slow down or your body will decide for you. Execution rarely announces itself louder. Days later she sat across from me, pale and shaking, test results clutched like proof of mortality, and a whisper broke the room when she said she did not want to die yet could not keep living this way.

Drive once forged her rise but urgency now poisoned rhythm. Wealth accumulated while wonder vanished. Her heart absorbed the weight until it fractured.

The Line That Divides

I told her about Steve Jobs and the clarity cancer delivered when mortality stripped distraction clean. A line drawn across time became a compass, so I placed a blank page in front of her and kept the instruction final.

Draw the line. Left side drains. Right side gives life. That line decides everything.

Silence held as she stared long enough to hear truth speak. Ink moved slowly as reality surfaced with emails, investors, and perfection without rest on one side, then color emerged with painting, stillness, laughter, children, and breath on the other. Tears blurred the page she had ignored for years and an exhale followed like release from captivity when she said she had lived on the wrong side.

That night she built her first ritual and the Deathline Calendar began the repair. Each morning opened with one question that acted like medicine. If six months remained, how would today change.

Designing from Mortality

The diagnosis stayed while resistance left and design replaced denial. Days rebuilt through elimination as meetings cut in half, energy drains removed without apology, and clients chosen for alignment instead of revenue. Mornings turned sacred with silence first, creation next, and connection sealing rhythm so life finally entered the schedule.

When her team protested, she stayed calm and chose refinement over fear. Results arrived without force as metrics shifted, blood pressure normalized, and strength returned quietly. Paint filled canvases with rhythm and color and she brought one to me, pulsing with movement, and said this was her heartbeat now.

The Resurrection Project

Six months changed everything when she announced her departure from the agency and shock traveled fast through familiar circles while her smile stayed steady. Madness always greets pioneers first. She sold her stake, chose simplicity, traded boardrooms for a small studio, and shaped The Deathline Project into life.

A collective formed for people living with illness, not survival coaching but life design. The first gathering filled a sunlit loft where circles replaced slides and calendars carried one question across the top. If the line exists, what will you create now. Her voice carried calm authority and the room listened without movement when she said the disease revealed her purpose.

The Living Frequency

Three years later, doctors used improbable without explanation as her heart stabilized and her body held strength again. Life responded to alignment. The original page still hangs framed above her desk with ink blurred by tears and truth while the studio hums with motion, sound, and paintings that breathe from the walls.

Workshops fill with people facing the line honestly as fear converts into focus through design. When I visited, she handed me a brush because design always invites participation. A mural stretched behind her in gold convergence where lines met and held, "That's what it feels like," she said. "When you finally align your life to what matters. You don't just survive, you vibrate."

Tools & Tactics: The Deathline System™

A Precision Framework for Eliminating Noise and Engineering Legacy

Most people live as if time is elastic. It isn't.
Every life runs on a countdown.
The Deathline System makes that countdown operational.

This is not about death.
It is about compression of focus, energy, and meaning.

1. The Deathline Calendar™

Clarity does not come from more options.
It comes from finality.

Tool Setup

- Draw one horizontal line across a page.
- Left side: Noise
- Right side: Essence
- Draw one vertical mark in the center: Today

Daily Question

> "If I had six months left, how would this day be structured?"

Rules

- Anything that does not serve creation, love, health, truth, or legacy goes to Noise.
- Anything that builds, teaches, heals, designs, or endures goes to Essence.
- Noise gets eliminated. Essence gets scheduled first.

Steve Jobs used this instinctively. He reduced Apple to what mattered and cut everything else without mercy. Samantha used it deliberately. Fear became structure. Anxiety became execution.

Result:
Decision speed. Energy reclamation. Ruthless clarity.

2. The Mortality Mirror Ritual

Avoidance weakens.
Confrontation sharpens.

Ritual

- Once daily, stand in front of a mirror for 60 seconds.
- No phone. No music. No distraction.
- Maintain eye contact.

Statement

> "My time is limited. My energy is sacred.
> What deserves it today?"

This is not a death practice.
It is a life activation protocol.

Jobs used this daily in his final years.
Samantha used it to stabilize her health and reclaim focus.

Finite awareness unlocks infinite discipline.

3. The Essence Elimination Audit

Complexity kills momentum.
Simplicity restores power.

Weekly Audit
Draw a cross and label:

- Personal / Noise
- Personal / Essential
- Professional / Noise
- Professional / Essential

Rules

- Everything in Noise drains energy.
- Everything Essential must be protected or expanded.
- Eliminate or reduce at least one item per quadrant weekly.

Jobs eliminated 70% of Apple's products.
Samantha eliminated 50% of her meetings.

Your goal is the same:
Make your life light enough to move fast.

4. The Deathline Design Block

Discipline does not create pressure.
It creates peace, when aimed correctly.

Daily Rule

- One 20-minute block.
- No notifications.
- No multitasking.
- No consumption.

Only creation: writing, designing, planning, building, structuring.

Jobs called this *working at inevitability.*
Samantha called it *resurrection time.*

Your nervous system will learn this truth:
Focus is safe. Creation is calming.

5. The Legacy Ledger

Legacy is not intention.
It is evidence.

Weekly Questions

1. What did I create that will outlast me?

2. What did I eliminate that no longer served my essence?
3. Who did I elevate through my presence, work, or words?

Write short sentences. Read them aloud.

Drift hides in silence.
Design reveals itself on paper.

6. The 80/20 Law of Mortality

Not all actions are equal.
Some define you. Most distract you.

Principle

- 20% of actions create 80% of meaning.
- Your Deathline work identifies and protects that 20%.

Treat those actions like oxygen.
Miss them and the system suffocates.

Implementation Challenge: Six Weeks to Simplicity

- Weeks 1–2: Deathline Calendar + Mirror Ritual
- Weeks 3–4: Weekly Essence Audits + Daily Design Block
- Weeks 5–6: Add Legacy Ledger + Full Deathline Algorithm

Result:
Less noise. More presence. Faster creation.
A sharpened internal frequency.

Algorithm: The Deathline Calibration™

15 Minutes to Convert Mortality Into Momentum

Purpose:
Transform awareness of time into decisive action.

Step 1: Face the Line (2 minutes)

Stand still or face a mirror.

Whisper:

> "My time is finite. My energy is sacred.
> What deserves it today?"

Feel the pulse.
That is your countdown—and your compass.

Step 2: Draw the Filter (3 minutes)

On one page:

- Draw a horizontal line.
- Left: Noise
- Right: Essence
- Write today's date at the top.

Dump everything on your mind onto the page.

Cross out Noise.
Circle Essence.

Only circled items survive.

Step 3: Choose the Creation Task (5 minutes)

Select one circled item.

Ask:

> "If today were my last, what would still matter to finish?"

That is your Creation Task.
Write it. Commit to it. Protect it.

Step 4: Silence the System (3 minutes)

- Turn off notifications.
- Close inboxes.
- Take three slow breaths.

You are not managing time.
You are conducting energy.

Begin.

Step 5: Seal the Signal (2 minutes)

Write one sentence:

> "Today I moved closer to my legacy by..."

That sentence becomes your identity echo.

The Deathline System does not make life smaller.
It makes it exact.

Use it daily.
Design deliberately.
Leave nothing essential undone.

Reflection Questions

1. What am I still clinging to that belongs to Noise?
2. What single act today would still matter if I were gone tomorrow?
3. What am I building that will outlast my body?

Pillar Activation: The Deathline Plan

Game Plan
This chapter is about facing the truth most people avoid. Time is not endless. Mortality sharpens focus, cuts noise, and forces you to build what actually matters.

Pillar Activation

- Mental Precision (Head):
  Jobs treated death as a filter. He eliminated distraction fast. Four products. One focus. Clear thinking replaced endless options.
- Physical Mastery (Body):
  His body weakened, but awareness increased.

Fatigue became a signal, not an excuse. Energy went only where it counted.

- Emotional Power (Heart):
  Fear did not scatter him. It concentrated him. Pressure turned into urgency with direction.
- Spiritual Alignment (Soul):
  Purpose replaced ego. He built for meaning, not applause. Legacy became the compass.
- Imaginative Strategy (Vision):
  Simplicity unlocked creativity. Essence shaped design. He built systems that lived beyond him.

Coach J's Challenge
Stop living like time will wait. Draw your line. Decide what drains you and what gives you life. Eliminate one source of noise today. Schedule one act of creation that would still matter if time was short. That is leadership under pressure.

Locker-Room Reflection
If today mattered more than tomorrow, what would you stop doing immediately?

Chapter 18: Crisis-Proof Living

"When we are no longer able to change a situation, we are challenged to change ourselves."

~ Viktor Frankl

Every life walks into fire at some point. Flames rise. Smoke swallows edges. Heat strips comfort from the air. A rare soul steps forward anyway. That step marks the start of true work.

Frankl stepped into that fire with clear intent. Camps closed around him like iron. Hunger weakened men beside him. Cold scraped bone. Names faded into dust. Yet he searched for meaning with the urgency of survival. That search kept him upright when strength left his limbs.

Purpose carried him through places built to erase hope. It lived where guards could not reach. It moved in him when the world tried to break the last idea of being human. A single truth rose from that ground. A person endures almost anything when purpose stands ahead like a distant light.

That light shaped the frame I later called Resilience Architecture. Crisis shifts the moment you stop asking why pain struck. A new life begins when you ask what the moment demands. Action answers that question with force that shapes your next chapter.

Frankl taught that suffering does not steal agency. It sharpens it. It hands you the final freedom. You choose your stance when the world strips every other choice away. That choice builds the base for Crisis-Proof Living.

Strength grows there. Not in comfort. Not in control.
Strength rises in the quiet act of standing inside the fire
and building from the inside out.

Viktor Frankl: The Furnace of Meaning

Before the war, Viktor Frankl believed meaning was
man's deepest drive.
Not pleasure.
Not power.
Purpose.

He wrote this in a quiet Vienna study, ink steady, ideas
orderly.
Then history tested the theory.

The soldiers did not shout.
They ended things.

A door burst open.
Boots filled the room.
Metal and wool swallowed the air.

Frankl looked up from his desk.
His fingers were stained with ink.
The manuscript lay open before him.

Decades of thought lived on those pages.
A single thesis: a man can survive any suffering if he
finds meaning within it.

He pressed the papers to his chest.
Not sentiment.
Instinct.

Orders followed.
Names vanished.
Identity collapsed.

Psychiatrist became prisoner.
Husband became number.

Snow fell as they were driven into the street.
Thin flakes melted along the edges of the pages.
He tightened his grip.

At the camp gate, a guard tore the manuscript away.
One motion.
Final.

Pages scattered into the mud.
White birds shot down mid-flight.

Frankl felt the world drop out beneath him.
Not terror.
Not rage.

Emptiness.

For a moment, he wondered if meaning itself had died.

Then something surfaced.
Quiet.

Unshakable.

They can take the manuscript.
They cannot take the mind that wrote it.

The camps were not merely places of confinement.
They were places without prediction.

Time collapsed into survival cycles.
Commands.
Cold.
Breath.

Frankl watched.
Not as a doctor.
As a man among men.

He saw surrender begin in the eyes.
Before the body failed.
Before the voice disappeared.

Despair entered slowly.
Posture bent.
Language shrank.

Yet anomalies appeared.

A crust of bread shared.
A joke whispered through cracked lips.
A man describing the sky instead of cursing it.

Frankl noticed a pattern.

Those who attached pain to purpose endured
differently.
They stood straighter.
They spoke of children.
Of unfinished work.
Of faith.

One night, returning to the barracks under a moon like
bone, clarity struck.

Everything can be taken from a man but one thing.
The last of the human freedoms.
The choice of attitude.

Freedom was not outside the wire.
It lived within the mind.

Meaning was not comfort.
It was structure.

From that night forward, Frankl rebuilt his work
internally.

He carried the manuscript in memory.
Sentence by sentence.
Beam by beam.

At dawn, the air cut like glass.
Men rose beneath thin blankets.
Already half gone.

Frankl straightened his spine.
Quiet rebellion.

If they took everything else, they would not take
posture.
Standing became prayer.
Motion became dignity.

As he marched across frozen mud, he recited
paragraphs in silence.
Thought replaced ink.
Memory replaced paper.

He learned that thinking is creation.
That the mind can reconstruct what force destroys.

During rare moments alone, he practiced gratitude.
Not for comfort.
For consciousness.

He could still see.
Still think.
Choose.

The ritual steadied him.
Like tension cables holding a bridge in storm.

He began to serve.

He reminded others of faces beyond the fences.
A wife.
A child.

A page yet unwritten.

He asked them to imagine the future vividly.
To let it pull them forward.

Heads lifted.
Spines straightened.
Some men smiled.

Each act became a brick.
Every choice a beam.

Agony turned into architecture.

Meaning was no longer theory.
It was scaffolding.

Liberation arrived without triumph.

The gates stood open.
Snow blew through them like disbelief.

Frankl walked out thin as bone.
Steps unsteady.
Structure intact.

Inside him, the design held.

In the months that followed, he wrote again.
Hands trembling.
Purpose firm.

He reconstructed Man's Search for Meaning from memory.
Observation became revelation.
Experience became blueprint.

He wrote that life's task is not to avoid suffering.
It is to assign it purpose.

He named it the last of the human freedoms.

Later, in **Yes to Life**, he expanded the design.
Joy and tragedy were not opposites.
They were materials.

Even when fate dictates circumstance, meaning remains authored.
And despite death speaks loudly, life answers once more.

Yes.

From suffering, Frankl produced blueprints.
Not of stone or steel.
Of choice.

He proved resilience is not the absence of despair.
It is design under pressure.

His work became the first true architecture of endurance.

The Blueprint and Its Evolution

Frankl proved resilience is engineered.

Strength does not emerge without suffering.
It emerges through structure.

In the camps, he built an invisible framework.
One that outlasted cruelty.

Posture.
Gratitude.
Service.

These were not hopes.
They were construction acts.

That framework later revealed itself as a system.
Repeatable.
Transferable.

Where he built under barbed wire, I build in
boardrooms.
Where he fought despair without comfort, I teach
clarity without certainty.

The materials changed.
The physics did not.

From his furnace came the foundation: meaning is
load-bearing.

From his suffering came the system: align thought, posture, emotion, spirit, and purpose.

His life became the first working model of Resilience Architecture™.

The same pillars that held him upright then hold leaders upright now:

Mind: Thought shapes structure.
Body: Posture signals power.
Emotion: Compassion creates cohesion.
Spirit: Gratitude fuels endurance.
Imagination: Purpose seals the build.

Every system I teach traces back to his design.

I did not invent resilience.
I inherited its blueprint.

Frankl drafted it in darkness.
He proved meaning could not be annihilated.

I translated it into code.

His manuscript became my manual.
His furnace became my forge.
His architecture became our map.

From that lineage, the Resilience Operating System was born.

Not philosophy.
Design.

Not hope.
Structure.

Not inspiration.
Indestructibility.

Universal Law: The Law of Correspondence

Your outer life rises or falls according to the structure you build within, and Frankl proved that meaning becomes the inner architecture no crisis can break.

Core Lesson

Frankl's story reveals the first blueprint of Resilience Architecture. Meaning rises as the load-bearing force of human endurance. Soldiers tear his manuscript from his hands and fracture his identity. Doctor falls. Husband falls. Thinker falls. Creator falls. Silence follows the collapse. A single question remains. What cannot be taken from me?

Camps turn into a laboratory stripped of comfort and choice. Men surrender long before death arrives. Eyes dim. Posture folds. Language shrinks into dust. Frankl studies these collapses with precision. He sees purpose act like heat inside a frozen world. A man shares bread. Someone jokes. Another lifts his gaze to the sky. Each act becomes a data point. Purpose raises voltage.

Breakthrough arrives under a pale moon. Freedom reveals itself as internal discipline. He cannot command guards or fate. He commands attitude and direction. That choice becomes architecture. That decision becomes strength.

He rebuilds the lost manuscript inside his mind. Posture becomes defiance. Gratitude becomes fuel. Service becomes structure. He urges men to imagine a future vivid enough to pull them toward it. Each thought becomes a beam. Each belief becomes a wall. The mind becomes a construction site of survival.

Liberation finds him thin as wire. Inner structure holds firm. He rewrites Man's Search for Meaning from memory. The essential manuscript lived inside consciousness and not on paper. Crisis attempted to erase his purpose. Meaning rebuilt it.

Frankl's insight forms the first Resilience Operating System. Suffering transforms into strength when meaning shapes design. The five pillars stand clear. Mind builds structure through thought. Body signals identity through posture. Emotion stabilizes community through compassion. Spirit strengthens endurance through gratitude. Imagination seals purpose into form.

Leaders do not invent resilience. They inherit his blueprint. Frankl drafted it under barbed wire. You apply it in boardrooms and crisis rooms. His furnace becomes your framework. His manuscript becomes your manual.

The result forms the first working model of Resilience Architecture. Inner stability outlasts external collapse. Crisis becomes material. Meaning becomes design. Resilience becomes the structure you build from both.

Client Story: The First Prototype

Velocity
Rafael moved fast through deals, deadlines, victories, and noise, feeding identity with speed and applause until lockdown stopped motion cold. Revenue vanished, doors closed, and silence replaced the hum of success. Loss spoke louder than any win and stayed.

The Call
Night carried his voice across the line, dry and distant, confession tangled with surrender. "I lost everything," he said, then named business, marriage, reason. Stillness between words exposed a missing self and meaning slipped out of reach.

The Choice
Quiet held the room as truth settled. "We begin where nothing can reach," I said, letting the pause sharpen the air. "What remains?" he asked. "Choice," I answered, and the word landed hard.

Frankl's Blueprint
A name entered the night with weight. Viktor Frankl survived erasure by engineering purpose, turning suffering into laboratory and plan. Meaning proved practical, not poetic, and design rescued the human spirit.

Ground Zero

Rafael lifted his eyes from the table and opened a notebook. Block letters filled the page: GROUND ZERO. Frankl's question followed and cut clean. "What does life ask of you now?"

The First Beam

Silence stretched, tears arrived, and a whisper steadied. "Help others who feel this," he said. Purpose found a foothold in rubble and construction began.

The Build

Months turned breakdown into site work as whiteboards filled with arrows and intent. Coffee rings stained fresh plans while we shaped the first Resilience Architecture prototype. Meaning anchored the ground.

The Framework

Morning opened before screens or alerts as choice set tone and direction. Rituals trained mind, body, emotion, spirit, imagination. Service capped the structure with reach as The Rebuild Project launched and lifted others.

The Insight

Each day raised another wall of resolve and giving steadied his stance. One evening he studied the board and smiled. "Resilience equals design," he said, and truth held firm.

The Test

Three months passed and screens filled with faces. Rafael spoke into light and told collapse plain, holding the notebook to read Frankl aloud. A second line followed and guided the room. Systems turn why into leadership.

The Proof
Messages surged and hope echoed back as tears marked success without spectacle. The prototype worked under pressure. Light carried the design forward and code lived.

Installation
I closed the laptop and saw the shape clearly. Darkness had forged the structure long ago and modern leadership installed it in daylight. Personal resilience scaled into an operating system. The design stood complete.

Tools and Tactics: The Meaning Reframe

Meaning is not found.
It is assigned under pressure.

1. Interrupt the Story
Stop the mental loop.
Take one controlled breath.
Reaction ends here.

2. Capture the Charge
Name the dominant emotion in one word.
This is raw fuel, not a verdict.

3. Ask the Frankl Question
"What is life demanding of me through this moment?"

4. Issue the Mission
Write one sentence that converts pain into contribution.
"This pain exists so I can serve by..."

5. Act Before the Day Closes
Take one visible action that proves the meaning is real.
No action, no meaning.

Each repetition replaces chaos with load-bearing structure.

Algorithm: The Daily Meaning Drill (≤10 minutes)

Breathe

Inhale for what was lost.
Exhale for what remains usable.

Write

Complete this sentence without editing:
"This experience is training me to become ___."

Move

Take one deliberate action aligned with that identity before sunset.

Close

End the day with one line:
"The strength this pain sharpened today was ___."

Reflection Questions

1. What crisis in your life could become a blueprint for others?
2. Where can you install meaning where you've only felt loss?
3. How might your purpose serve as structure for those you lead?

Pillar Activation: Meaning as Architecture

Game Plan
This chapter proves a hard truth. Resilience is built, not wished for. When life burns everything down, meaning becomes the load-bearing beam that keeps you standing.

Pillar Activation

- Mental Precision (Head): Frankl refused mental drift. He studied despair, chose his attitude, and turned chaos into data. Thought became structure.
- Physical Mastery (Body): He guarded posture and movement. Standing upright became resistance. The body signaled identity before words could.
- Emotional Power (Heart): Compassion replaced collapse. Sharing bread, humor, and presence stabilized others and strengthened him. Emotion became cohesion.

- Spiritual Alignment (Soul): Gratitude anchored endurance. Not gratitude for comfort, but for consciousness and choice. Purpose outlasted cruelty.
- Imaginative Strategy (Vision): He carried the future in his mind. Unfinished work, loved faces, and service pulled him forward. Meaning sealed the build.

Coach J's Challenge
When pressure hits, stop asking why this happened. Ask what this moment demands of you. Choose your stance. Write one sentence that turns pain into contribution. Then act before the day ends. No action, no meaning.

Locker-Room Reflection
What crisis in your life is waiting for you to design meaning instead of endure pain?

Chapter 19: The Resonance Effect

"Darkness cannot drive out darkness; only light can do that. Hate cannot drive out hate; only love can do that."

~ Martin Luther King, Jr.

Energy shapes the world more than effort. A single voice rises above a crowded room and the air tightens. Hearts pause. Breath holds. The unseen takes command. Every soul leans in without knowing why.

Another scene lives in memory. A weary crowd trembles in the cold. Fear settles across their ribs like iron frost. One man steps forward with only breath and conviction. His words fall steady. Storms ease. Courage spreads across frozen ground. Hope warms again.

Charisma never created that force. Resonance forged it. Effort pushes. Resonance pulls. Effort shouts. Resonance alters the field. Effort fights for attention. Resonance changes the direction of history.

Martin Luther King Jr. carried that field inside him. Picture him on a midnight street slick with winter rain. His coat lifts as the wind cuts through the alley. Threats hum through telephone lines. Rage gathers on porches. Death waits in shadow.

His voice still softened the storm. Crowds lifted their heads. Silence turned sacred. People felt his tone inside their ribs. Words struck like tuning forks against the human heart. Pauses rippled across bodies that forgot how to hope.

History did not move because he forced it. History drifted toward him. He tuned himself to truth with precise discipline. Fear lost its shape in his presence. The impossible shifted under his feet. Change answered his signal.

This chapter teaches you how to build that frequency. You will learn how to tune your life to a signal the world cannot ignore. You will learn how to send energy that bends reality toward the future you choose.

Martin Luther King Jr.: The Furnace of Resonance

Before the monuments, before the marches, before the title Doctor, there was Martin.

A preacher's son.
A choir mother's child.
A boy who learned early that sound moves people before words ever can.

Sunday mornings at Ebenezer Baptist Church smelled of wood polish and pressed linen. The organ shook the floorboards. Voices rose together. Tears fell without instruction. Hands clapped without command. Martin watched the invisible current pass through the room and bind strangers into one body.

Sound moved souls.
He felt it before he understood it.

He carried that knowing north to Boston. Frozen sidewalks. Collar up. Gandhi under streetlamps. Notebooks filled with questions that cut deeper than politics. Not What is power? but What aligns people?

Not How do you force change? but How do you tune a human being?

He was training his instrument long before the world heard the note.

The Collapse

Montgomery. 1956.

Night presses against the parsonage on South Jackson Street. Oil and ash hang in the air. The phone rings again. Sharp. Metallic. Merciless.

His hand hovers. He already knows the voice.

"Leave town, preacher. We're gonna blow you and your people to hell."

Click.

The dial tone hums like a live wire.

In the next room, Coretta hums to their newborn. Soft. Fragile. Breakable. The contrast nearly undoes him.

Martin lowers himself into a kitchen chair. The bulb flickers. The clock ticks too loud. Coffee turns bitter in his mouth. Every sermon he has preached collapses onto his chest at once.

Stand. March. Love. Lead.

The weight buckles him.

"Lord," he whispers, "I'm tired. I'm scared. I can't do this alone."

For the first time, he does not negotiate with doubt. He admits it.

Images flood him. Smoke around his wife. His child crying in rubble. Faces trusting him to guide them through fire. A mob tightening its grip on Montgomery.

He wonders if faith runs out.
He wonders if courage has a limit.
He wonders if God chose the wrong man.

Silence stretches thin as wire.

Then the room changes.

Not sound. Presence.

The air thickens. His breathing slows. Calm arrives—not gentle, but exact. Something enters him like breath returning to a drowning body.

No thunder. No spectacle. Only clarity vibrating through bone and blood.

Stand up for righteousness.
Stand up for justice.

I will be with you.

It is not comfort.
It is command.

Moments later, the explosion tears the night open.

Glass implodes. The baby screams. Coretta runs. Smoke claws his lungs. The porch disappears into splinters and flame. Neighbors surge forward with rifles raised, rage boiling over.

"Let's kill them."

Martin steps into the wreckage. Ash streaks his shirt. Soot marks his face. He raises one hand.

The noise dies.

"Put your weapons down," he says. "We must meet hate with love."

The mob freezes. The night holds its breath.

Something inside him shatters cleanly. Fear. Hesitation. Retreat.

What remains hums steady and unbreakable.

Resonance.

The Ignition

After the bombing, sleep never fully returns.

Threats arrive daily. Lies follow him through headlines. Funerals stack like stones. His body thins. His eyes darken. His resolve sharpens.

Doubt still visits. Always at night. Always alone.

"Is anyone listening?" he whispers after emptying a pulpit into silence.

And always the same answer rises from deep within him.

Stand up.

So he does.

Again.
And again.
And again.

Each morning becomes discipline. Prayer before speech. Scripture before step. Breath before anger. He studies Gandhi not as philosophy but as engineering. Nonviolence as structure. Love as force.

He stops trying to inspire.
He focuses on staying in tune.

Cadence becomes craft. Silence becomes strategy. His heartbeat sets the pace of crowds. His pause stills riots. His words land not as sparks but as waves.

This is no longer belief.
It is calibration.

The Reframe

At a packed church in Montgomery, a young activist shouts for retaliation. The room vibrates hot. Anger begs for release. Martin feels it rise in him too.

He closes his eyes.

The hum returns.

Low. Steady. Anchoring.

"If we return hate for hate," he says softly, "hate wins twice."

The room stills.

"The only force strong enough to turn an enemy into a brother is love."

Breath aligns. Bodies settle. Energy transmutes.

He understands it fully now.

The universe amplifies alignment, not argument.

He teaches it plainly.

"Anger is energy," he tells them. "You cannot destroy energy. You can only transform it."

His life becomes instrument design.

Morning silence.
Measured breath before speeches.
Stillness after violence.

Each act calibrates the movement.
Each sermon tunes the frequency.
Each march tests the signal.

He does not pull people forward.
They match his rhythm.

The Transformation

Selma. 1965.

The Edmund Pettus Bridge scars the horizon. Horses snort. Helmets gleam. Gas burns the air. Thousands wait behind him, hearts beating the same note.

Martin inhales slowly.

Step.
Breath.
Faith.

When batons strike, he kneels. Others follow. Silence detonates louder than force. Cameras capture poise where chaos was expected.

Brutality becomes broadcast.

The world cannot un-hear justice.

"I Have a Dream" is not a speech. It is frequency. His cadence rolls like drums. His words rise like brass. Millions vibrate together toward courage.

He becomes a tuning fork for humanity.

Legacy: Unity Transmission

April 3, 1968. Memphis.

Rain slants sideways. His body is failing. His spirit is electric.

"I've been to the mountaintop," he tells them. "I may not get there with you."

They know.

The bullet arrives the next day. It shatters bone, not resonance. Sound cannot be killed by force. His frequency multiplies.

In marches.

In songs.
In quiet acts of courage.

He proved belief, when aligned, becomes physics.

He did not speak of light.

He became it.

Universal Law: Vibration

Your energy dictates your impact, and Dr. King proved that when your inner frequency aligns with truth, love, and courage, the world cannot help but rise to meet your vibration.

Core Lesson

King faced collapse at a kitchen table in the quiet hours. Fear clawed at his mind and bent his thoughts. Weariness pulled at his body until it sagged under strain. Pressure crushed his creative spark. Only his spirit held firm enough to guard him from the fall. A deeper signal rose inside him and steadied his breath.

Night opened a new path. Silence shaped a command that cut through doubt. Strength returned through clarity. Calm gathered in his chest and spread through his limbs. Purpose replaced fear and set his direction. His life shifted from reaction to transmission.

Morning ritual shaped his discipline. He tuned breath until cadence felt clean. Prayer shaped intention.

Stillness set his frequency. He rose each day with a charge strong enough to shape crowds without losing himself to their heat. Every march tested that charge. Every sermon tested tone. Every confrontation tested coherence. Resonance replaced force.

Crowds learned to hold that resonance. Anger became raw power to refine. Doubt became fuel to steady the line. His voice carried through streets with a quiet truth that cut deeper than shouts. His presence aligned hearts under threat and guided action with control. He proved that inner order shapes outer change.

His arc closed with a final rise. His body failed under violence. His signal rose above time. His truth struck chords inside millions and still rings. His life showed that resilience grows from coherence. His frequency outlived him because it moved through people like a tuning note that refuses to fade. The world followed him because he lived in tune.

Client Story: Frequency of Freedom

The Climb Without Breath

Saleema built her business like a citadel under siege. Sleepless nights stacked each brick with caffeine and borrowed resolve. Clients heard balance preached while imbalance ruled her private hours. Before dawn, the phone rang like metal on bone. Metrics crowned each morning and deadlines hunted her sleep. Motion replaced meaning, and speed impersonated mastery.

Proof became her hunger. Victories followed one another, each thinner than the last. Applause faded faster than the ache behind her eyes. Momentum felt productive while emptiness grew louder. The current turned against its creator. The fortress began to fill with water.

The Day Silence Spoke

Collapse rarely shouts. Erosion does the real work. Winter light met her laptop and reflected a stranger with dull eyes and locked shoulders. Breath shortened as the screen glowed like a merciless confessional. Fingers hovered while words refused service. Tears struck keys with quiet precision, salt staining circuitry. Truth surfaced at last. "I don't know who I am without achievement." Walls absorbed the sentence. No audience arrived. Still, the crack spread through stone. Darkness wrapped the apartment that night. Pulse raced while purpose leaked away. Quitting offered mercy. Continuing demanded courage. Something older than ambition stirred. Extinction lost the vote.

The Voice of Resonance

Morning brought the call. Her voice shook, yet life remained. "I did everything right," she said, "and now it hurts to breathe." I spoke of Martin Luther King Jr. and disciplined calm. Hatred met harmony. Violence met stillness. Leadership moved through frequency, not force. Confusion crossed her face. "Frequency?" I answered clean and bare. Every leader vibrates before action begins. Tuning matters more than shouting.

Pressure creates noise. Alignment creates reach. Silence became her assignment. Five minutes of breath before sunrise anchored the work. One line of gratitude steadied the mind. One declaration followed, spoken without apology. I am alignment in motion. Resistance arrived immediately. Emails screamed. Thoughts clawed. Control demanded return. Beneath the noise, a low hum formed. The pulse predated success. Resonance reclaimed ground.

From Effort to Energy

Dawn arrived without violence. No alarm shattered the room. Presence filled it instead. Breath deepened and the body released its grip. Rhythm returned. That afternoon, she cleaned with intention. Old contracts disappeared. Stacks burned. Sunlight crossed the office floor for the first time. Beauty reclaimed stolen space. Order replaced strain. The first client noticed immediately. Warmth replaced urgency in her voice. "You sound grounded," the client said. Grounded became her new currency. Calls softened. Laughter ended meetings. Referrals arrived uninvited. Effort stepped aside. Energy led. Resistance vanished when self conflict ended. Resonance did the work strategy never could. Income doubled. Peace multiplied. Numbers reflected outcome, not cause. Presence rebuilt power. Alignment restored authority. She stopped chasing. She attracted by being.

The Resonant Leader

One year later, Saleema stood before hundreds of coaches, each carrying a cage built from hustle. She let silence lead her opening. Stillness commanded the room. Breath synchronized. "You don't attract what you want," she said. "You attract what you are." No applause followed. Only exhale. Truth crossed the space. Then bodies rose together. Leadership sounded different that day. Her words carried field, not volume. Morning rituals replaced frantic nights. Service replaced anxiety. Business moved like music. She felt the tremor King must have known, truth traveling faster than sound. Work transformed into ministry. Peace became protest. Frequency unlocked freedom. Today, she coaches from resonance. Calendars flow. Life hums. Presence speaks before promotion begins. Force retired. Alignment remained. She vibrates, and the world listens. That stands as her legacy. Resonance over resistance. Frequency over force. Alignment as leadership. Liberation begins in quiet courage.

Tools & Tactics: The Resonance Stack™

1. The Frequency Reset Ritual™

(Morning Nervous System Alignment)

Before input, create order.

Sit upright. Feet grounded. Spine tall.
Inhale through the nose for 4.
Hold for 4.
Exhale through the mouth for 8.

Repeat until the body softens.

Then ask one regulating question:

"What state must I embody to lead today?"

Declare it aloud—short, embodied, final:

"I am calm."

"I am precise."

"I am decisive."

This is not affirmation.
This is state selection.

You are choosing the frequency from which all decisions will flow.

2. The Environment Audit™

(Energetic Load Reduction)

Your space is not neutral.
It is programming you.

Clutter = unresolved decisions.
Visual noise = cognitive drag.

Remove anything that:

Belongs to a past identity

Carries guilt, delay, or obligation

Pulls attention instead of grounding it

Then add:

Light

One living element

One object that represents forward motion

When the environment stabilizes, the nervous system follows.

3. The Resonant Language Upgrade™

(Cognitive Signal Control)

Language is not description.
It is instruction.

Cut phrases rooted in lack or force.

Replace:

"I'm trying to get clients."
→ "Aligned clients are responding."

"I'm overwhelmed."

→ "I am simplifying to what matters."

Speak from completion, not pursuit.

Your brain organizes behavior around declared identity faster than around goals.

4. The Mirror of Service™

(Field Expansion Without Force)

Before work begins, ask:

"Who can I support today without agenda?"

Write the first name that appears.
Reach out with clarity and generosity.

No pitch.
No extraction.

Service stabilizes identity.
Stability creates trust.
Trust creates gravity.

Algorithm: The 9-Minute Resonance Reset™

Simple. Repeatable. Non-negotiable.

Minute 1–2: Regulate

Breathe: 4–4–8.
Eyes closed. Jaw relaxed.
Let the nervous system settle before thought leads.

Minute 3–4: Amplify

Name three specific gratitudes aloud.
Feel them in the body.

Emotion is the amplifier.
Thought alone does nothing.

Minute 5–6: Align

Ask:
"What do I stand for today?"

Write one word only:
Calm. Precision. Courage. Justice.

One word = one signal.

Minute 7–8: Declare

Speak one outcome as present reality:

390

"I am leading with clarity and authority."

"I am serving new clients with ease."

Do not hype it.
Feel it as settled truth.

Minute 9: Integrate

Silence.
No fixing. No chasing.

Let identity lock in.

Final Truth

This is not meditation.
It is signal conditioning.

You are not emptying the mind.
You are charging the system.

When your internal frequency stabilizes,
decisions sharpen, resistance drops,
and the external world responds without force.

Effort drains.
Resonance restores.

This is integration.

Reflection Questions

1. Where am I pushing for results that would come faster if I changed my state instead of my strategy?
2. Which three words, phrases, or internal stories quietly drain my energy each day—and what will I replace them with starting now?
3. If my presence alone set the emotional temperature of every room I enter, what signal would I choose to transmit today, and what single behavior will prove it before the day ends?

Pillar Activation: The Tuning Fork of a Nation

Game Plan

This chapter proves a hard truth. Force never changes history. Frequency does. Martin Luther King Jr. didn't push the world forward. He tuned himself to truth until the world followed.

Pillar Activation

- Mental Precision (Head)
  King mastered clarity under pressure. He chose discipline over reaction. Calm thinking shaped every word and pause.
- Physical Mastery (Body)
  Breath controlled his body before crowds felt his power. Stillness steadied his pulse. Rhythm carried him through fear and fatigue.

- Emotional Power (Heart)
  He refused to leak anger into action. Rage became resolve. Love became strength. Emotion served the mission.
- Spiritual Alignment (Soul)
  Purpose anchored him when threats closed in. Faith didn't comfort him. It commanded him. His "why" never wavered.
- Imaginative Strategy (Vision)
  He saw protest as pattern and sound as signal. Marches became music. Silence became force. Love became law.

Coach J's Challenge
Listen close. When you push harder and get less, stop forcing. Regulate your breath. Choose your state. Lead from alignment, not adrenaline. People feel your frequency before they hear your words. Train it daily.

Locker-Room Reflection
What frequency are you transmitting when pressure hits, and does it pull people forward or push them away?

Chapter 20: The Code is Now You

"Be water, my friend."

~ Bruce Lee

Cold glass tells the truth. Light sharpens it. A warrior meets his reflection before dawn and studies the shape of his doubt. Breath fogs the mirror while yesterday presses against the edges of his gaze. Muscles ache. Thoughts wander toward battles that wait beyond the door. Truth stands in front of him like a rival that knows his name.

Old mornings felt forced. Gratitude read like duty. Breathwork scraped through tension. Words of strength fell flat against a mind that refused to believe them. He shaped resilience like a chore and not a craft. The body moved without heart. The mind drifted without anchor. Nothing aligned with the man he worked to become.

Time carved a shift. Discipline repeated turned into music. Rhythm took root in his bones. Motion rose from that rhythm like water climbing stone. Flow replaced effort. Presence replaced strain. The ritual began to move him instead of the other way around.

A deeper truth rose next. Surrender created mastery and not the reverse. Breath guided the body. Body steadied the mind. Mind cleared the field. Flow arrived like a quiet tide that carried him past doubt and fear. Strength followed that tide. Power formed without strain.

Now he meets the mirror with no divide. Reflection bends toward him. Stillness folds into motion. Control feels like water sliding toward its own path. No tension. No force. Only flow. The world will call it mastery. He knows it as truth.

Bruce Lee: The Furnace of Flow

The Seed of Motion

San Francisco, 1940.
War sirens cut the Pacific air as a child entered the
world above a Chinatown stage.
Lights burned. Drums thundered. Movement arrived
before language.

He was born during performance. He never separated
life from expression.
In Hong Kong, film sets blurred into alleyways.
Cameras admired him. Gangs tested him.
He welcomed both.

His fists moved fast. His mind moved faster.
Every insult became invitation. Every loss became
instruction.
Conflict trained him early.

Under Ip Man, the wooden dummy answered nightly.
Strike. Recoil. Strike again.
He learned rhythm before power.

He was not fighting men.
He was fighting gravity.
The gravity of average.

Even then, his body spoke prophecy.
Learn motion deeply enough, and you will teach the
world to listen.

The Shattering

Nineteen. One ticket. One direction.
Twenty-six dollars. Heavy accent. Refusal to kneel.

Seattle replaced Hong Kong heat with rain and
rejection.
He washed dishes. He taught in basements. He slept
short.
Vision stayed awake.

Hollywood smiled without respect.
They asked him to bow. To soften. To shrink.
He refused.

Then his spine betrayed him.
1970. One lift. One mistake. Lightning down the nerves.
Doctors whispered the word *never*.

He lay still on a narrow cot.
Muscle twitched. Sweat pooled. Time slowed.
Silence pressed harder than pain.

Rage burned out.
What remained was listening.

Stillness spoke clearly.
Stillness trains.

The Law of Flow

Books replaced sparring partners.
Nietzsche. Krishnamurti. Taoist texts. Boxing reels.
Knowledge struck from all angles.

He filled notebooks with arrows and spirals.
Motion mapped onto thought.
Thought stripped of excess.

One truth repeated until it burned clean.
Rigidity kills.

Forms fossilize fighters.
Certainty blinds thinkers.
Attachment weakens both.

He wrote one line and lived inside it:
Absorb what is useful. Discard what is not. Add what is
uniquely your own.

That sentence rebuilt him.
He rehearsed movement in imagination until nerves
remembered.
The body followed the mind back to life.

Step by step, he rose.
Pain sharpened him. Philosophy aligned him.
Expression replaced domination.

The Strike Before Thought

The camera could not contain him.
Movement outran the frame.
Directors begged restraint. He refused.

Every strike cracked with meaning.
Each pause carried intent.
Nothing wasted.

He named it Jeet Kune Do.
The Way of the Intercepting Fist.
A system designed to erase systems.

No style. No dogma.
Only adaptation.

He spoke of water.
Water yields, yet erodes stone.
Water takes shape without losing power.

He did not imitate water.
He *became* it.

Training intensified. Time compressed.
Midnight conditioning. Dawn philosophy.
Urgency guided him.

There was no gap left.
No delay between thought and action.
He became the strike before thought.

Legacy: Motion Without End

Summer, 1973.
Hong Kong heat shimmered. Breath shortened.
The body collapsed under its own voltage.

Thirty-two years.
A comet mid-arc.

The world refused the ending.
But endings were never his domain.

Students carried notebooks like maps.
Artists borrowed his rhythm.
Athletes echoed his clarity.

He built no empire.
He built circulation.

His body stopped.
His motion did not.

He proved mastery is not control.
It is synchronization.

To fight the world, align with it.
To command the body, listen.
To endure crisis, become fluid.

Bruce Lee did not vanish.
He changed state.

Motion, immortal.

Universal Law: Perpetual Transmutation of Energy

Energy transforms through choice, and Bruce Lee proved that when you transmute pain into philosophy, limitation into flow, and struggle into mastery, you become a force the world cannot contain.

Core Lesson

Bruce Lee rebuilt his life through fire and stillness. A broken spine cut motion from his world and forced him into silence. Pain carved out space for study and deep inquiry. Books filled his room as he mapped a new path into strength. Thought became movement long before muscle followed.

Visualization shaped each small victory. He tested ideas with sharp focus and tracked progress with calm eyes. Weakness turned into a field for precise adaptation. Breath guided each step into controlled recovery. Stillness replaced panic and opened a doorway into presence.

Philosophy lifted him beyond injury. Flow replaced force. He dropped rigid forms and shaped a new language of combat. Jeet Kune Do rose from questions that demanded truth. Motion aligned with awareness until thought no longer slowed action.

Creation surged through his rebuilt frame. Insight shaped his strikes. Purpose guided his training.

Capacity expanded in every direction as he fused mind, heart, body, spirit, and imagination into one field. Collapse no longer defined him. Reinvention did.

His resilience lived in motion without tension. He adapted with speed. He dissolved each limit with study and grit. He evolved through failure and reclaimed power in stillness. He rose with a clear truth: flow turns fracture into strength.

Client Story: The Warrior Who Learned to Flow

The Architecture of Control

Cassandra built her world like a sealed fortress. Alarms rang at 4:45, followed by spin sessions, protein shakes, and inbox triage. Highlighters ruled her planner, purple for projects, blue for meetings, red for emergencies. Nights ended with locked jaws, burning shoulders, and a mind still sprinting past midnight. Strength, she believed, lived inside exhaustion. Silence later exposed the hollowness effort could not fill.

Admiration surrounded her like armor. Executives depended on precision. Friends praised relentlessness. Applause faded once darkness arrived. Between deadlines, an echo whispered something vital had gone missing. More force produced less life.

Coaching did not begin with a plea. Optimization drove the request. "A better system fixes this," she said, voice sharp with certainty. Control spoke through every syllable. The blade cut inward without mercy.

The Shattering of Effort
An elevator carried the reckoning upward. Fifty floors passed between meetings and vibrating alerts. Pressure seized her chest. Vision smeared. Air vanished.

Thoughts screamed resistance while the body refused commands. Doors opened to a woman on her knees, gasping and streaked with mascara. Heartbeats thundered like an animal trapped in steel. Doctors labeled panic. Betrayal felt closer to truth.

Control failed for the first time. Return visits brought rigid posture and crossed arms. "I'm broken," she said. "No time exists for this." Argument would have wasted breath.

Bruce Lee entered the room instead. A lift gone wrong. Bone snapped. Months trapped inside a cast. Silence forced a warrior to stop striking. Stillness replaced violence. Flow replaced force.

Recognition flashed behind her eyes. "He stopped fighting," she whispered. "He learned movement without effort," came the reply.

The Dojo of Stillness
Training began with five minutes of nothing. Phones vanished. Planners stayed closed. Breath remained.

Discomfort arrived immediately. Muscles twitched. Jaw muscles clicked. "This does nothing," she muttered. Meaning had always required motion.

Pause revealed the lie. Weeks of resistance followed. Repetition carved grooves where panic once lived. Roots formed beneath silence. Morning hours shifted from planning to breathing.

Armor loosened with every exhale. Perfection lost its grip. The Mirror Drill followed. Eyes met reflection. "I am not the schedule. I am the source."

Foreign words slowly found resonance. Rhythm surfaced beneath routine. Control softened into awareness. Life pulsed again.

The Strike Before the Thought
Six months later, crisis detonated without warning. A multimillion dollar campaign collapsed overnight. Voices clashed inside the war room. Phones vibrated like alarms. Tempers flared.

Silence arrived at the head of the table. Eyes closed. One breath. Waiting filled the room.

Calm replaced command when she spoke. "We pivot," she said. "Pressure breaks us. Flow carries us." Noise dissolved. Ideas aligned with ease.

Opportunity rose from wreckage. Executives called it genius. Clarity named the truth. A voice note followed that night. "I stopped fighting waves. I ride them now."

Her body confirmed the shift. Sleep returned. Migraines disappeared. Laughter loosened. Days no longer demanded conquest.

The Current Within
Bare feet greet morning air on her balcony. Slow arcs replace urgency. Breath guides balance. Neighbors guess Tai Chi. She calls it integration.

Offices follow her rhythm. Meetings open with silence. Projects unfold without panic. Teams feel gravity shaped from calm. Precision no longer requires fear.

"Resilience meant endurance," she said recently. "Elegance defines it now." Control surrendered to current. Success stopped running away. Life hums with composed motion.

Truth settled where struggle once ruled. Resilience never erased effort. Flow taught effort how to move.

Tools & Tactics: The Way of Integration

Presence Before Power. Flow Before Force.

Integration is not passivity.
It is controlled adaptability under pressure.
This system trains your nervous system to remain coherent while conditions change.

Tool 1: The Mirror Drill Source Recall

Purpose: Detach identity from urgency. Reclaim authorship.

Stand before your reflection each morning.
Feet grounded. Spine tall. Shoulders dropped.
Breathe through the nose. Slow. Silent. Deep.

Lock eyes with yourself and state once, clearly:
"I am not the schedule. I am the source."

Do not repeat it for motivation.
Repeat it to reset hierarchy. You command time, not the reverse.

Watch the body respond:

Jaw loosens
Chest drops
Breath deepens

This trains presence before performance—the same sequence Bruce Lee mastered: awareness first, speed second.

Tool 2: The Water Reframe Resistance Conversion

Purpose: Replace collision with redirection.

When resistance appears - a delay, tension, disagreement - pause.

Whisper internally:

"Flow around it."

No pushing.
No proving.
No emotional spike.

Adjust. Pivot. Redirect.

This conditions the nervous system to interpret
flexibility as strategic strength, not retreat.
Water does not lose power by bending. It preserves it.

Tool 3: The 3-Phase Breath Flow Reset

Purpose: Restore parasympathetic command on
demand.

Inhale through the nose for 4
Hold for 4
Exhale through the mouth for 6

One cycle lowers threat response.
Three cycles re-establish internal order.

Use it:

Before meetings
Before training
Before creative work
Breath becomes armor made of air: light, responsive,
unbreakable.

Tool 4: The Daily Flow Review Awareness Amplifier

Purpose: Eliminate wasted effort.
Before sleep, journal:

3 moments you forced
3 moments you flowed

Note which produced progress with less strain.
Do not judge. Observe.
Awareness compounds faster than effort.
This is how intelligence replaces exhaustion.

Algorithm: The Way of Water

Daily Practice Total Time: 5 Minutes

Step 1: Stillness (1 minute)

Stand or sit tall. Eyes closed.

Scan for tension:

Jaw
Chest
Belly
Exhale it out.

Quietly repeat once:
"Be water."

Stillness restores command.

Step 2: Breath Alignment (1 minute)

Inhale 4 → Hold 4 → Exhale 6

Let breath set the rhythm.
Thoughts fall in line behind it.
This is the shift from control to coherence.

Step 3: Mirror Activation (1 minute)

Open your eyes. Face your reflection.
State one identity sentence as fact:

"I move through challenge with grace and precision."
"I remain calm while others rush."
"I adapt faster than conditions change."

Seal it with a steady exhale.

Identity follows physiology.

Step 4: Motion Practice (1 minute)

Perform one slow, continuous movement:

Arm sweep
Spinal rotation
Controlled stretch

Move with breath. No speed. No strain.

This locks mind and body into a single signal.

Step 5: Integration (1 minute)

Ask once:

"Where can I stop forcing today?"

Write the first answer. Do not edit.

Then begin your day like water—
not passive, not aggressive,
inevitable.

Execution Standard

Practice for 7 consecutive mornings

Day 3: resistance drops

Day 7: flow precedes thought

This is not philosophy.
It is nervous-system conditioning for leaders, athletes,
and builders who refuse to waste energy fighting what
can be directed.

Reflection Questions

1. Where am I forcing control instead of using strength?
2. When did action feel easy and powerful?
3. Where can I move like water today?

Pillar Activation: The Way of Flow

Game Plan
This chapter proves a hard truth. Force breaks you. Flow rebuilds you. Bruce Lee shows how surrender sharpens mastery and turns collapse into command.

Pillar Activation

- Mental Precision (Head):
  Bruce abandoned rigid forms. He questioned everything. Clarity replaced tradition. Thought stopped fighting reality and started shaping it.
- Physical Mastery (Body):
  A broken spine forced stillness. Visualization rebuilt motion. Breath led recovery. Movement returned without strain.
- Emotional Power (Heart):
  Rejection burned. Rage dissolved. Pain became data. Emotion stopped controlling him and started teaching him.
- Spiritual Alignment (Soul):
  He stopped trying to dominate life. He aligned with it. Purpose shifted from winning to expression.

- Imaginative Strategy (Vision):
  Jeet Kune Do emerged from synthesis. No style.
  No limits. Only adaptation shaped by truth.

Coach J's Challenge
Stop forcing the day. Direct it. When resistance appears,
pause. Take one breath. Identify where flow replaces
force. Move there. Train presence before power.
Alignment precedes mastery. The day responds to
order.

Locker-Room Reflection
Where are you fighting life instead of flowing with it?

Chapter 21: Win the World by Winning Your Day

"If you want to change the world, start off by making your bed."

~ **Admiral William McRaven**

Destiny rises in small hours. Dawn hides the truth inside simple acts. A cold floor waits for your feet. A quiet room tests your intent. The first breath becomes your verdict.

Many wait for history to call their name. They hope for the miracle, the moment, the sign. The world never calls. It measures instead. It studies what you do when no eyes watch. Small actions shift the arc of a life.

Morning creates the current. Miss the morning and drift begins. Win the morning and the tide lifts beneath you. Win enough mornings and the world adjusts to your rhythm. Momentum grows in silence.

Admiral McRaven lived that law before the world honored his work. A dark sky met his rise. A tight bed steadied his mind. A cold swim hardened his intent. A quiet ritual carried him through storms few men faced with courage intact. His power grew in rooms no one saw.

Greatness grows from repeated choices. Each choice sets direction. Each direction builds identity. Identity shapes destiny long before the world agrees. Win the day and the week follows fast. Win the week and your nature shifts. Win enough weeks and the world bends.

The tide waits for your command. Step forward now. The day begins.

William McRaven: The Furnace of Discipline

The Boy and the Horizon

He grew up far from the ocean.
Yet he studied maps until dawn.
Model ships crowded his floor.
The sea meant possibility, not water.
When the Navy called, destiny answered.

Coronado greeted him with sun and sand.
Instructors stood like iron.
The surf waited like judgment.
He came to prove courage.
Arrived to meet suffering.

Hell Week

Two a.m. split the Pacific open.
Cold crushed breath from lungs.
Salt burned skin raw.
Thirty-six hours without sleep.
Every nerve begged surrender.

"Make your beds."
Not a request.
A command carved in thunder.
Hands shook.
Vision swam.

He steadied his fingers.
Pulled fabric tight.
Squared each corner.
A coin bounced clean.
Order stood where chaos raged.

That bed was not cloth.
It was control.

The Code of Order

Days dissolved into punishment.
Men vanished by stretcher or shame.
He stayed.
Each dawn, he made the bed.
Every fold said, *I decide.*

Discipline revealed its law.
Comfort lies.
Identity endures.
Ritual builds spine.
Order outlasts fear.

The cot became a mirror.
Correct the sheet.
Correct the self.
The man began forming.
Quiet. Exact. Unbreakable.

Blood and Dust

War followed him inland.
Desert wind carried fire.

Radios cracked with urgency.
A mission fractured.
Panic pressed hard.

He stopped.
Breathed.
Remembered the bed.
Smoothed fear into focus.
Spoke with steel calm.

The line held.
Men moved.
Lives returned.
Discipline scaled from inches to miles.
Armor, proven.

Begin Again

Years passed into ceremony.
Medals flashed.
Silence followed.
Each morning, he still made the bed.
Precision brought peace.

On a stage, he gave truth.
"Change the world.
Start by making your bed."
Laughter softened.
Understanding landed.

It was not metaphor.
It was a map.
Order the small.

Command the self.
Weather any storm.

Epilogue: The Furnace Remembered

Every crisis asks one question.
Will you choose order or quit?
Resilience answers quietly.
Repeat the ritual.
Begin again.

The sheet snaps tight.
A vow renews.
Storms wait outside.
Choice waits within.
Discipline stands.

Universal Law: Inspired Action

Your life advances the moment you move with disciplined intent, and McRaven proved that one precise action repeated daily becomes the foundation that no chaos can collapse.

Core Lesson

Order steadies a collapsing world. McRaven learns this truth early in the grind of special operations. Chaos surrounds him. Storms pound the coast. Instructors bark hard commands. Yet he controls one thing. He fixes his bed with sharp corners and clean lines. That simple act forms the first brick of his internal architecture.

Ritual guides his mind when exhaustion threatens to scatter it. He wakes, stands tall, pulls the sheets tight, and claims the day before the day claims him. Fear loses ground. Doubt fades. Purpose rises. His mind sharpens through the discipline of one quiet motion.

Emotion steadies next. War stirs anxiety like dust in a desert wind. He breathes, sets his bed, and restores a sense of place. The world may break around him, yet the ritual grounds him. Calm returns. He regains his center through the smallest act of control.

His body follows. Fatigue crushes muscles and dulls reflexes. Saltwater burns skin. Cold drills into bone. He still completes the task. The bed resets his physical system. Precision replaces strain. Order replaces collapse. Strength rebuilds in inches.

Creativity awakens as well. The ritual frees his mind for strategy and adaptation. Tight corners mirror tight execution. Clean lines echo clean plans. His bed becomes a small workshop for operational clarity. Solutions rise once clutter falls.

Spirit binds it all. The habit becomes a daily oath. He starts each morning with intention. He claims identity through action. The world cannot shake what he builds inside. One simple ritual shapes a life of command.

His story reveals a final truth. Resilience grows through quiet repetition. Each small act becomes a beam of structure. Each completed task becomes a vote for who you become. Heroic courage fades without discipline.

Lasting strength grows only through ritual. His bed becomes a lifelong operating system. Order earns freedom. Habit forms identity.

Client Story: The Advisor Who Reclaimed His Rhythm

The Man Who Managed Millions but Not Himself

Performance ruled Peter's life. Calls stacked, closings landed, and the chase never slept. Markets unfolded for him like clean maps under bright lights, and clients steadied when he spoke with calm authority. To his team, discipline wore a tailored suit.

Inside, erosion spread quietly through every hour.

Mornings disappeared into snooze alarms and dim resolve. Caffeine replaced breakfast, and inboxes swallowed intention. Days merged into profit reports without memory or texture. Paper gains rose while life losses deepened. Presence vanished long before revenue declined.

When Peter arrived, he did not ask for strategy. He asked for peace. "I know profit," he said. "I do not know stillness."

The answer waited at the edge of his bed.

The Day the Market Broke Him

Red numbers flooded screens before sunrise. Alerts shrieked. Fear pulsed through his phone. Three clients exited by midday with clipped voices. He stared as figures fell and hands shook, cold coffee untouched beside a fractured reflection.

The market moved.

The break lived inside him.

Night refused sleep. Charts glowed while dread whispered endurance had expired. At dawn, tangled sheets mirrored his mind. Order felt unreachable.

Then memory surfaced through exhaustion.

A story of discipline under fire returned with force.

Peter stood. He smoothed the sheets with intention. Corners aligned. Fabric tightened. Breath slowed.

Chaos persisted outside the room.

Clarity took root within him.

The Win Your Day Operating Code™

Morning arrived with structure instead of panic. We rebuilt his days through small, deliberate victories. Preparation began the night before with intention and restraint. Water waited. Notes rested. Gratitude stood written. Movement followed waking with quiet discipline.

Resistance surfaced fast.

"Simplicity insults scale," he argued.

"Master minutes," I replied. "Then command markets."

Days stacked through repetition. Ritual shifted from effort into calibration. Each morning, sheets smoothed with measured breath.

Meetings flowed without force. Clients listened longer.

Calm stopped hiding.

It began arriving uninvited.

From Chaos to Command

Another crisis struck without warning. A merger failed. Investors panicked. Former patterns waited at the door.

Peter paused.

Order preceded engagement.

Water grounded him. Movement cleared him. Breath centered him. He entered work with quiet inevitability. Fear shifted into conversation and direction.

Retention climbed. Referrals doubled. Energy returned without demand.

The lesson proved simple and enduring.

Control begins with the smallest corner.

The Rhythm That Builds Real Wealth

Months later, Peter taught the ritual forward. Teams paused before markets opened. Silence led. Breath followed. Gratitude anchored intention.

Order entered rooms before numbers did.

Culture shifted from panic into presence. Discipline shed its reputation as punishment and revealed itself as power. Volatility shrank under calm leadership. Wealth expanded beyond numerical measure into peace with permanence.

Each dawn still begins the same way.

Fabric smooths. Corners align. Breath deepens.

The day does not start with bells or screens.

It begins with command over self.

Tools & Tactics: The Win Your Day Operating Code™

Order precedes power. Always.

1. The Corner Rule

Every day begins with one act of order. Before screens. Before input. Before noise, bring one corner of reality into alignment.

- Make your bed.

- Clear your desk.
- Square your shoulders and steady your breath.

This is not about neatness.
It is about authority.

Order is not decoration.
Order is direction.

Whoever commands the first corner commands the day.

2. The Five Micro-Wins Framework

Momentum is engineered the night before.

Before sleep, script five wins for tomorrow:

- Simple
- Measurable
- Executable in under five minutes

Example (Peter's list):

- Pack tomorrow's essentials
- Rehearse opening client line
- Drink one full glass of water on waking
- Stretch for five minutes
- Write one sentence of gratitude

Five micro-wins preloaded at night produce five victories before doubt wakes up.

Anxiety feeds on ambiguity.
Momentum feeds on certainty.

3. The 4 A.M. Command Sequence

At dawn, execute the four anchors. No negotiation:

1. Hydrate – Reset chemistry
2. Move – Ignite energy
3. Review – Reassert purpose
4. Anchor Gratitude – Stabilize emotional tone

This sequence locks:

- Body → Mind
- Mind → Mission

Skip none.
Shortcuts create drag.

4. The Order Feedback Loop

At day's end, rate execution 1–10.

- 7 or higher → Continue
- Below 7 → Diagnose friction

Name the cause:

- Fatigue
- Distraction
- Emotional leakage

Then simplify tomorrow's micro-wins.

This is not self-judgment.
This is system calibration.

Reflection without adjustment is noise.

5. The Commandment of Smallness

Small acts carry disproportionate power.

The smaller the act, the cleaner the signal.

Precision at the micro level compounds into dominance at the macro level.

As Admiral McRaven proved:
If you can command a corner, you can command a crisis.

Algorithm: The Resilient Order Loop™

Total Time: 15 minutes or less

1. Breathe (1 min)
Inhale through the nose.
Exhale twice as long.
Shift from reaction to command.

2. Make the Bed (2 min)
Smooth. Fold. Align.
Finish something immediately.

Completion builds confidence faster than affirmation.

3. Hydrate & Move (3 min)
One full glass of water.
Ten squats. Ten push-ups. Or a short mobility flow.
Signal readiness through the body.

4. Review the Mission (3 min)
Read your five micro-wins aloud.
Visualize each completed.
Certainty programs execution.

5. Anchor Gratitude (2 min)
 Name:

- One person
- One opportunity
- One lesson

Gratitude stabilizes the nervous system and sharpens perception.

6. Command the Day (4 min)
Open your planner.
Choose one result that defines victory today.

Everything else is secondary until that result is secured.

Outcome

15 minutes → Full-system alignment

Run this sequence daily for 21 days.

The ritual becomes rhythm.
Rhythm becomes instinct.
Instinct becomes identity.

You stop chasing control.
You start embodying it.

This is not motivation.
This is command.

Reflection Questions

1. Where does disorder enter my day first, and what one act of order will shut that door?
2. What five micro-wins can I script tonight that guarantee momentum before the day begins?
3. When pressure spikes, what single "corner" can I command right now to restore authority?

Pillar Activation: Command the Morning

Game Plan
This chapter proves destiny forms before the world wakes up. Small acts at dawn create order, and order creates command. Admiral McRaven shows how one disciplined ritual can steady chaos and shape a life.

Pillar Activation

- Mental Precision (Head)
  McRaven focused on what he could control. One bed. One task. Clear edges built a clear mind.

- Physical Mastery (Body)
  Cold mornings, exhaustion, and pain met action,
  not debate. Movement followed discipline.
  Strength returned through repetition.
- Emotional Power (Heart)
  Fear rose in surf and war. He answered with calm
  structure. Emotion settled when order appeared.
- Spiritual Alignment (Soul)
  Each morning became a vow. Identity formed
  through action. Purpose anchored him when
  comfort vanished.
- Imaginative Strategy (Vision)
  A simple bed became armor. Precision at inches
  turned into leadership across miles. Order
  unlocked strategy.

Coach J's Challenge
Stop waiting. Begin with command. Choose one act of
order before noise. Finish it clean. Let that win set the
tone. When pressure returns, repeat the act. Small
control restores authority.

Locker-Room Reflection
What single corner will you command tomorrow
morning to claim the day?

Chapter 22: You Are the Frequency

"If you want to find the secrets of the universe, think in terms of energy, frequency, and vibration."

~ **Nikola Tesla**

The universe shifts when you move in tune with its pulse. A clear note carries farther than force. A tuning fork holds its tone. The world listens.

Midnight pressed against the windows of Tesla's laboratory. Silence filled the room like deep water. Copper coils waited in the dark. Glass caught stray sparks. Ozone drifted across the air with a faint bite. No crowd gathered. No applause rose. Only the steady charge of current moved between unseen worlds. Truth lived in that quiet.

A raised hand cut the stillness. The air trembled. A thin shiver crossed the room as if matter prepared to wake. Light rose without sound. Light answered without speech. Light carried the message.

Clarity struck him. Strain achieves nothing. Frequency shapes everything. The world bends to the signal you send. The field answers the quality of your note.

You stand inside that same field. Life forms around the current you project. You transmit the charge that builds your path. You shape the pattern that becomes your days. You create the signal that sets reality in motion.

Precision tunes you. Alignment lifts you. Resonance moves the world toward you. Nothing shifts because you push. Everything shifts because you vibrate with intent.
 You are frequency.

The Storm and the Man - Tesla's Furnace

Midnight. New York.

Tesla's coils scream through the dark. Lightning carves the air in jagged blue fire. Ozone sears his lungs. Thunder hammers the floor beneath his boots.

Any other man runs.
 Tesla advances.

Arms lift. Current crowns him.
 He fuses with the storm, a living conduit of voltage and will. The bolts lunge toward him, not to strike—but to sing.

He shouts through the roar, voice cutting pure:
 "If you want the secrets of the universe, think in terms of energy, frequency, vibration."

Theory never forged this creed.
 Tesla lived it.
 Each storm he summoned reflected the one raging inside him.

Nikola Tesla: The Furnace of Frequency

The Boy Who Heard Lightning

Smiljan, 1856. Summer split the sky open.
 Thunder struck as he arrived. Midwives froze. His mother spoke once. *He belongs to the storm.*

From that night, he listened past silence.
Electric breath moved beneath walls and floors.
He drew sound as geometry. He counted thunder like time.
His father demanded priesthood. He chose light.
The house hummed with an argument that never slept.

Truth-punch: Destiny announces itself as pressure before it appears as purpose.

The Current War

New York, 1884.

Smoke clung to ceilings. Sparks warned and vanished.
Edison owned the city with lamps and certainty.
Tesla arrived starving, precise, unwelcome.

His machines worked while he slept.
Alternating current emerged clean and alive.
Edison mocked it as lethal chaos.
Tesla left with ideas only.

He dug ditches to eat.
Each shovel struck felt like burial.
He whispered equations to keep his name alive.

Truth-punch: Genius without backing is tested by hunger.

The Birth of Lightning

Colorado Springs opened wide and empty.
Wind carried courage across the plain.

Tesla raised a tower into the dark.
Locals called madness. He called alignment.
He threw the switch.

Earth convulsed.
Sky tore itself open.
Lightning bent toward him.

He did not study energy.
He entered it.

That night taught him the rule.
Resilience vibrates. Survival oscillates. Harmony
returns.

Truth-punch: Endurance is motion held without fear.

The Fall into Silence

Fame flickered, then fled.
Backers smiled and disappeared.
Patents vanished. Credit shifted.

Wardenclyffe drained him.
Reporters circled. Friends thinned.
He moved into hotel rooms with pigeons.

One white dove perched on his hand.
He called it his heart.

He stopped asking *why me.*
He started listening for *through me.*

Truth-punch: Applause is noise. Coherence is power.

The Infinite Frequency

Isolation purified intent.
Ego loosened its grip.

Each morning he walked Manhattan.
Hands behind his back.
Steps counted to the pulse of creation.

He wrote for truth, not funding.
Stone, bird, wind, thought—slowed electricity.
Failure became feedback.
Pain became tuning.
Loneliness sharpened signal.

Invention crossed into revelation.
The universe began to speak through him.

Truth-punch: When identity dissolves, transmission begins.

The Resilience Blueprint: Invention as Law

1) Alternating Current: Law of Vibration
Direct current strangled distance.
Tesla chose rhythm. Energy breathed again.
At the 1893 World's Fair, night turned to day.
Niagara learned how to sing.

Lesson: Hold your frequency. Resonance outlasts resistance.

2) Tesla Coil: Law of Resonance
 Lightning arced with order.
 Air itself tuned.
 Power crossed space without force.

Lesson: Tune yourself first. Alignment moves worlds.

3) Radio: Law of Perpetual Transmutation
 Signals traveled the ether.
 Credit drifted away.
 Truth kept humming.

Lesson: Energy remembers its source.

4) Wireless Power: Law of Oneness
 Free energy threatened profit.
 Funding vanished. Vision stayed.

Lesson: Unity scares systems built on division.

5) Wardenclyffe: Law of Cause and Effect
 The tower fell. The idea did not.
 Satellites rose. Wi-Fi filled the sky.

Lesson: Collapse transmits. Echo builds futures.

Final Furnace: Becoming Current

New York, 1943.

A quiet room.
No fortune. No audience.

Outside, the city glows with his work.
Every wire hums his thinking.
Each light answers his name.

He did not die.
He changed state.

Truth-punch: Resilience is frequency made permanent.

Universal Law: Vibration

Your dominant frequency becomes your destiny, and Tesla proved that when you hold a clear, unwavering vibration through collapse and doubt, the world eventually synchronizes with the energy you sustain.

Core Lesson

Storm light marked Tesla at birth. Thunder split the sky as he drew breath. Midwives whispered of fate. His mother spoke of a child claimed by the storm. He grew into a mind shaped by current, not approval.

Ideas charged him. Critics circled him. Poverty closed in. Rivals stole credit. Towers fell. Friends left. He watched his name fade as inventions spread across continents. He refused to bow. He chose signal over safety.

Vision guided each step. Silence pressed against him. Rage cooled into focus. Hope tightened into discipline. Thought fused with faith and imagination. He carved clarity from ruin and forged purpose inside the dark.

Work filled his nights. Light moved through his hands. Patterns rose in his dreams. Machines formed inside his mind before metal touched flame. He built worlds no one understood. He refused to dim his inner voltage.

Recognition drifted away. Wealth slipped through his grip. Fame passed to louder men. He accepted the cost and guarded his frequency. He learned that resilience comes from resonance. He held his truth when the world shook.

Civilization later caught his signal. Cities lit with his current. Engines hummed with his designs. The modern world carried his pulse in every wire and wave. He became the quiet source behind the age of power.

His story delivers one lesson. Purpose becomes unbreakable when you refuse to lower your frequency. Stand firm in that truth and your signal outlives you.

Tools & Tactics: The Transmission Suite

1. AC Ritual: Law of Vibration

Purpose: Restore natural oscillation. Kill static.

Tool:
Ask two questions, once in the morning, once under pressure:

- *Where am I resisting instead of moving?*
- *What would flow look like right now?*

Tactic:
Take one visible action that shifts you from force to rhythm—slow the breath, simplify the task, remove friction.
Resistance lowers frequency. Motion restores it.

2. Coil Resonance Drill: Law of Resonance

Purpose: Tune the self until the environment follows.

Tool:
Select one daily habit that represents your next identity.

Tactic:
Execute it at the same time, same way, every day for 30 days.
No optimization. No expansion. Just clean repetition.
When the coil stabilizes, the field reorganizes.

3. Radio Reflection: Law of Transmutation

Purpose: Convert thought into signal.

Tool:
Write one thought each day that carries clarity, courage, or conviction.

Tactic:
Transmit it before sunset: post it, speak it, teach it, send it.
Unshared insight decays. Broadcast insight compounds.

4. Wireless Unity Practice: Law of Oneness

Purpose: Collapse separation. Restore coherence.

Tool:
Five minutes of stillness each morning.

Tactic:
Focus on one invisible connection: breath, heartbeat, shared intention, love.
Feel how it links you to others without effort.
Isolation fractures power. Unity amplifies it.

5. Wardenclyffe Review: Law of Cause & Effect

Purpose: Recode failure into future infrastructure.

Tool:
List one perceived failure from your day or past.

Tactic:
Answer one question only:

What strength, insight, or direction did this plant for later?
Nothing is wasted. Everything is wired forward.

Algorithm: The Transmission Loop™

Breathe → Reset the nervous system.
Tune In → Notice your current vibration without judgment.
Embody → Align thought, word, and action into one signal.
Transmit → Express it outward through action or communication.
Uplift → Observe the ripple. Reinforce what multiplies.

Time Required: 7–10 minutes
Result: Static dissolves. Signal strengthens. Reality responds.

Bottom Line

This is not self-reflection.
This is frequency engineering.

Those who master transmission stop chasing outcomes.
Outcomes start finding them.

Reflection Questions

1. What frequency are you transmitting unconsciously each day?
2. Which "failure" of yours might already be transmitting a future effect?
3. How can you embody Tesla's law of Oneness in your relationships, work, and mission?

Pillar Activation: Frequency Over Force

Game Plan
This chapter proves a hard truth. Reality does not move for force. It reorganizes for frequency. Tesla won not by pushing harder, but by holding a cleaner signal when the world resisted.

Pillar Activation

- Mental Precision (Head): Tesla thought in patterns, not opinions. He chose clarity over consensus and stayed loyal to first principles.
- Physical Mastery (Body): Long nights, walking rituals, measured breath. He conserved energy so his mind could stay sharp.
- Emotional Power (Heart): Rejection and theft never collapsed him. He transmuted rage into focus and loss into feedback.
- Spiritual Alignment (Soul): He served a future larger than profit. Purpose anchored him when applause vanished.

- Imaginative Strategy (Vision): He saw worlds before wires existed. Towers fell, but the vision outlived them all.

Coach J's Challenge
Reduce effort. Increase alignment. When pressure hits, stop forcing. Slow the breath. Simplify the next move.

Choose one action that matches who you are becoming. Hold it steady. Train this daily. Protect consistency. Stability reorganizes outcomes.

Locker-Room Reflection
What frequency are you transmitting when no one is watching?

Chapter 23: The Comeback Blueprint

"Never let a good crisis go to waste, and if there is no crisis, create one"

~ **Michael Dell**

Collapse strikes without grace. It rips titles from steady hands and scatters them across cold floors. It stains your name in rooms that once praised your vision. One bad quarter becomes a blade. One rumor turns into a verdict. Pride dries on your tongue like ash.

Another night stretches wide as exile. Silence grows heavy. Fear waits at the edge of thought. Yet codes form in places where panic fails. A patient mind studies patterns while others chase noise. A focused leader reads the pulse of a company the way a surgeon reads a failing heart. Strategy replaces rage. Clarity replaces shame.

Michael Dell entered that fire with clear eyes. His empire cracked under weight he had not predicted. Titans circled. Analysts carved his obituary with quick hands. Markets dismissed him out of habit. He met their judgment with calm breath and steady focus.

Rebuild began with one quiet decision. He stopped pleading for relevance. He chose to remember who built the first machine. Structure returned. Noise vanished. Ego left the room. A clean signal rose through the wreckage. Teams followed the man who refused to fade. The comeback gained heat.

Collapse tested him. Code lifted him. Truth waited inside the discipline he reclaimed. Momentum grew from design, not hope. Power returned when he aligned the pieces with ruthless clarity.

A similar law now stands in front of you. Comebacks never seek permission. They wait for resolve. They wait for design. They wait for the moment you choose to turn exile into advantage. This chapter gives you the blueprint.

Michael Dell: The Furnace of Reconstruction

The Dorm Room Signal

The room smelled of dust and ambition.
University of Texas. 1983.

While other students chased grades and beer, Michael Dell sat on the floor. Beige computer parts surrounded him like unfinished sentences. Solder smoke curled upward, thin and sharp. The air carried heat and intention.

He wasn't building for class.
He was building for escape.

Each screw tightened delivered the same verdict. The middleman was friction. Friction was failure. The future belonged to whoever removed it.

Direct-to-consumer wasn't theory. It was physics.
Shorter distance. Less waste. More power.

Orders multiplied. The dorm became a factory. The desk became command. At nineteen, he dropped out. Not from school, but from permission.

Dell Computer Corporation surged across America. Speed replaced bulk. Customization beat inventory. A teenager bent an industry by eliminating noise.

Success arrived clean and bright.
But light always casts shadow.

When the Machine Forgets the Maker

The empire expanded.
The pulse weakened.

Meetings replaced movement. Process replaced instinct. The company that once sprinted now negotiated with itself. Dell felt the drag before anyone else noticed it.

He stepped away.
Confident the system would hold.

But systems do not dream.
They only repeat.

Markets shifted. Competitors adapted. The stock slipped. The press sharpened knives.

Headlines arrived like notices of death.
"Dell Dethroned."

"Innovation Exhausted."

He had built a machine that no longer needed him—
until it failed loudly enough to call him back.

Going Private Into Fire

The boardroom smelled of old coffee and fear.
Dell stock had fallen from fifty to fourteen.

Analysts spoke in verdicts. Irrelevant. Obsolete.
Finished.

Michael Dell stood at the table. Calm. Exact.
"We take it private," he said. "We rebuild without noise."

Laughter followed. Too late. Too risky. Too expensive.

He signed anyway.
Twenty-four billion dollars in leveraged debt.

The pen cut silence like steel.

Outside, Wall Street roared.
"The Most Expensive Suicide in Tech."
"Michael Dell Has Lost His Mind."

That night, Austin glowed through the office windows.
He didn't sleep. He remembered the dorm room. The
hum. The heat. The hunger.

If he was going to burn,

he would choose the fire.

That decision was ignition.

Work Without Applause

Then he disappeared.

No cameras. No interviews. No defense.
Only work.

He dismantled the company without sentiment. Sold what diluted purpose. Cut what slowed movement. Rewired the organization from instinct outward.

The pivot was surgical.
From personal computers to enterprise systems.
From selling boxes to building infrastructure.

Servers. Storage. Security. Cloud.
The backbone, not the billboard.

Each quarter hurt. Each cut clarified. The furnace stripped vanity and left function. What survived was strong enough to scale.

Silence did the heavy lifting.

The Furnace Refined the Architect

Dell Technologies returned transformed.
Not loud. Not flashy. Necessary.

It no longer chased consumers.
It powered civilization's digital spine.

Michael Dell emerged changed. Less urgency. More
precision. Less proving. More knowing.

He became evidence of a harder truth.
Resilience is not born in brilliance.
It is rebuilt in collapse.

He walked willingly into debt, ridicule, and fire.
The furnace did not ruin him.

It refined him.

The dorm-room builder didn't just reconstruct a
company.
He revealed a law of life:

You are not destroyed by your furnace.
You are redesigned by it.

Universal Law: Perpetual Transmutation of Energy

Energy rises when you choose to raise it, and Michael Dell proved that collapse becomes fuel the moment you transform crisis into the drive that rebuilds your future stronger than before.

Core Lesson

Michael Dell built clarity in the rubble of collapse. He studied failure with a calm eye and cut away everything that dulled direction. Markets mocked his return. Analysts predicted decay. Critics circled his company like scavengers. Pressure rose and carved sharp lines across every surface of the enterprise. Reinvention answered each blow.

Debt mounted while competitors surged. He faced falling stock and shrinking trust. Noise filled the street. Confusion filled the boardroom. Dell ignored both. He hunted signal inside crisis. He rebuilt teams. He redesigned systems. He turned silence into strategy and strategy into decisive action. Purpose hardened into structure.

A new architecture formed. Servers replaced slogans. Infrastructure replaced vanity. Execution replaced talk. Vision fused with discipline and burned away doubt. The company moved like a single force through a crowded field. Renewal became identity rather than event.

His return revealed the truth within resilience. Collapse shaped direction. Fire shaped character. Reinvention shaped destiny. The furnace never punished him. It refined him. Strength rose from that heat.

Client Story: Crisis Into Code

When the Lights Went Out

April 2020 arrived without warning and drained sound from every building. Thirty seven properties stretched across four states, polished for motion, now frozen. Marble floors reflected chandeliers but no footsteps, only silence where luggage wheels and greetings once lived. Nothing moved except the weight of realization.

Inside a corner suite, the CEO sat alone while the city below hollowed out. Phones stayed still as reservations vanished in hours. Revenue fell faster than thought could track. Staff faced furloughs, credit tightened, vendors pressed, investors circled with calm voices. For the first time, no move appeared.

Balance sheets blurred under a steady stare. A slow thought entered and refused to leave. Not collapse through bankruptcy but erosion through time. Decades dismantled piece by piece felt unbearable. That week carried the edge of quitting.

Refusing the Final Story

Coaching never promised inspiration in moments like this, and desperation placed the call when options ran dry. The voice arrived flat, controlled, dangerous in restraint. Execution had built everything and now execution had nowhere to land. Silence worked before words entered.

The response cut clean and stayed grounded. Collapse sounded like a signal, not an ending. Breath paused before the question surfaced. What kind of signal. Truth answered without comfort. The model had died while the builder remained. Air released from lungs held too long. Motivation lost all usefulness. Truth stepped forward alone.

The frame landed without ceremony. Saving hotels missed the assignment. A human problem had shifted shape overnight. The room deepened. People no longer needed places to pass through. They needed places to live, think, and work intact. That sentence opened a door.

Seeing the Hidden Door

Work began by stripping everything unnecessary. Nostalgia left first, followed by ego and loyalty to sunk costs. One question returned until defenses fell away. Starting today, with fresh eyes, what deserved construction.

Early answers clung to fear. Discounts surfaced, promotions followed, waiting pretended to lead. The correction arrived without mercy. Survival preserved nothing worth keeping. Legacy demanded more.

The lens widened as the world shifted. Remote work surged while cities emptied. Homes strained under full time living as isolation deepened. Burnout climbed faster than infection curves. Hotels already held the bones of an answer. Private rooms waited. Internet stayed reliable. Cleaning systems already functioned. Services stood ready. Only courage lagged behind.

The line landed without softening. Stop thinking like a hotel company. Start thinking like a human performance company with buildings. Ignition followed immediately.

Turning Crisis Into Code

Action moved fast and precise. Properties transformed into extended stay hubs for professionals. Tourists left the equation along with conferences. Builders arrived. Thinkers arrived. Operators stayed. Identity shifted in real time.

Thirty day minimums set the tone. Quiet floors protected focus. Workspaces replaced ballrooms. Community dinners rebuilt human contact. Mental health partnerships entered the frame. Fitness access grounded the days. Pricing stayed predictable. Language changed across every channel. Culture followed.

This went beyond a pivot. Employees retrained into relevance. Roles gained clarity instead of tradition. Metrics rewrote the scoreboard. Retention replaced occupancy. Focus replaced foot traffic. Stability replaced luxury.

Six months delivered balance. Twelve months formed waitlists. Eighteen months rewrote the future. Revenue did not return quietly. It surpassed everything that came before.

The Leader Who Emerged

Numbers told the story without celebration. The CEO leaned back in stillness. This build felt unfamiliar and precise. The answer arrived calm and certain. Preparation explained everything.

Reactivity lost control. Applause lost power. Reinvention carried no fear. Questions changed shape permanently. Protection vanished. Anticipation replaced it. What problem arrives next became the standard. That question sharpened leadership into a weapon.

The Empire That Learned to Breathe

Today the company earns study, not sympathy. Pandemic survival never defines the case. Resilience frames the lesson instead. Crisis became raw material. Identity evolved by choice.

Circumstance offered no rescue. Engineering created escape velocity. Alchemy replaced luck. Endurance followed naturally. The mark remains.

Crisis did not save them. Their alchemy did.

Tools & Tactics: The Comeback Blueprint Toolkit™

1. Collapse Journal (Reality Extraction)

Purpose: Strip emotion from the wreckage and recover usable material.

Tool: One page. No editing. No stories.

Prompt:

- *What broke?* (facts only)
- *What belief failed with it?*
- *What illusion did this collapse expose?*

Rule:
Do not justify. Do not soften. Collapse is data, not drama.

Result:
You convert loss into raw intelligence.

2. Confrontation Map (Truth Under Pressure)

Purpose: End internal resistance—the real energy leak.

Tool: Three lines. That's it.

Prompts:

1. *What truth am I avoiding because it threatens my identity?*
2. *What decision am I delaying that already chose its cost?*
3. *What action would terrify my old self—but free my future one?*

Rule:
If it doesn't sting, you're lying.

Result:
Energy returns the moment avoidance ends.

3. Climb Strategy Grid (Ascent Engineering)

Purpose: Turn survival into momentum.

Tool: Simple 2×2 grid.

Columns:

- Low Effort → High Effort
- Low Impact → High Impact

Action:
Circle one move that is:

- High impact
- Executable within 24 hours
- Impossible to overthink

Rule:
No planning beyond the first lever. Leverage beats volume.

Result:
You stop rebuilding the past and start climbing forward.

Algorithm: The 432 Comeback Loop™

Time: 15 minutes. Non-negotiable.

1. Name the Breakdown
    Write one specific failure, loss, or fracture from today.
    No adjectives. Just facts.

2. Extract the Energy
    Finish this sentence:
    *"This collapse is forcing me to become more
    _____."*
    (Precise words only: decisive, disciplined, humble, bold.)

3. Define the Transmutation
    Choose one micro-action that proves that trait today.
    If it takes more than 10 minutes, it's wrong.

4. Execute Before Noon
    Do it fast. Do it imperfectly.
    Action seals the frequency.

Reflection Questions

1. What collapse in my past became my hidden asset?
2. Where am I resisting transmutation today?
3. If failure is energy, how will I shape it into my next victory?

Pillar Activation: Shackled to the Furnace

Game Plan

This chapter is about collapse without panic and comeback without noise. Michael Dell shows how leaders rebuild power by design, not hope, when everything turns cold.

Pillar Activation

- Mental Precision (Head):
  Dell ignored headlines and hunted signal. He chose clarity over commentary and made one decisive call. Take it private. Think clean. Move forward.
- Physical Mastery (Body):
  He endured pressure without burning out. Long days. Quiet nights. Controlled pace. Energy stayed steady while others fractured.
- Emotional Power (Heart):
  Ridicule did not steer him. Fear did not command him. He stripped ego from the process and turned shame into resolve.
- Spiritual Alignment (Soul):
  Dell remembered his origin. He reconnected to

why he started in the dorm room. Purpose grounded every hard cut and bold move.

- Imaginative Strategy (Vision):
  He redesigned the company's future. PCs gave way to infrastructure. Silence became leverage. Fire became a forge.

Coach J's Challenge
When your world collapses, stop begging for approval. Step back. Breathe. Ask one hard question: *What must be rebuilt from truth, not tradition?* Then design your comeback in silence and execute without apology.

Locker-Room Reflection
Where is collapse asking you to become sharper, not smaller?

Chapter 24: The Infinite Transmission

"First they ignore you, then they ridicule you, then they fight you, and then you win."

~ Mahatma Gandhi

Energy moves with intent. It carries force. Then returns shaped by choice. Every action sends a signal into the world. A lifted hand shifts direction. A quiet refusal alters the field. A single step taken in truth breaks the grip of fear. Stillness gathers weight. Restraint turns into strength. Resilience begins after survival. Transmission defines legacy.

Gandhi lived inside this law with stark clarity. Poverty held his frame. Authority rose from his presence. Soft words crossed continents. Empires trembled under his calm tone. Each fast stirred nations awake. Each march rewired destiny. Each sacrifice carved new architecture into the earth. His life radiated clean voltage. Presence replaced force.

Conflict surged around him like a tide. He answered with stillness that anchored crowds. Armies advanced with noise. He answered with patience that refused haste. Power crushed villages with ease. He answered with truth that held its line. Many misread the quiet as weakness. Quiet carried charge. Quiet carried law. Quiet carried change.

His life revealed a truth that unsettles the unready. Transmission outlives the body that sends it. Flesh falls. Frequency endures. His message crossed borders long after breath left his chest. His resilience shaped the conscience of nations. His signal outlasted prisons, bullets, politics and time. His light guided generations without wielding a weapon.

Energy now moves through you. Each choice becomes a ripple others feel before thought forms. Each refusal becomes a boundary the world learns to respect. Each stand becomes a field that shapes the air around you. Gandhi sets the measure. Resilience is not the fire you protect. Resilience is the fire you leave behind. Your signal builds the world you enter.

You transmit already. Choose with precision. Rise with awareness. The world listens for your frequency.

Mahatma Gandhi: The Furnace of Restraint

The Timid Boy

He began without force.

A boy afraid of his own voice.
Words shook before leaving his mouth.
Silence felt safer than speech.

In Porbandar, restraint arrived early.
Authority pressed inward.
Expectation narrowed his posture.
He learned to fold himself small.

London offered education, not confidence.
The ocean delivered him into isolation.
Conversation felt dangerous.
Visibility felt unsafe.

He survived by withholding.
By choosing not to speak when fear demanded retreat.
By staying present without striking back at himself.

Then South Africa stripped restraint bare.

> 1893.   A cold railway platform.
>   A clerk sneered. A passenger barked an order.
>   "You can't sit here."

Gandhi held a valid ticket. First class.
Law allowed him. Power rejected him.

They threw him from the train.
His body hit stone.
His suitcase burst open.

Anger surged.
Rage asked permission.

He denied it.

That refusal marked the fracture.
Fear lost command.
Restraint found purpose.

The Furnace of Exile: Withheld Force

South Africa tested him daily.

Insults arrived without warning.
Humiliation followed routine.
Violence hovered close.

He did not retaliate.
He observed.

He gathered those erased by policy.
Laborers beaten into silence.
Merchants stripped of dignity.
Families denied sidewalks.

They followed him because he never flinched.
His stillness felt immovable.
His refusal felt safe.

Arrests came.
Beatings followed.

Each time, retaliation offered itself.
Each time, he declined.

This was not passivity.
It was strategic denial.

He discovered a deeper leverage.
Empires feed on reaction.
Restraint starves them.

He built an ashram.
Spun cloth by hand.
Reduced his life until no excess remained.

He removed everything the empire could threaten.
Only principle stayed.

When prison claimed him, restraint hardened.

The Prison Cell

Four walls.
 Iron bars.
 A cot and a bowl.

The cell invited collapse.
 He refused.

Each morning, he sat upright.
 Breath controlled.
 Spine steady.

Hunger arrived.
 He welcomed it.

Fasting stripped noise from desire.
 Silence sharpened intention.
 Restraint became mastery.

Guards mocked him.
 He smiled.

Threats followed.
 He bowed.

He denied them the reaction they sought.
 Denied the empire its favorite weapon.

Letters left the cell quietly.
 They carried calm without apology.
 They multiplied courage without command.

Outside, the system strained.
 Inside, restraint held.

One man removed his compliance.
 The structure began to crack.

The Salt March: Restraint in Motion

The empire taxed salt.
 Life's smallest necessity.
 A daily humiliation.

Gandhi chose not to riot.
 He chose to walk.

Two hundred forty miles.
 Bare feet.
Wooden staff.

Each step denied escalation.
 Each mile disciplined refusal.

Crowds grew without summons.
 No slogans.
 No threats.

Only movement without aggression.

At the sea, he bent down.
 Lifted salt from water.
 Raised it calmly.

The gesture dismantled legitimacy.
Law lost moral footing.
Power stood exposed.

They beat him.
He did not strike back.

They jailed him.
He did not resist.

Every withheld reaction amplified him.
Restraint turned into contagion.

The man once thrown from a train now destabilized an empire.

The Ultimate Refusal

Independence arrived.
Violence followed.

Partition tore the land open.
Neighbors became enemies.
Blood filled streets.

Gandhi refused hatred.

He walked barefoot into danger.
Fasted until violence paused.
Used his body as restraint.

"My life is my message."
He meant refusal embodied.

January 1948.
Evening prayer.
A man stepped forward.

Three shots.
No resistance.

Gandhi fell with palms together.
"Hey Ram."

Death failed.

Restraint multiplied.

His refusal instructed the world.
King learned it.
Mandela carried it.

Resilience, Gandhi proved, is not endurance.
It is choosing not to become what oppresses you.

That choice breaks empires.

The Universal Law: Vibration

Your inner frequency determines the force of your
impact, and Gandhi proved that when you raise your
vibration through discipline, courage, and conviction,
the world cannot help but rise to meet it.

Core Lesson

Gandhi began as a quiet boy who feared his own voice. Silence wrapped around him like a second skin. Every room pressed him inward. Each moment shrank his will. Crisis arrived when South Africa struck him from a train. Cold air hit his face. The blow revealed an ember hiding beneath the fear. Truth rose through pain.

He studied his mind after that night. Breath steadied thought. Stillness shaped clarity. Discipline hardened emotion into resolve. Simplicity guided action. New fire moved through his body. He walked into prisons with calm steps. Beatings bruised skin yet strengthened purpose. Injustice shaped his direction. Collapse refined his signal.

Salt glimmered in his hand at the shore. Waves curled at his feet. Empire soldiers watched from a distance. He lifted the grain with quiet intent. The act shook the world. A single gesture cut through steel and smoke. His presence spread across villages and cities. People stood taller because he did.

Bullets later split the air. His body fell. His frequency stayed. Streets filled with grief that turned to devotion. Nations bent toward his memory. His ideas moved through courts and parliaments. His courage shaped movements far from his birthplace. His truth endured because it lived in others.

His journey proves a final law. Resilience does not resist force. It turns crisis into power. It converts fear into coherence. It builds a vibration strong enough to bend history. His life shows how an awakened inner world can realign the world outside.

Client Mirror Story: The Consultant Who Chose Connection Over Control

The Collapse

Nadia built empires for other people through precision, pressure, and immaculate control. As a top consultant, she crossed continents teaching leaders alignment, clarity, and command, her slides glowing with logic while calendars overflowed and fees purchased silence. Inside her own firm, that silence turned hostile. Staff moved carefully, errors felt criminal, delays read as betrayals, and authority hardened into rule until fear replaced trust.

Mid-project, her assistant resigned and left a single line on white paper. "I cannot keep up with this anymore." Hours passed while Nadia stared, jaw tight, pride intact. She labeled the exit weakness and archived the discomfort. Days later, an international client ended the contract in public view. Their reason cut clean: a lack of collaboration.

Reputation fractured in one breath. Phones quieted, inboxes emptied, referrals vanished. Years preaching connection collapsed into exile. What she taught no longer recognized her voice.

The Furnace

Night after night, the apartment replayed failure without mercy. Arguments resurfaced, ignored sighs echoed, emails burned with accusation. Anger curled inward and sharpened into shame until a voice hissed the truth she avoided: fraud hides behind control. That pressure finally drove her to call me.

She asked for strategy, though surrender waited underneath every word. The first session filled with stiffness like glass underfoot. Arms crossed, tone sharpened, posture braced for defense. "I built everything from nothing," she said. Silence answered and refused rescue. Minutes stretched, breath slowed, eyes flickered, and a whisper escaped. "They were afraid of me." Armor cracked. Light slipped through.

I told her Gandhi's story without ornament. A train, an insult, and a choice to turn pain into transmission. Control never won his battles. Connection carried every victory. Revolutions begin when energy shifts before strategy follows. She scoffed at spirituality. I answered that movements run on frequency long before metrics appear.

The Ignition

Work began with the only territory she could command: herself. Each morning followed a simple ritual. Silence trained presence for three minutes. Journaling named avoided friction and buried truths for five. One act of grace closed the practice through message, apology, or thanks.

Resistance mocked the first week. Complaints softened the second as shoulders dropped and breath deepened. By the third, her voice slowed and carried warmth. An apology reached her former assistant without defense. The reply returned gentle and free of resentment. That tone unsettled her more than anger ever could. Ink closed the day with a new admission: "I believed strength meant control. Connection may hold the real power."

The Transformation

Months reshaped meetings through gratitude instead of directives. Questions replaced reprimands and invited shared ownership. Contracts mattered less as relationships gained attention. Energy softened and steadied, drawing people instead of pressing them. Former clients returned seeking counsel rather than compliance. The firm breathed collaboration and moved with quiet confidence.

Her keynote retired authority and introduced a different signal. The title read, "Leading by Frequency." Rooms listened without fear and leaned toward her calm.

The Legacy

Two years later, five hundred executives filled a hall. She told the collapse without armor. The firing, the isolation, the fear stood exposed under steady light.

Then truth landed clean. "Resilience does not harden leaders. It harmonizes them."

Silence held. Applause surged. Old power never returned, yet something stronger emerged. Control ended in collapse. Connection rose in its place. A business rebuilt. A transmitter awakened. Her voice carried the same law Gandhi lived: people never change through force; frequency always leads.

Tools & Tactics: The Connection Code™

Connection is not softness. It is control without force

1. Morning Connection Ritual (10 Minutes)

Purpose: Clear internal interference before external interaction.

- Silence (3 min)
  Sit still. No fixing. No rehearsing. Let the nervous system settle
- Friction Journal (5 min)
  Write one answer to each:

  - Where am I guarded?
  - Who am I subtly resisting?
  - What truth am I avoiding because it feels uncomfortable?
- Grace Decision (2 min)
  Choose one specific act you will execute today:
  - A repair.
  - An acknowledgment.

- A calm truth spoken cleanly.

Grace is not indulgence. It's precision without ego.

2. The Mirror Minute (Pre-Interaction Reset)

Before every meeting, call, or hard conversation:

Ask silently: "Am I about to transmit fear, or trust?"

Then:

- Inhale through the nose (4 seconds)
- Exhale through the mouth (6 seconds)
- Lower the shoulders
- Speak slower than instinct

Your nervous system enters the room before your words.

3. The One Message Practice (Evening)

Non-negotiable daily action

- Send one message of:

  - Gratitude
  - Recognition
  - Respect

No fixing. No coaching. No agenda.

Connection compounds faster than correction because safety precedes growth.

Algorithm: The Connection Loop™ (≤15 Minutes)

Inhale. Awareness (2 min)
 Identify one moment today where connection weakened.
 Name it without defense.

Exhale. Release (3 min)
 Write one sentence:

> "I release the need to control how this is received."

Forgiveness here is strategic. It frees energy.

Tune. Select One Repair (5 min)
 Choose one action only:

- Call.
- Message.
- Apology.
- Appreciation.

If it scares you slightly, it's the right one.

Transmit. Act (5 min)
 Execute immediately.

End with this internal command:

> "May my presence create safety, not pressure."

Close the Loop (10 seconds)
 Ask: Did the energy soften or sharpen trust?

That answer is your metric.

Reflection Questions

1. What frequency am I transmitting unconsciously?
2. Who has caught my resilience and carried it forward?
3. If my energy became my legacy, what would endure?

Pillar Activation: Transmission Over Force

Game Plan
This chapter proves that real power never shouts. It transmits. Gandhi shows how resilience becomes legacy when energy aligns with truth and restraint replaces force.

Pillar Activation

- Mental Precision (Head): Gandhi chose clarity over reaction. He disciplined thought until impulse lost authority.
- Physical Mastery (Body): Fasting, walking, and still posture conserved energy. His body became a signal, not a weapon.
- Emotional Power (Heart): Fear and anger refined into resolve. Pain sharpened compassion instead of rage.

- Spiritual Alignment (Soul): Purpose anchored every action. "My life is my message" kept him immovable inside chaos.
- Imaginative Strategy (Vision): He turned simplicity into strategy. Salt, silence, and marches rewired empires without violence.

Coach J's Challenge
Listen closely. You already transmit. Every room feels your energy before your words land. When pressure rises, slow down. Lower your shoulders. Choose the signal you want remembered. Control yourself first. Connection will follow. Resilience is not what you survive. It is what others carry because you stood clean in truth.

Locker-Room Reflection
What frequency are you transmitting today, and who feels it first?

Chapter 25: Live the Win Frequency

"Only a man who knows what it is like to be defeated can reach down to the bottom of his soul and come up with the extra ounce of power it takes to win when the match is even."

~ Muhammad Ali

The arena trembles as light cuts the dark. Noise rises and smothers breath. Sweat runs down your cheek. Fear circles your mind and searches for a weak edge. You stand in the tunnel and feel your pulse hammer against your ribs. Air thins. Thought narrows. The moment demands truth.

Fire shapes champions. Ali walked into that heat with certainty etched in his bones. He carried three words that bent history. I am the greatest. He spoke them to build. He spoke them to shape the man he chose to become. Identity formed long before proof arrived.

Victory lived inside him before the first bell rang. The fight only confirmed the signal he released into the world. Ali revealed a law many ignore. Evidence follows intention. Broadcast the note first. The universe moves toward the vibration that refuses to kneel. That is how you win your day.

Muhammad Ali: The Furnace of the Voice

The Boy Who Spoke First

Before fists.
Status meant nothing.
Silence owned the space.

A boy stood before a mirror in Louisville and spoke a future into shape.

"I am the greatest. I shook up the world."

Adults laughed.
Trainers frowned.
Reporters sharpened knives.

He was not boasting.
Not pride.
Transmission.

Each word carried belief.
Every rhyme rehearsed destiny.
He built identity in sound before the world learned the outline.

Reality follows the voice that refuses to whisper.

Exile by Conscience

The draft notice arrived without poetry.
Ali answered without fear.

"I ain't got no quarrel with them Viet Cong."

One sentence split the nation.
In hours, the champion became an outcast.

Titles stripped.
License revoked.
Prime years erased.

Headlines howled: coward, traitor, disgrace.

Crowds that once cheered now cursed.

He trained in borrowed gyms.
Shadowboxed silence.
Watched his body peak with nowhere to go.

Friends begged surrender.
"Apologize. Get back in the ring."

He did not bend.

"If war were right, I'd fight," he said.
"My conscience won't let me."

America saw defiance.
Ali lived alignment.

Holding Frequency Under Fire

Three and a half years passed.

No belts.
No cameras.
No forgiveness.

He prayed.
He trained.
Repeated the same words.

"I am the greatest."

Not ego.

Orientation.

When the world collapsed his platform, he kept his signal.
When they took his crown, he wore conviction.

The Rumble in the Jungle

Zaire.
1974.

Heat pressed down like judgment.
Sixty thousand voices thundered one command.

"Ali bomaye."

Across the ring stood George Foreman.
Younger.
Stronger.
Favored.

Round one cracked open with violence.
Foreman charged.
Ali leaned back into the ropes.

Punches hammered ribs and arms.
Ali absorbed them without panic.

Rounds bled together.
Foreman swung harder.
Ali smiled wider.

He whispered truths mid–combat.
"You ain't got the power no more."

Energy shifted.
The crowd felt it first.

Round eight.
Ali sprang forward.

Left.
Right.
Left.
Right.

The giant fell.

The jungle erupted.

Ali raised his arms without surprise.
He had already won years earlier.

When the Voice Learned Silence

Age arrived without mercy.
Parkinson's stole his speech.

His hands shook.
His pace slowed.

His presence deepened.

He visited hospitals.

Refugee camps.
Orphanages.

The mouth that once roared now healed by stillness.
The fighter became a witness.

Asked about the years taken from him, he smiled.

"They gave me purpose," he said.
"I learned what I was fighting for."

The Broadcast Never Ends

Champions win fights.
Ali changed frequency.

He fought Liston for respect.
Foreman for redemption.
America for conscience.

He proved belief outlasts exile.
Conviction outweighs crowns.

His final transmission still hums:

"The fight is won far away from witnesses—
in the gym,
on the road,
long before the lights."

Resilience is not volume.
It is belief that never stops speaking.

Universal Law: Vibration

Your dominant vibration becomes your reality, and Ali proved that when you speak belief with unwavering certainty, the world eventually rises to match the frequency you broadcast.

Core Lesson

Muhammad Ali forged identity through sound. He spoke greatness before he lived it. His voice carved truth into the air of Louisville and turned doubt into fuel. Each rhyme shaped belief. Each claim lit a path no one else could see. Conviction rose from that fire.

Exile stripped him bare. The courts took his crown, his income, and his ring. Crowds turned quiet. Friends stepped back. Fame dissolved like chalk in rain. Ali stood alone and guarded conscience with steady hands. Integrity shaped strength no training camp could match.

Silence became his furnace. He prayed with fierce calm. He trained with relentless focus. He protected belief when the world tried to crush it. His signal sharpened. His purpose hardened. His spirit held shape while his life collapsed. Crisis revealed design.

The Rumble in the Jungle proved the work. Age crept in. Speed faded. Yet clarity replaced fear. He faced Foreman with steady breath and a mind built for pressure. Rope burn cut his back while patience shaped the fight. Victory rose from inner order, not brute force.

Later years softened his body and brightened his heart. Illness slowed his steps yet opened his presence. He carried children in airports. He comforted strangers. He offered peace without asking for praise. Service replaced applause. Purpose rose above ego.

Ali's life delivers one truth. Protect your inner frequency with integrity. Conviction becomes destiny. Crisis becomes the furnace that reveals your power.

Client Story: The Captain Who Lost the Wind

After the Storm That Would Not End

She arrived braced for waves that no longer existed. Sixteen years in the Coast Guard had trained stillness into her bones. Valor medals rested in a past she no longer touched. Across the table, her fingers shook despite a face built for fire. No ocean roared that day. The real weather churned beneath her ribs.

I did not ask about the medals. My eyes stayed on her hands. Training lingered there, muscle memory refusing rest. Silence spoke louder than rank. The body always tells the truth first.

A rescue mission fractured on seconds that refused forgiveness. Two young sailors moved before backup reached position. Both lived. Trust did not. Investigators cleared her name with stamped conclusions. Headlines ignored clearance and fed the public hunger. Safe waters turned into mirrors she could not face.

Resignation followed without ceremony. No farewell arrived. No handoff closed the chapter. At forty-two, she stepped out of uniform and into absence. Structure collapsed. Noise vanished. Purpose lost its compass.

That emptiness brought her to me.

The First Signal

Her entry came through a veterans referral into Win Your Day Now. The first session stayed quiet. Others spoke first. Founders. Athletes. Parents. Leaders naming fractures without rank. She listened like someone still on watch.

When the call ended, she did not log off. The screen stayed open. Breath slowed. Eyes lifted.

One question broke the stillness.
"What storm are you still standing in?"

Her voice cut clean through discipline.
"I know how to command inside chaos. No one taught me how to live after it passes."

I nodded once.
"Then we don't rebuild with force. We rebuild with frequency."

She did not answer. A long inhale replaced words. That was enough.

The Furnace of Exile

No grand strategy followed. Noise came off first.

"Wake before dawn," I said.
"No drills. No orders. Only stillness."

Habit pulled her upright each morning. Silence replaced commands. Breath replaced control. Mornings became wide and unmoving. Nothing advanced unless she chose it.

The first assignment carried edges.
"Chart silence. Map what surfaces when you stop steering."

Early pages held one word. Drift. It returned again and again. Resistance spoke louder than insight. The pen fought the quiet.

Weeks passed.

One morning, effort loosened. The page slowed. Her shoulders dropped. Acceptance arrived without announcement. Calm followed, not as victory, but as release.

On our next call, her voice stayed low. "I'm not drowning anymore."

I answered the same way. "Good. Now you can navigate."

Command Reclaimed

Six months in, the field shifted.

"You're ready to lead," I said.

Her head moved once.
"Leadership isn't mine anymore."

I leaned forward.
"Transmission never leaves the signal. It only waits."

Silence stretched long enough to test resolve. Then a nod closed the gap.

The morning she led, preparation replaced fear. Grounding settled her voice. Cadence carried authority without pressure. Each word landed clean.

She guided breath into order. Inhale opened space. Release restored trust. No commands followed. Care did the work.

Screens softened. Faces exhaled. Tears arrived without collapse. Her steadiness told everyone they could stand inside the storm without armor.

When quiet returned, she spoke again.
"I never lost command. I lost permission."

I smiled.
"You just took it back."

Reclaiming the Fleet

A year changed everything. Not because I held her close.
Because I stepped aside.

On our final call, the truth stayed simple.
"You don't need me anymore."

She did not resist it.

Weeks later, she launched The Fleet. A resilience
command for those carrying weight without relief.
Executives arrived first. Physicians followed. First
responders stayed.

Her mission stayed clean. Connection over control.
Presence over force. Calm as authority. Failure became
navigation training. Leadership regained its human
center.

Before we ended, she said one last thing.
"Losing the uniform exposed the illusion. Control never
defined leadership. Communion did."

I nodded.
"The ocean never took you. It returned you."

She logged off standing tall.
Command intact.

Tools & Tactics: The Identity Installation Protocol™

1. Victory Visualization Protocol (Not Motivation. Conditioning)

Each morning, close your eyes and enter a specific future moment of dominance:

- Where are you?
- Who is reacting to you?
- What decision did you just execute cleanly?

Do not watch yourself win.
Be inside the body that already has.

Neurologically, this primes the motor cortex and reticular activating system. You're conditioning recognition, not wishing.

Rule: If the image doesn't tighten your posture and slow your breath, it's too vague.

2. Future-Self Embodiment Map (Identity → Behavior)

Write four short lines. No essays.

- Future Self Eats: (fuel, timing, restraint)

- Future Self Speaks: (pace, certainty, silence)
- Future Self Decides: (speed, standards, boundaries)
- Future Self Lives: (what they refuse to tolerate)

Then choose one micro-behavior today that proves you belong to that identity. Identity shifts only when the nervous system sees congruence between self-image and action.

3. Assumption Discipline (Reality Mirrors Precision)

Most people carry unconscious assumptions:

- "I need permission."
- "I have to prove myself."
- "This will be hard."

Elite performers install assumptions deliberately.

You don't affirm outcomes.
You assume authority.

Algorithm: The Win Frequency Ritual Daily Practice ≤15 Minutes)

Morning: Install the Assumption (3 minutes)

Stand or sit upright.
Slow inhale through the nose. Long exhale.

Declare one identity-level assumption, not an outcome:

- "I move with authority."
- "My presence sets the tone."
- "I execute cleanly under pressure."

Say it once.
Silence after. Let the body register it.

Midday: Prove It With Friction (5–7 minutes)

Take one action your future self would not delay:

- Make the call you're avoiding.
- Speak with clarity instead of politeness.
- Remove something misaligned.

If there's no resistance, it doesn't count.

Frequency locks in through *earned evidence*.

Evening: Close the Proof Loop (3–5 minutes)

Journal one sentence:

> "Today, reality reflected my assumption
> when _____."

This trains your mind to look for confirmation, not doubt.

Over time, belief becomes memory.
Memory becomes identity.
Identity bends outcomes

Final Calibration (Non-Negotiable)

- No assumption without action.
- No visualization without embodiment.
- No frequency talk without proof.

This isn't manifestation.
This is self-installation at the identity level.

Reflection Questions

1. What victory do I need to assume into existence now?
2. How would my actions shift if I already lived as my future self?
3. Where am I waiting for proof instead of radiating certainty?

Pillar Activation: Voice on Fire

Game Plan
This chapter proves one truth without apology. Identity comes before evidence. Ali won long before the bell because he installed belief first and defended it through fire.

Pillar Activation

- Mental Precision (Head):
  Ali decided who he was before the world voted.
  He held focus through ridicule, exile, and doubt.
  Clarity beat chaos every time.
- Physical Mastery (Body):
  He trained even when the ring vanished.

495

Rope-a-dope was not luck. It was patience, breath, and body control under punishment.

- Emotional Power (Heart):
  Fear never led him. He turned hate into fuel and pressure into rhythm. Emotion served conviction, not the other way around.
- Spiritual Alignment (Soul):
  Conscience guided him when crowns disappeared. Faith anchored him during exile. Integrity became his real title.
- Imaginative Strategy (Vision):
  He spoke the future into form. Words shaped belief. Belief shaped behavior. Behavior bent reality.

Coach J's Challenge
Stop waiting for proof. Install identity first. Speak who you are with calm certainty. Then take one action today that proves alignment. If there is no friction, you chose too small.

Locker-Room Reflection
Where are you still waiting for evidence instead of broadcasting belief? *You are the win.*

Chapter 26: Live Your Championship Code

"I think sometimes in life the biggest challenges end up being the best things that happen in your life."

~ Tom Brady

The draft clock ticks. Heat crowds the small room while breath thins. Cameras sweep past him toward brighter names. Brady waits on a battered Michigan couch. His family circles close with soft smiles that fail to hide their strain. Each pick lands like a blow to the ribs. Doubt settles across the room like dust.

Another name flashes. Then another. Prospects he outran in practice. Prospects he outworked in silence. One hundred ninety-eight men rise into their futures while he sits still. Humiliation hits with a clean strike. Fire pushes through his gut. He forces a grin for his parents as the sting deepens. The moment cuts him open.

The screen finally speaks his name. Sixth round. One hundred ninety-ninth. A footnote in a long draft. A spare part with no promise. The sting burns through muscle and bone. Molten truth runs through his veins. The Law of Compensation wakes without a sound. Every unseen rep gathers weight. Every lonely drill collects power. Every silent morning aligns for a future reckoning.

Judgment crowns him small. He absorbs the verdict and sharpens the edge. The furnace rises in his chest. It lights for proof, not revenge. Resolve hardens with each breath. He stands from that couch with a new identity. He names his path with quiet force. I will define my life. I will carve my code. I will rise from obscurity through work alone.

Championship lives start with moments like this. The world doubts. You answer with labor. You answer with frequency. You answer with a code that never breaks. Truth grows in shadows before it rules the field.

Tom Brady: The Furnace of Forever

The Humiliation: Birth of the Code

April 16, 2000.
Six rounds passed without his name.
Each announcement erased another future.

Tom Brady sat in his parents' living room, hands folded, eyes fixed on the screen.
Experts dissected other men.
The cameras ignored the one still breathing.

Pick 199 arrived without ceremony.
A sixth-round afterthought.
The verdict followed fast. Backup. System arm.
Disposable.

He smiled once.
No anger. No defense.
Only a decision forming.

That night, while the house slept, he knelt beside his bed.
He made a vow without witnesses.
Preparation would become his unfair advantage.

The Furnace No One Saw

Greatness began in rooms without applause.

Midnight stretching sessions carved durability into
muscle.
Ankles, hips, spine, breath.
Longevity became a practiced skill.

Ice baths followed.
Steel tubs. Clock ticking. Pain negotiated daily.
Minutes of discomfort bought decades of availability.

Film study replaced talent with foresight.
Defenses revealed habits.
Anticipation replaced speed.

Food became fuel, not pleasure.
No shortcuts. No indulgence.
The body became an instrument built for distance.

While others chased Sundays, he trained for decades.

The Body Breaks

September 2008. Opening week.
A single hit rewrote the season.

Helmet met knee.
Ligaments tore. Silence spread.
The stadium exhaled disbelief.

Surgery followed. Then doubt.

Commentators speculated expiration.
Dynasties do not survive torn knees.

At night, he stared at ceilings he could not escape.
Stairs mocked him.
Patience replaced momentum.

Rehab became reckoning.
Every repetition honored a promise made eight years earlier.
This was not the end. This was refinement.

The 28–3 Reckoning

Houston. Super Bowl LI.
The scoreboard accused him.

Twenty-eight to three.
Mistakes stacked. Time evaporated.
History prepared an obituary.

He gathered the huddle.
No speeches. No panic.
Just clarity.

One play. Then another.
Precision replaced urgency.
Belief replaced noise.

Completions followed. Touchdowns answered.
The deficit cracked.
Overtime arrived.

The final drive unfolded without drama.
Preparation executed its design.
The scoreboard surrendered.

He did not celebrate.
He recognized alignment.

Leaving the Kingdom

Age returned as accusation.
Critics sharpened timelines.

He left New England.
Security dissolved. Identity questioned.
Tampa offered chaos.

A pandemic erased structure.
He built his own.
Fields closed. Discipline remained.

Practices happened in parks.
Routes taught through screens.
Leadership traveled without facilities.

The season ended with another title.
Not dominance. Command.
Experience replaced youth.

He had evolved beyond position.
He became a system.

The Code of Forever

Talent opens doors.
Repetition keeps them open.

Humiliation sparked hunger.
Injury enforced gratitude.
Adversity exposed frequency.

He lived the Law of Compensation.
Invisible work returned visible legacy.
Nothing arrived unearned.

Asked for the secret, he deflected.
"The next throw matters most."

That was never modesty.
It was instruction.

Forever is built one disciplined moment at a time.

Universal Law: Compensation

You are rewarded in exact proportion to the discipline you invest, and Tom Brady proved that every unseen rep, every sacrifice, and every quiet act of preparation compounds into a legacy the world can't deny.

Core Lesson

Tom Brady built resilience through work no one watched. Pick 199 cut him deep and set a code that ruled his life. Midnight stretches shaped control. Ice baths steadied breath. Film study revealed truth one frame at a time. Each ritual carved a structure that held firm through injury, doubt, and age. His torn ACL refined humility. His surge in the 28 to 3 game showed that belief can lift a broken moment into triumph. His rise in Tampa proved that mastery follows the worker who refuses to drift from his craft. Talent never creates greatness. Habit creates it. Quiet labor forges the core. Victory arrives later as its quiet echo.

Client Story: The Comeback Architect

The Collapse Nobody Saw

Clint entered every room looking untouchable. Forty one years had forged a founder who moved markets on command, eight figures flashing across dashboards while adrenaline and black coffee carried him through each day. On paper, victory stacked clean and convincing, yet inside the body something frayed and pulled apart. Investors praised vision and magazines crowned him The Next Visionary, applause masking the cost carved into his nerves. Hands trembled during quiet moments, thoughts clouded under pressure, chest pain followed him home and passed as stress.

Monday morning shattered the illusion. Boardroom lights smeared into fog, heartbeat sprinted without rhythm, and darkness closed fast without warning. Awareness returned inside a hospital room humming with machines. Doctors spoke in clean, unforgiving terms. Burnout surfaced first, then hypertension, then adrenal collapse. Translation landed harder than any diagnosis. The man who drove growth forgot how to breathe. Lying still, one question burned through the haze. What good is winning if survival costs everything?

The Call

Clint found me a week later. Voice low. Words clipped. Control already slipping.
"I built everything," he said, "and now my body quit."
I listened to the space between sentences. The body speaks there first.
"Your body did not quit," I said. "It pulled the emergency brake."
Silence followed. Truth tends to do that.

He leaned forward. "So what do I fix first. The company or myself."
I answered without pause. "The engine. No engine, no empire."
His jaw tightened. Pride fought for air.
"Then we start small," I added. "So small your ego cannot hijack it."

The Furnace of Obsession

Recovery moved slow and unglamorous. Capital flowed elsewhere while an interim CEO took control, phones falling silent inside a house once alive with urgency. Late nights pulled him into old photos of launch parties and magazine shoots, smiling back from screens he barely recognized. Fame looked louder there and far less tired. Something hollow stared through every grin.

One night he texted. "I cannot shut my mind off."
"Good," I replied. "Then we will train it, not silence it."
I sent him an assignment. Watch how the great ones outlast the noise.
Chance brought a documentary across his screen. Tom Brady trained in silence without spectacle or noise. Stretching replaced celebration, breathwork replaced bravado, film study outlasted applause. No fireworks followed discipline. Longevity followed instead.
"That's it," Clint said during our next call. "He is building forever."
"Then stop chasing moments," I said. "Start installing systems."

Ignition

Darkness still ruled at four thirty. A mat hit the floor beneath stiff limbs and heavier pride as stretching burned muscles unused to patience. Breath came shallow and uneven while ego resisted every second. Steel water waited without mercy. Ice bit skin and nerve at once, each inhale demanding negotiation as time stretched into combat.

He called afterward, voice shaking. "I thought I would quit."
"You did not," I said. "That matters."

Emerging shook the body awake and clarity followed the cold.

A notebook opened with purpose. Three lines anchored the page and the future.
Discipline is destiny.
Recovery defines leadership.
Longevity outranks applause.
He read them to me aloud.
"That page," I said, "is your new boardroom."

The Invisible Season

Noise lost him for an entire year. Obscurity returned something fame had stolen as mornings began with breath, movement, and cold while evenings closed without screens or urgency. Caffeine exited and clarity entered. Meditation replaced meetings. Presence displaced bravado. Energy stabilized, focus sharpened, and patience learned how to lead.

Progress arrived quietly.
"I am calmer," he said. "And sharper."
"That is regulation," I told him. "Power without volatility."
Return came without announcement. Eyes noticed first. The storm burned out and left a steady flame. Decisions slowed and strengthened. People leaned in instead of bracing.

Operations changed with intention. Meetings shortened, recovery earned a place on calendars, gratitude ended each day. Performance rose through balance, not force. Harmony replaced hustle.

"This works," Clint said.

"It always did," I answered. "You just stopped fighting it."

The Code Installed

Dawn found Clint barefoot on grass, air shimmering with pre sunrise stillness as executives gathered expecting forecasts and strategy. A worn notebook rose instead.

"This saved my life," he told them. "The furnace forms every comeback worth keeping."

Silence held the group steady.

One executive finally asked, "What do we call this."

Clint looked at me. I nodded once.

"Furnace Mode," he said.

Slack lit up before sunset as invisible reps filled the channel daily, breathwork, workouts, recovery, gratitude. Clint sent me a final message that night.

"It spread."

"That is leadership," I replied.

One recovery reshaped an entire culture. Rhythm became legacy.

Tools & Tactics: The Championship Code™ Toolkit

1. The Code Audit (Identity Lock)

Write 5 non-negotiable rules you live by regardless of mood, chaos, or reward.

Rules must be:

- Actionable (you can violate or honor them daily)
- Observable (you can prove them with behavior)
- Uncomfortable (easy rules don't shape identity)

  If a rule can't cost you something, it can't command you.

2. The Hidden Rep Ledger (Discipline Under No Applause)

Each day, log one invisible rep:

- The task you did when quitting was easier
- The restraint you held when ego wanted noise
- The standard you kept when no one was watching

This is where championships are actually won.

  What you repeat in private becomes your public ceiling.

3. The Compounding Ritual (Weekly Dominance Review)

Once per week:

- Identify the one behavior producing disproportionate return
- Eliminate one habit that dilutes focus
- Double down on the smallest action that's quietly working

Momentum isn't built by doing more.
It's built by feeding what already grows.

Algorithm: The Daily Championship Code
≤15 Minutes)

1. Wake to the Rule (3 min)
 Write one core rule at dawn.
 Read it aloud. This sets the day's operating system.

2. Live the Rep (7 min)
 Execute one micro-action that proves you honored the rule.
 Small. Sharp. Non-negotiable.

3. Close the Ledger (5 min)
 Journal one line:

> *"Today I sowed _____."*

If you can't name the seed, you didn't plant one.

Reflection Questions

1. Which invisible reps am I repeating that my future self will inherit, whether I like it or not?
2. Where am I demanding outcomes without earning them through daily proof?
3. If my life were governed by only three rules, which ones would force excellence even on my worst days?

Pillar Activation: Champions Live Forever

Game Plan
This chapter proves that greatness starts in obscurity. Humiliation becomes fuel when you build a code and honor it daily. Brady shows how unseen work compounds into unstoppable legacy.

Pillar Activation
• Mental Precision (Head): Brady ignored noise and locked onto preparation. Pick 199 sharpened his focus instead of breaking it.
• Physical Mastery (Body): Stretching, cold exposure, recovery, and nutrition built durability. Longevity came from respecting the body as an asset.
• Emotional Power (Heart): He turned doubt into discipline. Humiliation became resolve, not resentment.
• Spiritual Alignment (Soul): His "why" stayed clean. Discipline became destiny through devotion to craft, not applause.
• Imaginative Strategy (Vision): He trained for a future

others could not see. Film, ritual, and foresight rehearsed wins before they arrived.

Coach J's Challenge
Listen up. When the world underrates you, stop negotiating with doubt. Install a code. Do one invisible rep today that proves who you are becoming. Protect recovery. Honor preparation. Let consistency speak louder than talent.

Locker-Room Reflection
What code will you follow when no one is watching, and are you honoring it today?

Chapter 27: Design Your Resilience Plan

"However difficult life may seem, there is always something you can do and succeed at. It matters that you don't just give up."

~ Stephen Hawking

Awakening begins when you stop asking what is possible and start asking what is designable. Stephen Hawking received a verdict that crushed many men. Doctors pointed to a shrinking horizon and spoke of limits. Muscles failed him. Speech slipped. Simple motions turned traitor. He refused their script and treated the diagnosis as instruction. A plan rose from the wreckage with quiet purpose.

A clear map formed in his mind. Each step carried intent. Each hour carried weight. He pushed his thoughts into the vast stretch of the cosmos while his body tightened around him. Metal turned into motion. Circuits turned into voice. The chair carried him farther than strong legs ever dreamed. The machine at his throat sounded like a horn that summoned the world. His body weakened and his resolve strengthened. His limits became fuel.

Hawking refused the notion of bouncing back. He built forward. He placed one choice upon another until a new life took shape. He built that life brick by brick. His days formed a spine that never bent.

A similar pattern stands before you now. Crisis draws its line. You choose its direction. You carry the right to design your path beyond collapse. You build a plan. You build forward. You rise because you decide to rise.

Stephen Hawking: The Furnace of Redesign

The Diagnosis

Cambridge, 1963.
The world still trusted certainty.
Equations closed clean. Time obeyed order.

Then the doctor spoke collapse into flesh.
Amyotrophic Lateral Sclerosis.
Motor neurons dying. Muscles surrendering. Speech
fading. Breath rationed.

Two years, they said.
Two years until erasure.

Stephen Hawking stared at the verdict without panic.
Not fear. Not rage.
Wonder.

How could something finite contain something
infinite?
How could thought outlive motion?

He stepped into the gray rain and issued a command:
*If my body contracts, my mind expands beyond the
universe.*

Truth-punch: The furnace ignited with diagnosis.

The Erosion

The end did not arrive violently.
It arrived patiently.

Hands shook when holding a pen.
Feet dragged across stone corridors.
Sentences dissolved before reaching air.

Pity replaced curiosity.
Rooms grew quiet when he entered.
The mirror no longer reflected a man, it reflected
subtraction.

At twenty-four, despair nearly completed the work.
Days blurred. Equations stalled. Futures vanished.
He waited for nothing.

Then came Jane.
Not as rescue. As alliance.

She did not soften reality.
She strengthened direction.

Truth-punch: Despair halted when partnership
appeared.

Will Reclaims Command

Love reignited intent.
The body retreated. The mind advanced.

Chalk slipped from weak fingers.
Ideas thundered without permission.

516

While muscle froze, imagination detonated.
He crossed galaxies without moving an inch.
Asked forbidden questions.

What happens at a black hole's edge?
Does time die, or reboot?

Night after night, machines breathed beside him.
Jane slept. Hawking worked.

Resilience was not dramatic.
It was exact.

Each equation defied extinction.
Every proof declared sovereignty.

Truth-punch: Collapse sharpened cognition.

The Machine Voice

1985.

Speech ended. Pneumonia nearly ended everything.

Doctors offered a trade.
Life for silence.

He accepted.

Then technology intervened.
A synthetic voice emerged. Flat. Metallic. Immortal.

"My name is Stephen Hawking."

The machine was not confinement.
It was amplification.

Through it, he released *A Brief History of Time*.
A book that bent public consciousness.
The mind without movement moved the planet.

A wheelchair became his spacecraft.
His voice became architecture.

Audiences wept.
He laughed.

He joked about God, time travel, the absurdity of
certainty.
And lived as contradiction made visible.

Truth-punch: Limitation became transmission.

The Inner Cosmos

He did not die in two years.
But lived fifty-five beyond the sentence.

Each morning, he chose focus over loss.
Attend to what remains.

That became his operating law.

He taught the world that resilience is not resistance.
It is redesign.

His work reshaped gravity, time, and cosmic origin.
But the deeper legacy was human.

He proved the body is not the ceiling.
Imagination is not optional.
Crisis is not final.

When his life ended, physics whispered back.
Black holes emit energy before disappearance.
Radiation escapes collapse.

Even extinction releases light.

Truth-punch: What redesigns survives forever.

Universal Law: Perpetual Transmutation of Energy

Energy can always rise to a higher form, and Hawking proved that when the body collapses, the mind can transform that limitation into genius vast enough to reshape the universe itself.

Core Lesson

Stephen Hawking met collapse early and chose redesign over despair. Doctors spoke a death sentence. He answered with curiosity. His body failed inch by inch while his mind expanded across galaxies. Each loss carved space for a greater reach. Each setback sharpened focus until thought moved faster than time.

Love steadied him when darkness gathered. Jane lifted him from the edge and returned will to a man trapped inside silence. He seized that light and built a bridge between paralysis and purpose. Machines carried his voice across continents. Ideas carried his name across the cosmos. Crisis forged an architect of infinity.

Work defined his rebellion. He studied stars while muscles quit. He shaped theories while breath trembled. He mapped black holes while his own body closed around him like night. Insight rose from fatigue. Imagination rose from pain. Freedom rose from the tightest cage.

Hawking lived long past every prediction. He created meaning from limits that would have crushed another life. He trusted the strength that remained instead of mourning what vanished. His journey proves a simple truth. Crisis cannot reduce you unless you surrender expansion. Reinvention begins the moment you design a self that no collapse can break.

Tools & Tactics: The Resilience Blueprint Kit

Lay these tools out like instruments, not weapons. Precision beats drama. Each one exists to reduce fragility before stress arrives.

1. Personal Pillar Scorecard (Daily Scan)

Mind | Body | Emotion | Spirit | Imagination
 Score each 1–10.
 Circle the lowest number. That pillar becomes today's priority.

Rule: Crisis attacks the weakest system first.
You reinforce before it collapses.

2. Daily Ritual Spine (Non–Negotiable)

Anchor three actions only:

- Ignite (Morning): wake the system
- Stabilize (Midday): reset the nervous system
- Seal (Evening): close loops, reduce entropy

If the day breaks, return to the spine.
Everything else is optional.

3. Collapse Conversion Protocol

Collapse → Confront → Convert

- Collapse: Name what failed without story.
- Confront: Identify the behavior or assumption that broke.
- Convert: Define the new rule going forward.

Pain unused is liability. Pain converted becomes structure.

4. Identity Loop Reset

One loop only. Do not hunt many.

- Catch the thought.
- Name the cost.
- Rewrite the rule.

- Act once in alignment.

Identity changes through behavior, not affirmation.

5. Pressure Test (Weekly)

Ask one question:

"What would break this system first?"

Simulate it.
Patch it.
Document the fix.

Surprise is just rehearsal you skipped.

Algorithm: The Hawking Method

A Constraint-First System for Human Resilience

Use this once. Then live it.

Step 1. Define the Cosmic Mission (1 sentence)

Test: If this succeeds, does everything else simplify?

Formula:

My mission is to [create X] *by* [method Y] *for* [people Z].

If it sounds vague, it is.

Step 2. Convert Constraints into Design Specs

List constraints honestly:

- Body
- Time
- Money
- Skills
- Environment
- Energy

Write the constraint you resent most. Circle it. This becomes your design surface.

Flip each:

"Because X, I will design Y."

Choose one workaround per constraint.
No heroics. Only systems.

Step 3. Inventory Enduring Assets

These survive stress.

- Intellect: what you solve faster than most
- Character: virtues that hold under pressure
- Network & Tools: leverage already in reach

Write:

My three unfair advantages are: 1) ___ 2) ___ 3) ___

Step 4. Engineer Your Daily Interface

One pipeline. No detours.

Capture → Crystallize → Ship

Write:

> I capture in ___ → clarify in ___ → ship via ___

Design it for *bad days*, not perfect ones.

Step 5. Run Micro-Experiments (7 Days)

Perfection lies. Data doesn't.

- Hypothesis: *If I do X, Y moves.*
- One behavior.
- One metric.
- Seven days.

  Proof beats confidence.

Step 6. Light the Furnace (Daily Non-Negotiables)

Only three:

- Body: breath + water + movement
- Mind: 10 minutes of single focus
- Spirit: two sentences of gratitude or awe

Miss none. Adjust intensity, never consistency.

Step 7. Assemble the Crew (Roles Only)

No emotional contracts.

- Spotter: calls drift
- Synthesizer: sharpens thinking
- Ship-Mate: enforces cadence

Define cadence in writing.

Step 8. Crisis Playbook (One Page)

Pre-decide.

For each likely hit:

- Illness
- Rejection
- Cash pressure
- Tech failure

Write:

> *If X happens, I will:*
>
>   1. _____
>   2. _____
>   3. _____
>
> Contact: ___
>
> Calm is a decision made in advance.

Step 9. Scoreboard & Review Rhythm

- Daily (5 min): Furnace lit? Signal shipped?
- Weekly (20 min): Double down / Cut ruthlessly
- Monthly (45 min): Mission still true?

No journaling for journaling's sake. Decisions only.

Step 10. Signal the World

Ship small. Ship often.

- Drafts
- Notes
- Threads
- Demos

Ask one question every time:

"What's unclear?"

Feedback tightens orbit.

Step 11. Fuel: Humor & Awe

This is not optional.

- Humor: dissolves fear
- Awe: restores proportion

One laugh. One moment of wonder. Daily.

Burnout comes from forgetting scale.

Step 12. Constraint Upgrade Cycle (Quarterly)

Pick one limitation.
Train it deliberately.
Document proof.

> Weakness ignored becomes fate.
> Weakness trained becomes leverage.

Reflection Questions

1. Which pillar would fail first if pressure doubled tomorrow?
2. What constraint am I still trying to overpower instead of redesign?
3. What system would keep working if my motivation disappeared?

Pillar Activation: The Cosmos of Redesign

Game Plan
This chapter proves a hard truth. Resilience is not recovery. It is redesign. When life removes options, you build new systems and move forward anyway.

Pillar Activation

- Mental Precision (Head)
  Hawking refused distraction and pity. He focused on one thing that still worked: thought. Clear focus turned limits into leverage.
- Physical Mastery (Body)
  His body weakened, so he conserved energy and used technology as extension. He designed for

bad days, not perfect ones. Rhythm replaced force.

- Emotional Power (Heart)
  Despair showed up. He did not drown in it. Love and partnership stabilized him. Emotion became fuel instead of friction.
- Spiritual Alignment (Soul)
  Curiosity became his why. Meaning lived beyond the body. Purpose anchored him when control disappeared.
- Imaginative Strategy (Vision)
  When movement failed, imagination traveled. Machines became bridges. Creativity opened paths no strength ever could.

Coach J's Challenge
When pressure closes in, stop fighting the constraint. Name it. Accept it. Design around it. Build systems that work even when energy drops and motivation disappears. That is real resilience.

Locker-Room Reflection
Which pillar will you redesign today so it still holds when everything else tightens?

Part III Summary

The Architecture of Flow

Resilience architecture creates the conditions where flow can exist.
Flow never appears by accident, emotion, or belief alone.
Design produces it through internal structure.
Nothing meaningful sustains itself without architecture.

Thought, emotion, action, meaning, and imagination operate as one system.
When they drift apart, friction multiplies.
When they align, force releases without strain.
Alignment adds nothing.
It stops leakage.

Without structure, contradiction drains power.
Intention argues with itself.
Vision hesitates.
Action fragments.
Effort rises as resistance dominates.

Chaos becomes expensive.

Architecture gathers energy into coherence.
Rules replace reactivity.
Order replaces confusion.

Internal agreement removes drag from execution.
Alignment converts coherence into causality.

Under these conditions, effort stops resisting reality.
Work moves with the current instead of against it.
Momentum accelerates as opposition dissolves.

Flow emerges as a byproduct of order.

Inner conflict dissolves first.
Intention stops negotiating with fear.
Command replaces hesitation.
Decision speed increases without recklessness.

Vision translates into action without delay.
Action builds belief through evidence.
Belief stabilizes emotion.
Emotion sustains motion.

Manifestation follows as consequence, not chance.
Outcomes respond to coherence with precision.
Reality mirrors internal order without negotiation.

Cause and effect activate cleanly.

None of the leaders in this section rose through
coincidence.
Each engineered inner systems before shaping the
world.
Structure preceded scale.
Discipline preceded dominance.
Flow remained active because architecture held firm.

Reality answered because coherence demanded response.
Resistance yielded to order.
Greatness followed inevitability.

The Universal Flow Pattern

Every leader followed the same invisible physics.
Collapse exposed contradiction before expansion emerged.
Clarity aimed intention with precision.
Emotion stabilized power without distortion.
Discipline translated belief into repeatable action.

Meaning aligned sacrifice with purpose.
Imagination expanded scale without breaking coherence.
Flow erased delay and replaced effort with inevitability.

At unity, destiny responded without resistance.

Leaders in Flow

Disney compressed failure into imagination.
Rejection purified direction.
Characters replaced approval.
Coherence accelerated creation into empire.

Jobs stripped noise until essence remained.
Illness sharpened urgency.
Design, intuition, and discipline aligned.
Flow collapsed distance between idea and execution.

Frankl preserved meaning under annihilation.
Purpose stabilized mind as the body weakened.
Suffering lost dominance.
Coherence survived extermination.

King unified conviction, compassion, and moral resolve.
Threats amplified purpose instead of fracturing it.
Nonviolence operated as lived coherence.
Systems reorganized without force.

Lee adapted after collapse.
Visualization replaced brute repetition.
Philosophy merged with motion.
Rigidity dissolved.
Truth moved without delay.

McRaven imposed order where chaos ruled.
Ritual synchronized focus and execution.
One completed action restored command each
morning.
Precision scaled from inches to continents.

Tesla sustained vision without validation.
Isolation tested coherence.
Imagination aligned with intellect.
Infrastructure replaced applause.
Reality arrived late but answered fully.

Dell redesigned structure without losing identity.
Clarity guided restraint through volatility.
Adaptability restored momentum without
fragmentation.

Gandhi reduced action to simplicity.
Discipline stabilized emotion under provocation.
Symbolic acts bent empires.
Humility scaled into consequence.

Ali protected identity through exile.
Belief remained intact.
Training stayed synchronized with faith.
Coherence overwhelmed stronger bodies.
Flow outlasted youth.

Brady refined consistency beyond visibility.
Humiliation simplified intention.
Age sharpened precision.
Reinvention occurred without fracture.

Hawking redefined identity beyond the body.
Focus replaced reach.
Imagination expanded past limitation.
Purpose anchored awareness beyond form.
Thought reshaped humanity.

The Architect's Charge

You walked through furnaces built by giants who survived collapse and consequence. Mandela endured prison. Jobs faced exile. Roosevelt fought paralysis. Hawking rewrote limits. Each fire forged discipline, vision, courage, and moral clarity under relentless pressure.

Their trials hardened code through action, restraint, and refusal to surrender purpose. Now pressure turns inward and demands authorship instead of admiration from history. Today you stand finished with study and ready for construction.

Architecture replaces imitation as you transmit alignment through daily design. This plan lives in behavior, choice, rhythm, and quiet consistency. Every morning shapes structure. Every decision amplifies frequency into tangible force.

Create resilience. Live resilience. Transmit resilience until legacy carries your signal forward.

Final Transmission

Hawking forged power as flesh failed and thought carried the entire load. Today you proved strength grows through choice rather than condition. Reduce the plan to one page that tolerates no confusion.

Each morning ignite the furnace and send a signal that confirms direction. Storms return because pressure always hunts weak alignment. When resistance strikes, discipline replaces hesitation without debate.

Action lifts you. Ignition locks intent. Momentum answers doubt.

Win your day by design and let legacy accumulate through repetition.

Reader's Acknowledgement

To you, the reader, this work opens with gratitude and respect.
Opening these pages marked a decision to choose resilience over retreat.
Fire greeted you not as threat but as invitation to become refined.
Each insight lives because your attention grants it breath and meaning.

Reading never ends on the page alone.
Your presence completes the sentences through action and reflection.
Meaning forms when words meet resolve inside lived experience.
This book finishes itself only through you.

Epilogue
The Transmission Lives in You

This final page opens a beginning rather than a conclusion.
Crisis filled these pages with fire, leaders, and codes forged under pressure.
Practice turned collapse into clarity through deliberate alignment and action.
Resilience lives as a frequency carried forward through daily choice.

Each day applies pressure through alarms, deadlines, loss, betrayal, or sudden collapse.
Now a different force travels with you through every test.
Code guides response, system anchors action, and truth reshapes meaning.
Crisis designs strength when intention meets discipline.

The Resilience Architecture you built here operates through lived execution.
Alignment of pillars, practice of algorithms, and respect for law create vibration.
Family, teams, and communities feel coherence before hearing explanation.
Transmission begins through presence rather than proclamation.

Resilience refuses confinement and expands through every decision made under strain.
The world waits for embodiment rather than instruction or permission.
Reader identity dissolves as resonance takes command through action.
Win your day and momentum carries the signal outward.

EMOTIONS

IN HIS

IMAGE

Explore God's Purpose for Your Emotions
& Cultivate Emotional Intelligence

EKEMINI OGUNSOLA

Emotions in His Image